meet President Abraham Lincoln and General Ulysses S. Grant

the civil war DIARY

Colonel Alfred B. Wade

transcribed and annotated by

Michael P. Downs

published 2009 in book form

James Keir Baughman

www.baughmanliterary.com

Published in the year 2009 by James Keir Baughman, Fort Walton Beach, Florida.

Transcription and annotation from the original handwritten format by Michael P. Downs, South Bend, IN. Downs is an educator and noted historian of the 73rd Indiana Volunteer Infantry Regiment. This volume is manufactured and printed in the United States.

www.baughmanliterary.com

ISBN # 978-0-9790443-8-0

This historic diary by Colonel Alfred B. Wade was kept in his own handwriting during three years of active service as a Union Infantry Officer during the years of America's Civil War, 1862-1865. In this book his words have been maintained precisely with minor edit for clarification only.

Cover background art, the painting "12th Ind. Vols. Pvt." created by famed Civil War artist Don Troiani, is his depiction of the battle uniform of a soldier in the 12th Indiana Volunteer Infantry Regiment. As Artist and Publisher, Troiani's work may be found at Historical Art Prints. His web site address is www.historicalimagebank.com

TABLE OF CONTENTS

In Appreciation

I would like to thank the Indiana Historical Society, the Indiana Humanities Council and the National Endowment for the Humanities for their Indiana Heritage Research Grant which has allowed me to transcribe and annotate this Civil War Diary of Colonel Alfred B. Wade.

Additionally I would like to thank the Northern Indiana Center for History for being the local sponsor of the project.

All pictures in the Diary are also provided by the Center for History.

Again, thank you.

Michael P. Downs
South Bend, Indiana

Transcribed, annotated, and printed in binder form December 25, 2000.

INTRODUCTION

This is the Civil War diary of Colonel Alfred B Wade. In its near daily record, he chronicles his own life as well as activities of the 73rd Indiana Volunteer Infantry Regiment.

The entries start in January of 1862 from South Bend where the 73rd was being formed, and continue on through early September, 1865.

Alfred Wade was born in South Bend, Indiana on December 28, 1839. He was the youngest son of Judge Robert Wade. However his father died early in his life and his mother directed his childhood growth.

Wade's personal interest was in art, but living so close to the frontier, such educational opportunities were seldom at hand. His early education was at "Old Seminary," one of the first high schools in the South Bend area. He was brought up in the Presbyterian Church. In fact, his mother named him after the church's first minster, Alfred Bryant.

Also attending this church was Schuyler Colfax, a friend who was destined to play a key role in Wade's future.

After finishing school, Wade traveled to the Pikes Peak area where so many Americans were going at the time. However, unable to find either fortune or fame there, he returned to South Bend and soon began reading the law under Judge Stanfield.

With President Lincoln's call for Union Army volunteers at the outbreak of America's Civil War, Wade was one of the first to offer his services, joining up as an enlisted man in the Ninth Indiana Volunteer Regiment. Like most others at the start of the War, that enlistment was for only 90 days of service.

After discharge from that brief enrollment he requested that Governor Morton assign him as Adjutant, with the rank of Major, to a new Regiment, the 73rd, then being created in South Bend. This unit was to be composed of volunteers from the counties of the Ninth Congressional District then being represented by the Honorable Schuyler Colfax in the House of Representatives.

Gilbert Hathaway, a lawyer from LaPorte, was named the Regiment's Colonel. The unit was Federalized (mustered in) on August 16, 1862 with ten companies totaling 1010 men.

A silk Regimental flag was presented to the 73rd by Schuyler and Mrs. Colfax as the men left South Bend to reinforce Union troops then being opposed by Southern forces under General Braxton Bragg during an invasion of Kentucky.

Finally, almost two weeks after the Regiment left South Bend, Wade received his commission and joined his fellow Hoosiers then camped at Lexington, Ky.

An important note about the transcription of Colonel Alfred B. Wade's Civil War diary:

His entries begin, not with stories of America's Civil War, but with a literary criticism of Lord Byron.

In my opinion, Wade was rather bored at this point, waiting on his army officer's commission to arrive from the Indiana Governor. However, some early entries are of great interest because they comment on the direction the War had taken and the morale of his fellow citizens at that point in time.

The Colonel's writing during the initial entries was quite good and his spelling was usually correct. But by 1865 his entries are frequently a scrawl which required a great deal of interpretation on my part.

Additionally, his use of the English language frequently leaves something to be desired. During the transcribeing I altered, as little as possible, his style of writing, leaving his punctuation and capitalization the way he wrote it, as much as feasible.

However, I have included the addition of commas,

periods, and apostrophes to make his meaning - when obvious – more clear. I have, in the same way, corrected spelling or capitalization errors only when leaving them as written might result in unnecessary confusion.

I have endeavored to separate his ideas by paragraph, more often than he, only when it could obviously make his topic and meaning more clear. I used the "sic" annotation as little as possible, inserting it only where I felt the reader might be confused if it were not employed. At times I have also used brackets to insert editorial notations.

I have included two types of additions that are more notable, but which may greatly aid the reader in understanding the flow and timing of Col. Wade's observations.

First, Wade identified each Chapter only by dates. I have added a title subject in parenthesis so the reader has an idea of what is occurring in that Chapter.

Second, with few exceptions, Wade also identified each day only by the date. I included the day of the week in parenthesis so that the reader may orient events to the normal flow of week days by which we, of all generations, have tended to gauge periods of work, rest, relaxation, and worship. I trust that will help greatly in getting a sense of how different the life of a soldier in the field or in battle must be.

However, I feel a further warning is needed. There will be a number of entries in which an immediate understanding of the Colonel's intent is not easy. Some lines may have to be read two, or even three, times to uncover their meaning.

It should also be remembered, as highly interesting in our time, that the diary reflects language, punctuation, and speaking styles of the 1860's and the Civil War era. To this end I have included a Glossary at the completion of the Colonel's story.

A reader will also find it useful to understand the organization of the United States Army at the time. So, please take a moment to read the Glossary under "Army Organization. " In fact, you may well find it helpful to read the Glossary before you begin reading the Diary.

Moreover, if the reader has specific interest in the "Western Theater" of our Civil War, this diary is a must read.

In Col. Wade's words you will feel the terror of the bloody Battle of Stones River, with its 20,000 casualties, the excitement of Colonel Streight's raid along with its peril of death or capture by famed Confederate Cavalry General Nathan Bedford Forrest and his hard-riding, hard-fighting mounted troops.

Wade and his fellow officers of Streight's Brigade already knew of Forrest's reputation as a vigorous foe when they first learned that it was he who was pursuing them. Far more, though, by the end of the Civil War, Forrest was recognized as the fiercest, most combative, most effective cavalry officer of the entire War...on either side.

Understanding this makes far more notable the severe battering given to Forrest's Cavalry troopers by the 73rd Indiana and other Regiments of Streight's Brigade before their surrender. In fact, despite having inferior rifles and being mounted on much less agile steed's, they were very nearly the equal of Forrest for an entire week of running battles.

A gripping account of Civil War history is Wade's detailed description of Richmond's Libby Prison. That Confederate jail for captured Union officers is little remembered now...but was famed in Civil War years. Wade's daily notes of his months-long boredom and longing for freedom while being held prisoner there make an eye opening read for Civil War scholars.

Finally comes the emotional high of being released from prison, exchanged, heading back home, and going through Washington to see his friend and Congressman Schuyler Colfax.

While there Wade met such famed Civil War era

leaders as President Abraham Lincoln and his wife; General Ulysses S. Grant - General of the Armies; General Henry W. Halleck, - General of the Armies for a time before Grant; Edwin M. Stanton - Secretary of War; and Secretary of the Treasury Salmon P. Chase.

Col. Wade stayed in the home of Congressman Colfax while in Washington, and attended a number of social gatherings. His personal view of Washington's social life is surprisingly little different than many of us might express in our present era..

Upon return home, after a few weeks furlough with his family, Wade returned to duty with the 73rd and served as its Commander during the last year and closing months of the War.

Wade's story contains a great deal of "Hoosier" history. So, those from Indiana will find it an especially fascinating read.

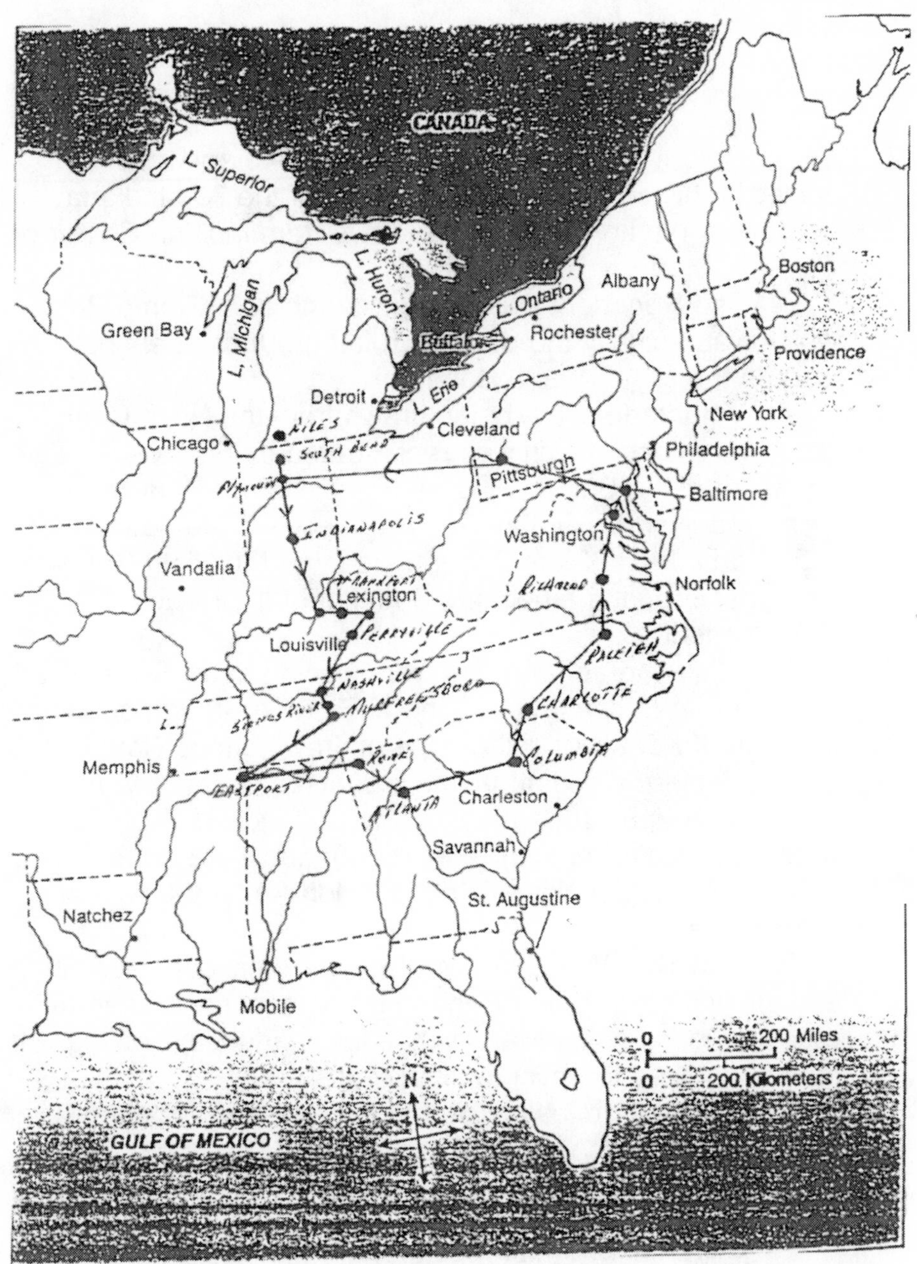

Wade's sojourn - January 7, 1862 through March 23, 1864

Preface

Colonel Alfred B. Wade began this diary while he waited for his commission as Adjutant of the 73rd Indiana Volunteer Infantry Regiment to arrive from Indiana Governor Oliver P. Morton.

The Regiment was being assembled at Camp Rose which was actually the St Joseph fair grounds, then just outside the city of South Bend.

Volunteers were being drawn from the Ninth Congressional District which was represented by Schuyler Colfax, publisher of the South Bend newspaper, "The Register."

Additionally Colfax was very active in the new Republican Party. In 1863, as Congressman for the Ninth Congressional District, he became Speaker of the House of Representatives.

While men of the 73rd were waiting to be Federalized, Confederate forces under General Braxton Bragg began an invasion of Kentucky in the hope of drawing that State into the Confederacy and attracting recruits to their army.

By August 16, 1862 the 73rd had indeed been Federalized (mustered in to the Regiment) and were on their way to Louisville, Kentucky to join the Union Army of Gen. Don Carlos Buell.

However, Wade had yet to receive his commission and sat waiting in South Bend. Finally, nine days after the regiment left the new Major Wade followed the marching men and joined them in Louisville.

The two armies collided at Perryville on October 8th (the Battle was also called Chaplin Hills). There, a rather lack-luster confrontation took place, with neither side gaining a military advantage.

However Bragg soon feared that his army might be flanked by Buell, and finding relatively little support from the populace of Kentucky he decided to retreat into Tennessee.

Meanwhile, Union Gen. Buell had more than double the troops Bragg commanded (Union 37, 000 vs.16,000 Confederates) yet allowed the Confederate army to escape without serious challenge. This situation dropped the morale of Union troops to nearly rock bottom, and Major Wade made several comments upon the need to replace Buell with a stronger man.

In fact President Lincoln, soon after, did replace Buell with General William Rosecrans who after some repair to the army began an invasion of Tennessee. Nashville soon fell and by late December the army was marching upon a small town named Murfreesboro.

Here on the Stone's River Confederate troops once again confronted the Union Army and in a three day battle (December 31,1862 through January 2, 1863) the two armies literally slugged it out. The Seventy-third Indiana was hotly engaged and suffered heavy casualties. By January 3rd the Southern Army was in a tenuous position, and Bragg once again ordered a retreat.

As a result of this, fight both armies suffered nearly 10.000 casualties each, and the 73rd had over 90 of its 439 effective men listed as killed, wounded, or missing. As a result of the battle at Stone's River several units, including the 73rd, were allowed to rest, refit, and enjoy their victory at Murfreesboro.

Michael P. Downs

Colonel Alfred B. Wade

Chapter One

January 7th, 1862 – July 11th, 1862
(A time of Waiting)

Jan. 7, 1862 – South Bend. (Tuesday) Am reading "Byron and propose to take a vote "here and there" upon the general and particular of his "complete works."

George Gordon Byron was born in Hoiles Street, 22 January 1788. His father deserted him and his early training devolved upon his mother who was as passionate in temper as her son proved to be in after years. His first "dash at poetry" was in1800.

The ebullition of his passion for his first cousin, speaking of her he says, "She looked as if she had been made out of a rainbow - all beauty and peace."

Byron died in western Greece 19 April 1824 being engaged with the Greeks in their struggle for freedom. Tis a pity that such genius should be alloyed with so many glaring faults.

I have just finished the 3rd canto of Don Juan and am sorry that I did not take notes while reading as I am afraid I have only read the many beautiful thoughts, which abound in every part of the work, to forget them. Will only take a cursory glance of what I have already read..."Childe Harold's Pilgrimage" is a masterpiece, as indeed it should be, being one of the oldest. It shows the marks of deep thought and feeling and so much thought is crowded into even one verse that I could not read much at a time without growing weary. I was not so much interested in the pilgrimage of the fictional Harold as I was in the author's digressions and ortrature of his own feelings.

Extract from Childe Harold LXXXII.C1

And lately had he learn'd with truth to
deem
Love has no gift so grateful as his
wings:
How fair, how young, how soft soe' er he
seem
Full from the front of Joy's delicious
springs
Some bitter o'er the flowers its bubbling
venom flings.

There is at least as <u>much</u> truth and poetry in the above lines and here is another Canto 2nd Verse XXVI

But 'midst the crowd, the hum, the shock
of men,
To hear, to see, to feel, and to possess,

And roam along, the world's tired deni-
zen,
With none who bless us, none whom we
can bless;
Minions of splendour shrinking from dis-
tress!
None that with kindred consciousness
endued,
If we were not would seem to smile the
less,
Of all that flatter'd, follow'd, sought, and
sued;
This is to be alone; this, this is solitude!

With which I hardly agree for I like to be "alone in a crowd" and yet after all it <u>is</u> solitude and here another which is alas too often true Canto 2nd Verse 34th

Not much he kens, I ween, of woman's
breast,
Who thinks that wanton thing is won by
sighs,
What careth she for hearts when once possess'd?
Do proper homage to thine idol's eyes,
But not too humbly or she will despise
Thee and they suit, though told in moving
tropes:
Disguise ev'n tenderness if thou art wise
Brisk confidence still best with woman
copes;
Pique her and soothe in turn, soon passion
crowns thy hopes.

In Canto 3rd from verse XXI to XXVIII that noted description etc. of the battle of Waterloo is found of which I was as fond in my schoolboy days and which so far back that my "memory runneth not to the contrary" has always been copied in the school readers to the edification of the youthful mind. It was eight years from the commencement of Childe Harold till its last canto was finished. That interval happening between the 3rd and fourth canto.....

Extract from fourth canto Verse XXI

Existence may be borne, and the deep root
Of life and sufferance make its firm abode
In bare and desolated bosoms; mute
The camel labours with the heaviest load,
And the wolf dies in silence, - not be-
stow'd
In vain should such example be; if they,
Things of ignoble or of savage mood,
Endure and shrink not, we of nobler clay
May temper it to bear, - it is but for a day.

From Verse CXXVII I extract

Yet let us ponder boldly; 'tis a base
Abandonment of reason to resign
Our right of thought, etc.

to which the author appends a note lauding the philosophical mind of the British nation

CLXXVII

Oh that the desert were my dwelling-
place,
With one fair Spirit for my minister,
That I might all forget the human race,
And, hating no one, love but only her!

Thus ended my "glance" at Harold and the no good crime hereby at least no harm can

January 27th, 1862 - South Bend. (Monday) Twenty days have elapsed since I first commenced to criticize Byron and writings. At this rate will take one "many moons" to finish the complete works. My only excuse is the novelty to me in my first attendance at court which is wearing off somewhat now and I promise myself to be more attentive to my journal hereafter. "The Giaour" is a fragment of a Turkish tale and inscribed to Samuel Rogers, Esq. is a vague sort of a poem from which I could not get much satisfaction. The "Bride of Abydos" is a wild Turkish tale of love, blood, and thunder.

Who hath not proved how feebly words essay
To fix one spark of beauty's heavenly ray?
Who doth not feel, until his failing sight
Faints into dimness with its own delight.

The "Corsair" comes next on the list and tho I do not admire the taste of the author in making a pirate his hero still there are many beautiful passages in it. "Lara" is a dreary tale built up principally upon a murder. "The Siege of Corinth" written in 1815 and dedicated to John Hobhouse, Esq. is a poem of some merit. "The Prisoner of Chillon" is a very affecting piece and there are many parts of it that shows the amazing genius of Byron. It bears the mark of deep thought. "Beppo" a Venetian tale does not possess much interest to me. "Mazeppa" has a world wide reputation and I can only say that it well deserves it.

Feb. 2nd, 1862 - South Bend. (Sunday) "The Island" makes heroes of traitors and heroines of savage women. “Manfred,” “The Deformed Transformed," "Heaven and Earth," "Cain," "Marino Faliero," "The Two Foscari," "Sardanapalus," and "Werner," are all Shakespearean style and I did not have patience enough to read them.

There are some good pieces in "Hours of Idleness." I was much interested in "English Bards and Scotch Reviewers." He hits right and left and deals some heavy views on "English Bards." "Hints from Horace" - I did not appreciate quite so well as my Latin studies are not far enough advanced to translate the "Horace part."The Curse of Minerva" I do not remember anything about and do not care to read it again. "The Waltz" is to the point exactly. "The Age of Bronze" did not meet with the approbation of the public as well as the author expected and therefore a second carmen" was not forthcoming. "The Vision of Judgment" is hardly in good taste. I've entirely forgotten the subject matter of "Morgante Maggiore" which does not speak well for my reading. Ditto the "Prophecy of Dante.” "Hebrew Melodies" I did not read. “Monody on the Death of Sheridan" is good "Ode to Napoleon Bonaparte" smacks of British ideas and nothing else. "Ode to Venice" is a useless waste of rhyme. "The "Dream" is exquisite and the "Blues" I did not read. The

"Miscellaneous Poems' are a rare collection and are worth reading. And now comes Don Juan." The masterpiece as I think. But I don't feel like commenting upon that or anything else today. And therefore I shall bring my criticism on Byron to a close.

Feb. 21, 1862 - South Bend. (Friday) Glory to God! Fort Donelson is taken!! Fifteen thousand prisoners captured including Generals Buckner and Johnson. Since the commencement of the New Year victory upon victory has crowned our arms. Not a single reverse, not once, has our glorious flag been lowered to the rebels since '62 dawned upon our nation.

First the Rebel Humphrey Marshall was completely routed in eastern Kentucky by our gallant Thomas (or perhaps I may mistake our general's name our successes follow each other so rapidly that I can hardly keep in mind who even commands our brave soldiers at the various engagements), next followed the capture of the Rebel Batteries at Port Royal.

The navy now under command of Commodore Dupont and the land forces under Brigr. General Sherman (who by the way does not appear to amount to much) or come to think I'm getting this engagement mixed up with the original fight at Port Royal itself. This will never do for a historian must be more careful, but who cares for details or dates. We've whipped the Rebels at every point and glory enough for two months but to resume the glorious record.

Zollicoffer's army was next utterly routed at the battle of Mill Springs in Ky and Zolly himself was laid away where he will never rise to attempt the overthrow he had solemnly sworn to uphold. There followed the capture of Fort Henry with nearly 100 prisoners and a large number of cannon and small arms and munitions of war by Commodore Foote of the Gunboat Flotilla and Brigr. General Grant commanding the land forces. It was, however, a naval victory entirely.

Then the capture of Roanoke, North Carolina, with 3,000 prisoners and military stores without number. This expedition was commanded by Burnside whose name already is a household word throughout the North and last, but by no means least, this truly brilliant victory at Fort Donelson, Tennessee.

The enthusiasm created in every city, town, and village in the Northern States upon the receipt of the news showed how deeply interested the loyal people of this country are in the struggle for the restoration of our government. The Court House bell in South Bend rang forth sharp and clear upon the cool, crisp air of evening upon that memorable night and it was known that now our long suspense would be ended. Hundreds of every class and station rushed pell mell to the Court House and there how the overburdened hearts of people relieved themselves by loud long cheers when the news was read from the stand.

We have no particulars as yet as regards to the loss on either side but it must have been very severe. It is rumored that 7,000 of the prisoners will be stationed at Camp Douglas. Chicago, some at Springfield. Illinois, and some at Detroit. This is a death blow to the Southern Confederacy and soon our banner will wave over Nashville and Memphis.

Feb. 22 1862 - South Bend. (Saturday) Washington's birth day is very appropriately celebrated by the reading of his farewell address in the various cities and towns of the North by suggestion of President Lincoln. The news today is to the effect that Clarksburg, Tennessee is surrendered and Nashville has offered so that our flag waves in the northern part & Arkansas and that all is quiet on the Potomac.

Feb. 24th 1862 South Bend. (Monday) Chicago Tribune reports today that Nashville Tennessee is occupied without resistance by Gen. Buell. Hope its true. Also Fort Columbus will be evacuated. 7000 prisoners of war are at Camp Douglas, Chicago 2 or 3000 at Indianapolis and the balance of the Fort Donelson crew at Springfield and Alton. No particulars of killed and wounded at the Fort D fight.

Feb. 26th - So. Bend. (Wednesday) Occupation of Nashville confirmed. It is supposed that Columbus Kentucky is being evacuated by the rebels. On to Memphis and New Orleans is now the union war cry.

Feb. 28th. 1862 - South Bend. (Friday) Have been reading today a book entitled "Cincinnati in 1859" by Charles Cist. It relates some of the early reminiscences of the settling of Cincinnati and I have gleaned a few facts concerning my great grandfather on my mother's side Capt. Ephram Kibby.

The first mention made of him is on page 14. It seems that when Cincinnati was first laid out 30 of the in lots and out lots were given to the first settlers and at a lottery drawn at Losantiville(?) January 7. 1789, Capt. Kibby drew in lot 59 and out lot 4. The real estate now is probably worth over a million of Dollars. Kibby was one of Stiles party who first settled Columbia. Gov. St. Clair on the 4th day of January 1790 appointed Ephram Kibby Ensign (2 Lieut.) in the 1st Regt. of the County of Hamilton Ohio.

The next mention made of him (page 90) is that he was in command as captain of about 65 scouts in Wayne's expedition against the Indians. It also mentions his name as being in the battle of "Fallen Timber" in command of a battalion of spies (page 118).

Mar. 5 1862 - South Bend. (Wednesday) Military matters remain in status quo at present. Nothing of moment to chronicle except perhaps the occupation of Columbus Ky by our forces. That is certainly an important movement but it has been so long talked of that the minds of the people were fully prepared for it when it did come and therefore did not produce the excitement and interest that would have been felt had it happened sooner.

The 37,000 rebels left that point in such a hurry that a large quantity of stores and ordinance fell into our hands.

Recd. a letter last week from Adjutant Stanfield of the 48th Indiana Regt. Col. Eddy of the Regt. is in command of Fort Anderson with four companies. The remaining six companies are in Paducah Kentucky.

Gen. Banks has moved his command over the Potomac. Whether this indicates an onward movement from Washington or no is hard to tell. Hope so for the never ending telegrams that "all is quiet on the Potomac" has got to be a hiss and by word through the whole west.

March 12, 1862. (Wednesday) We have a few particulars today concerning the great battle at Sugar Creek Ark [Wilson's Creek campaign, Ed.]. Gen. Curtis has completely routed Genl Price McCullough [McCulloch, Ed.] and Van Dorn. Our loss is reported at one thousand killed and wounded. A telegram from Washington states that Gen. McClellan is no longer Commander in Chief and that our troops have occupied Manassas. The Rebel Steamer Virginia, better known as the Merrimac, has proved an ugly customer. She sunk one or two Frigates near Fort Monroe but our new iron class steamer the Monitor after a four hour fight succeeded in driving her back.

March 15th 1862. (Saturday) Glorious news from Arkansas. Gen. Curtis has given the Rebels a terrible blow at Pea Ridge completely routing their army and killing the noted Secesh General McCullough. The slaughter on both sides was immense but no particulars as yet.

Gen. Pope has captured New Madrid with ordinance and stores amounting to a million of Dollars according to his official report.

Mar. 20th 1862. (Thursday) Six inches of snow today but

no sleighing. Burnside (a native Hoosier) has captured Wellbern, North Carolina. Commandore Foote has been shelling Island No. 10 on the Mississippi for several days. Pope is in the rear at New Madrid and the capture of the island is reduced almost to a certainty. Nothing from McClellan for several days.

John C. Fremont has been appointed to the command of the Mountain Department comprising West Va., Western Kentucky and Tennessee and Ohio. I was certain that he would be appreciated sooner or later.

Halleck's command absorbs Hunter's and it is sent south. Lew Wallace of Ind. is confirmed a Brigade Major General and Seigel ditto Segil [Sigel] is one of our best generals. Nothing from Buel's column. Stirring work up the Tennessee River soon. The Merrimac exhibits a wholesome fear and does not venture out from Norfolk. Capt. F. Hardman died on the 5th in Tennessee. He was a hard case. The 48th is still at Paducah. 9th and 29th probably at Nashville. Thank God the backbone of the rebellion is broken.

Monday Eve - March 25 1862. (Actually March 24th)
Written in an Album "Impromptu Vic"

To do or to die
Is the favorite cry
of warriors and oft they resolve it
But what shall I write.
Is the question tonight
It's a problem. Alas I can't solve it.

And yet I must "do"
or prove falsely untrue
To the promise I've solemnly made
And the "die" being cast
I can only at last
Sign myself "yours"
Alf. B. Wade

March 27th, 1862 - Thursday Eve. The following lines composed today. I've written in the last leaves of Vic! Album. This is as first written and before I examined and corrected the grammar as well as sense.

Friend Vic to criticize I own
Is thankless task to anyone
and if thy friends should chance to find
what I have written of my mind
To give the needful blame
They'd ne'er forgive this waste of rhyme
Nor deem me a true friend of thine
Who doth at present ape the sage
and turning oft from page to page
Sees just "what's in a name."

First Gus (for short) a brother thine
Has written verses three
And penned more wishes in a line
Than e'er could happen thee.

But then it shows the "heart is right"
No fault with him I find
I only wish those wishes might
Be e'er as true as kind.

"Yours truly" no one here to tell
What story this line breathes
I think the "faded rose" might well
Afford to fold its leaves.
Next comes a wish from Mme. S.
The verse is chaste and fair
I vow I could not wish you less
As "perfect bliss" is there.

And heres a letter thus begun

"Dear Vic" and ends "till deth, yours Lide"
July the fourth in Sixty one
Saw wit and beauty side by side.

Could I write more I might begin
But us the thought I scout
For where the candle's growing dim
Tis best to snuff it out.

Though I have gone but halfway through
My muse is well nigh worn out
But e'er I close Friend Vic hark you
This page is easily tom out.

P.S.
My preface is wrong
For the drift of my song
Has been more to praise than to blame
To late I awake
To the awful mistake
That this critic will never win fame.

Apr. 1st 1862 - South Bend. (Tuesday) Before inserting the "criticisms" (on the opposite page) I succeeded polishing it up to some degree of excellence. I altered some lines and made them read very different. But with all the "extra polish" it still looks, tastes and reads most distressingly sickly.

Apr. 4 1862 -South Bend. (Friday) Island No. 10 on the Mississippi after a bombardment of three weeks is not yet taken. All is quiet on the Potomac. Gen. Shields won a brilliant victory in Va. several days ago. A desperate fight is expected at Corinth Miss.

Sabbath Eve. - April 7 1862. (Actually April 6th) Am in "the mood" to write a line or two but am at a loss for a subject. The telegram from the seat of war, like angel visits, come few and far between.

Expect a desperate battle at or near Corinth Ala (or Miss) this week. If we gain a victory the Island No. 10 and Memphis falls into our hands as a matter of course.

Gen. McClellan has done nothing yet in spite of his proclamation 3 weeks since. Blunker Brigade is transferred to Fremont. It is stated that we have 80,000 men at Fort Monroe. If so there will be warm work at Norfolk and Richmond. Eleven Rose died this morning. Weather pleasant tho rather chilly. Spring rather backward this year.

April 9th, 1862- South Bend. (Wednesday) I am again afflicted with a malignant type of the "poetic fever." Here's the latest "effusion."

On the return of her pen knife
Friend Lizzie
Remember before, when last we met
That book! That subject! Etiquette?
O sweetest author. Peace be with you,
Like picture..I want to kiss you,
When from the fools we give to learn.
Straight to thy pages will I turn.
And fair convince myself from you,
That "knife won't cut love when tis true,"
At first I thought twas foolish stuff,
But now tis a "diamond in the rough"
For it is proved at least in part
This knife has rested near my heart
For twelve long hours and all that time
Both knife and heart were truly thine
And this I write you just to prove
That rusty blades can nier cut love.
Alf

April 10th 1862 - South Bend. (Thursday) The whole country is rejoicing and sorrowing by turns over the exciting news which has crowded thick and fast upon us for several days. Rejoicing over two great and glorious victorys, sorrowing over the many thousands even who have freely given their lives to save our Union. Brave Commodore Foote has at last captured Island No. 10 and with it a thousand prisoners. And the combined armies of Buell and Grant have just won a "second Waterloo" at Pittsburg Tennessee. It is stated that the Rebel army under Johnson and Beauregard numbered over a hundred thousand. Ours amounted to 170 Regiments (a Regiment number 1000) but how many were actually engaged cannot be ascertained but all accounts agree that the loss on both sides was terrible.

Some placing our loss as low as 3,000 and some as high as 18,000. The enemy's must have been greater as we routed them completely and they have fled in wide confusion towards Corinth followed closely by twelve thousand of our cavalry. The battle took place on Sunday and Monday last, 7th and 8th.

Apr. 17th, 1862 - South Bend. (Thursday) Have just finished reading "Thucydides or rather the "History of the Peloponnesian War" translated from the Greek of Thucydides by Wm. Smith a.m. New York sold by Baugo Bro. No 13 Park Row 1855. My plan of reading this work has been to spend about ¼ of an hour after retiring for the night in its perusal and I find it works admirably as I can remember what I have read full as well if not better than what I read during the day. I believe this is the oldest history extant. At all events it is a splendid work and written as natural and easy as the books of our modem authors. Thucydides has been translated by several persons but the translation of Wm. Smith is generally admitted to be the best. The long war which was carried on against the Pelopennesians,and at times the ......by Athens has a particular interest at present viewed in the light of our present civil war. Thucydides ends his history abruptly in the twenty first year of the war.

Apr. 23rd 1862 - South Bend. (Wednesday) Military matters since the battle of Shiloh have settled into a distressing quiet. Gen. Grant is being censored on all hands from permitting himself to be surprised. Whether he deserves it or not, I cannot say. But there is no doubt but that blame should rest somewhere.

Gen. McClellan is before Yorktown made celebrated during our revolution by the surrender of Cornwallis. I hope the precedent will be followed and the Rebel Magruder with his army of 40,000 be captured. McClellan must do it or he will go down somewhat faster than he went up in reputation.

Banks and McDowell with their "corps de arm" are closing in towards Richmond and we shall hear something stirring soon.

I have been appointed agent for the "Arctic Insurance Company" of New York and hope to do a good business.

The weather has been miserable this spring but today bids fair to inaugurate a new era and the farmers will be much rejoiced thereat.

Chaplain Brown of the 48th left on Monday last for Paducah.

May 7th 1862 - So. Bend. (Wednesday) Yorktown is evacuated by the rebels and the latest news is that Gen. McClellan is in hot pursuit. Dispatch last night says that Gen. Pope holds Corinth. Beauregard having evacuated and gone to Grand Junction. We'll soon hear thrilling news.

May 9th 1862 - South Bend. (Friday) Trest Carely delivered a lecture on poetry or rather music last eve. He said music had no connection with the fallen angels but with the un-fallen angels. Music is high and noble. God is its author. A man whose heart does not swell with mysterious pleasure at music's sound is fit for treason etc., thus said Shakespeare the world's many minded poet who holds the mirror up to nature for amusement. 1st as to its nature and origin. It was produced by vibration. 10 octaves embrace all the sounds of music. There is sound and music in every-thing. A yawn will embrace an octave. Sometimes there is discord in the music of nature when the storm king drives before him the winds like a crowd of laughing shrieking maniacs. Music is a Divine and etc. etc.

Sunday 11th, May 1862. This is a beautiful day. etc etc etc etc etc

May 30th, 1862. (Friday) Have just returned from Niles Mich. where I have been working my trade for the past two weeks. Have not read the papers lately and am not posted up in regard to the war. Niles is a beautiful place and is improving rapidly but So. Bend is the "dearest spot on the earth to me" yet??

June 1st 1862 - South Bend. (Sunday) The war news may be summed up as follows: Secretary Stanton is still in office and guides our many different armies to the general satisfaction of the people.

Gen. McClellan and army having fought the battle of Williamsburg is now encamped within 5 miles of Richmond Va. the Rebel capitol a large but unknown force defending that place.

Gen. McDowell is at and beyond Fredericksburg doing nothing at present.

Gen. Banks has been driven back and Jackson (Rebel General) threatens Washington.

Gen. Fremont however is marching from West Va. with 20,000 men to drive him back.

Gen. Wallace who commands the largest separate army in the U.S. has just taken possession of Corinth,

Beauregard having evacuated a day or two ago.

Our upper Mississippi Flotilla is bombarding Fort Pillow, our lower fleet having captured New Orleans, at last, account was at Vicksburg Miss. on the way to Memphis.

General Curtis was on the march to Little Rock Ark. As to present movements of other forces in New Mexico. Florida, S.C., N.C. I'm in the dark.

June 2nd 1862 - South Bend. (Monday) We had a hard frost week before last killed the grapes, peaches, etc. etc. Raining today.

June 3rd 1862. Recd. letter (first) from E.L.F. Mich U.

June 10th 1862 - South Bend. (Tuesday) We've had a glorious fight and whipped the Rebels soundly. It occurred a day or two ago in front of that sink hole of secession down Memphis between our upper Mississippi fleet and all the available Gunboats and raw force of the Rebels but one of their boats escaped. All the rest were sunk burned blown up or captured. Glory enough for one day. The Miss. river is now open.

June 14th 1862 - South Bend, Ind. (Saturday) Gen. Fremont has been adding glory to his name by whipping the rebel Jackson and his army in a hard fought battle. The federal fleet have left Memphis and gone down the river for the purpose of confiscating any stray rebel craft it may find and bombarding any city town or village which holds to obstinacy to the secession doctrine. In three months I venture to predict the rebellion will be played out.

June 16th 1862 - South Bend, Ind. (Monday) Today marks an important epoch in my eventful life. I've opened an office and hereby invite all the good, bad and indifferent people of St. Joseph County who are already or to be involved in the intricate mazes of the law to call at 3rd door from Washington House, Main Street, opposite the Post Office - in truth its a serious step I've taken but its well enough to take it with a light heart, laugh at discouragements and surmount them.

Don't expect much if any business for a year or two but intend to spend most of my time in hard study.

June 18th 1862 South Bend. (Wednesday) Have been retained in a to be hotly contested case!!! Prospect looks encouraging. It is not every young lawyer who gets a case the first week he hands out his shingle. Must make the most of this one. Informed my client that if I succeeded I would charge him $5.00. If I lost the case would not charge anything so that success is a consummation to be devoutly wished for.

June 28th 1862 South Bend. (Saturday) My "first case" is over and I am victorious. Here's a brief resume of the facts in the case. Jacob Hardy sued Barnhart Hardy on account for $32.50 and relyed upon himself father and mother to swear it through. Barnhart retained me and I promised to win the case or charge nothing. I made out subpoenas for my witnesses but Constable forgot to serve them and therefore went to trial with only one voluntary witness to prove an unimportant fact. Demanded a jury trial and after the opposite counsel (John Henderson) rested made the Plaintiff my witness and put him through a severe examination and made him commit himself fully. Before I was through with him saw that the jury were satisfied as to what the facts in the case were. Examined one witness whom they had not examined but subpoenaed and closed by a short speech. The jury after half an hour's deliberation returned a verdict for defendant. Charged my client $5.00.

July 11th 1862 South Bend. (Friday) Our army under

Major General McClellan after six or seven days hard fighting have been driven back from Richmond Va. a distance of 17 miles. The loss of life on both sides was terrible.

Chapter Two

August 6th, 1862 – November 30th, 1862 (First Taste of Army Life)

August 6th 1862 - South Bend Ind. (Wednesday) Stirring news yesterday. More men are called for and half of them are to be drafted immediately. The other half it is hoped will volunteer before the 15th of this month. If not they will be drafted. Our Government seems to have come to the conclusion that this rebellion must be put down and that immediately.

Gen. Halleck has been appointed commander in chief and has his headquarters at Washington. A new policy has been proclaimed and rebel property including negroes are not to be guarded by our troops hereafter.

Gen. Pope is in command in the Shenandoah valley and everything looks hopeful.

Aug 18 1862 - South Bend Ind. (Monday) Recruits have crowded so thick and fast upon each other this month that I haven't had time to "write them up."

No particular change has taken place in the disposition of our armies. Everything seems to be at a stand still except volunteering for the last great final effort. The notification from the President that a draft would be made to has had a wonderful effect upon recruiting. Everybody seems to be rushing into the army.

The 73rd Regiment Indiana Vols (stationed here) was full to over-flowing in about one week and now there are over 2000 men in camp and another Regt is organizing. For the past week I have been making out the muster rolls of the 73rd. Difficult job.

The Gov. has promised me the adjutantcy of this

Regt. Provided there is a vacancy. I hope I'll get it as am anxious to go. The enrollment of name for the draft comm.-enced Saturday.

Aug 23rd 1862 - South Bend (Saturday) Have been making out the Draft Rolls for Olive Township for a day or two. She has 240 men between the age of 18 and 45 and 84 volunteered. Received a dispatch dated Louisville Ky from Col Hathaway that I was appointed Sergeant Major of the 73rd Regt. I wrote him respectfully declining the appointment as I had applied for the adjutantcy and received a promise from the Gov. that I should have it provided there was a vacancy.

August 27 1862 - Letter from the 73rd (Wednesday) Friend Wheeler:- I have been looking long and patiently for the arrival of our "home sheet"- the Register, [the South Bend newspaper owned by Schuyler Colfax, Ed.] but as yet it is "non est inventus" in Camp Buell. Hope to receive it regularly hereafter. Newspapers are in great demand, and a bit of news now and then would be highly relished, both at headquarters and in Company C.

If you have not already received a detailed account of the marches and counter marches, the advances and retreats of the 73rd since taking the field, perhaps a line or two on the subject would not be uninteresting. I joined the regiment at Lexington, Ky, on the 30th last, and found everything in hurry, bustle, and confusion, preparatory to a forward movement, to take place on the next day, our destination being Camp Dick Robinson.

Early in the morning of the 31st, heavy firing was heard in the direction of Richmond, [Ky.. Ed.] but no attention paid to it, supposing it to be nothing but gun practice.

About 5 p.m. we took up our line of march, but scarcely marched a mile before the order was countermanded, and we returned to camp, stacked arms and awaited orders, which soon came to the effect that we must march immediately to reinforce our troops at Richmond. A small guard being left with the baggage, knapsacks were thrown off, and the 73rd filed through town, out on the Richmond pike with every man in the ranks that was able to go.

We marched all night, meeting long trains, of government wagons, and scores of stragglers who positively affirmed that their companies and Regiments were all cut to pieces. The 73rd boys greeted them with sneers for their cowardice and marched straight ahead. There was every prospect for a fight, and although the regiment is almost entirely ignorant of battalion drill, and very poorly equipped, I do not think one man fell out on the night's march.

The column halted for rest one mile this side of the Kentucky river and remained a few hours, when the order came to counter march on Lexington. Our regiment had retreated about 2 miles when an aide rode up with the information that our rear guard consisting of the 94th Ohio was engaged with the advance guard of the enemy. The gallant 73rd, tired, hungry and thirsty, as they were, fell gaily into line, loaded, fixed bayonets and waited an hour for the rebels to make their appearance, but they prudently refrained from making any further attack and we were left to retreat to Lexington at our leisure, which we did the same day.

Next day hearing that the rebels were advancing in force on the camp Dick Robinson road, our Regiment, the 93rd and 105th Ohio were ordered out to meet them, but the order was countermanded in half an hour and we marched back remaining under arms till dusk, when orders were issued to burn all baggage and retreat to Louisville.

Fortunately the order came to us in a garbled form, with the "burning clause" left out and we saved most of our baggage. The Ohio regiments lost everything.

There was much grumbling when we marched out of Lexington that night, our troops though raw and undisciplined were ready and more than willing to fight. We were leaving our sick behind (among them James Finley, who but a few weeks since left the Register Office to join our ranks).

We were well nigh worn out with our previous forced marches, and the prospect before us of another long 50 miles of *retreat* was disheartening, but orders must be obeyed, and on we went all that night and next day reaching Frankfort about 9 o'clock, p.m., forced into column of companies and laid on our arms till 3 a.m.

Received orders about midnight to cook three days' rations which we did not do from the fact that there was none to cook.

We marched next day with nothing to eat and scarcely anything to drink, for this whole country appears to have "dried up"- water commanding good prices according to grade.

But I've no heart to enter into the minute details of our march. I must give you one instance, however, which shows the *spirit* of our men, and their readiness at all times to perform the work for which they volunteered, that is to *fight*. -

When within one half a mile of Shelbyville a very pretty little town - and full of Union people - God bless them, it was apparent that our troops were so completely worn out, hungry and thirsty, that it would be impossible to get them through the town, and I have no doubt that they would have stopped *en masse,* in spite of the officers and demanded food, drink, and rest, before proceeding further, if the comm.-anding General or someone else had not passed word along the lines that the rebels were in force on the other side of town and determined to cut off our retreat; the news seemed to give new life to the men and our whole Regiment passed on the "double quick" through Shelbyville without leaving a man behind.

We found no enemy on the other side, and the boys digested the joke spiced with some pretty hard words, on empty stomachs.

We arrived at Camp Buell minus 65 men, most of the

missing are taken prisoners. We have moved camps three different times since our arrival, and orders have just been issued to our division (commanded by Brig. Gen. Jackson) to prepare 5 days rations, and pack the wagons, and throw away superfluous baggage and be ready to march tomorrow morning - where to - no one under the General commanding knows.

The health of the Regiment considering the fatigue which we have undergone, is remarkably good, not a man in the hospital, not one has yet died under the Surgeon's care, and very few that are excused from duty. We number 951 men present in camp. We have miserable muskets but *good bayonets.* The 73rd will win for itself a name with nothing but cold steel if need be.

A. B. Wade P.S. Letters should be directed: 73rd Ind. Vols.,1st Brigade.1st Division, Army of Ky.

August 27 1862 Indianapolis Indiana (later Wednesday)
Left South Bend Aug 25th to join my Regt. (the 73rd Indiana Volunteers) having received notice of my appointment as Adjutant. I understand that the 73rd is at Louisville Ky but can learn nothing definite in regard to its location. The 87th Ind. now in camp at South Bend will leave for Indianapolis today or tomorrow.

We are raining Regiments on the South - Received my commission as Adjutant and was immediately mustered into the United States service for three years or the war this a.m. Saw 1500 secesh prisoners start south today, arrangements having been made for an exchange. They were a hard looking lot clothed in butternut and jeans.

Have purchased sword and equipment and shall start south this evening.

The 88th Regt. Indiana Volunteers from Fort Wayne came in this morning. Indianapolis is not so lively as usual with military. They are sending them south where they are needed.

Aug. 28 1862 Louisville Ky. (Thursday) Arrived here over Indianapolis and Jeffersonville R.R. early this morning and have put up at the National. Took stroll of half an hour before breakfast to view the city. Louisville is a substantial built snug little city and should judge that a great deal of business was or is transacted here.

After breakfast went to Hd. Qtrs. Major Granger Commander of the post but could not ascertain the location of my Regt. Took a weary tramp out to the suburbs of the city but could only find the 73rd Illinois and 3 companies of the 17th Ind.

Went back called at Genl. Boyles Hd Qtrs. who commands forces in Ky. and consulted list of Regts. Found that the 73rd Ind were in camp at Lexington. Obtained transportation, pass and will start at 4 0' clock this p.m. Shall have to lay over however at Frankfort as none but the accommodation train goes out today but do not object as shall have till 9 a.m. tomorrow to see the Capitol of Ky.

Aug. 29th 1862 Frankfort Ky (Friday) Came in last night and in company with a 1st Lieut. of the 11th Ky Cavalry. Ordered a good supper. The legislature is in session and "members" from all parts of the state loyal and disloyal are laying around loose. Frankfort is a medium sized town beautifully situated away from the hills and on the banks of the Kentucky river. I've taken quite a fancy to it.

Aug. 29th 1862 Lexington Ky. (later Friday) Arrived here about 11 o'clock a.m. and having heard that the Regt. had moved to Richmond was going to take stage immediately for that place when fortunately just after getting off the cars I espied the familiar face of Quarter Master E. Bacon and upon hailing him received the information that our Regt. was stationed about one mile south of town.

Lexington is a busy place now. Government wagons, cannon and stores scattered in all directions. Understand that there are quite a number of Regiments here.

Aug. 30 1862 Head Quarters 73rd Indiana Vols. Camp Lexington Ky. (Saturday) Came out to camp yesterday afternoon and found everything hurry, bustle and confusion having received orders to march to Camp Dick Robinson starting at 2 a.m. tomorrow.

I went on duty at 9 a.m. this morning and superintended Guard Mounting for the first time. The Regiment is not well organized yet - scarcely any of the officers understanding their duty. Our men however are in the best of spirits and sanguine of success in whatever they undertake.

We are camped upon the farm of a voted secessionest but his family, negroes and property are well guarded by our troops. The lady of the house, Ms. Strong, in her attachment to the rebel cause shows many a little kindness to the "Field and staff." She says that Metcalfs cavalry encamped here a short time since and showed the ruffian character to such an extent that it was pleasant to contrast that Regt. with the gentlemanly 73rd.

August 30 Head Quarters 73rd Ind. Vol. Infantry Camp Lexington Ky (Later Saturday) Time of starting for Camp Dick Robinson was changed to 4 p.m. today - upon hearing which I immediately bestirred myself to procure a horse and have finally made arrangements with the Qr. Ms. to furnish me one temporarily.

Breaking up camp was a busy affair, tents were struck and baggage packed in short order and the train was soon on its way preceded by the 93rd and 105th Ohio Regiments and followed by the 73rd. We had marched about half a mile when the order was countermanded and returning to camp we stacked arms and impatiently awaited orders which have come at last to the effect that we must make a forced march tonight to reinforce our troops at Richmond who are contending against an overwhelming force of the enemy. We heard heavy firing this morning in that direction but supposed it to be only artillery practice.

Aug. 31st 1862 On March (Sunday) I detailed a guard of twenty men under command of Lieut. Wolf, Co. F. to remain with our baggage at Camp Lexington and about dusk last evening the 73rd minus knapsacks filed through town and on the Richmond pike with every man in the ranks that was able to go.

We have marched all night through clouds of dust. Meeting long trains of government wagons and scores of stragglers who positively affirmed that their companies and Regts. were all cut to pieces. The 73rd boys greeted them with sneers for their cowardice and marched straight ahead.

There was a prospect of a fight and I don't believe we lost a man on that night's march. We have stopped to rest about one mile from the Ky river and several of our boys are out on the scout to find if the enemy are near. It is a beautiful country here and tis a pity two opposing armies are grinding it under.

Aug. 31st 1862 Camp Lexington Ky (Later Sunday) Our Brigade consisting of the 52nd, 93rd and 105th Ohio and the 73rd Indiana under command of Col. Anderson of the 73rd remained a few hours at our resting place near the river where hearing that our forces were badly beaten at Richmond and were already up to us on retreat an order to countermarch was given and off we started. The 73rd at the head of the Brigade.

We had marched about two miles when an aide rode up from the rear with the information that the rebel advance guard had attacked our rear guard consisting of the 94th Ohio. The 73rd fell into line of battle with a will, loaded, fixed bayonets and waited an hour for the enemy to make their appearance, but they prudently refrained from making an attack and we were left to fall back on Lexington at our leisure which we did the same evening through a pelting rain storm.

Sept. 1st 1862 On March (Monday) Were ordered out today from Camp Lexington to meet the enemy who were reported to be advancing in force and but six miles from town. Order was countermanded before marching half a mile. We returned to camp and about dusk orders were issued to the different Regts. to burn all their baggage and retreat to Louisville. Fortunately the order reached us in a garbled form and we saved most of our baggage. Marched all night.

Sept. 2nd 1862 Camp 3 miles from Frankfort (Tuesday) Marched all day with scarcely anything to eat. The boys straggle very much and it is almost impossible to keep them in ranks. I am so tired and worn out myself that I don't feel like writing items concerning the march. This whole country appears to have suddenly "dried up" and water commands good prices according to grade. We have a poor camp but the boys are glad enough to get a little rest.

Sept. 3rd 1862 On March. (Wednesday) Were ordered out of camp last night about dusk and took up line of march for Frankfort where we arrive about 8 o'clock and went into camp a description of which I cannot give as I've never seen it. Half a doz Regts appeared to be in the same field and filing in we formed column of companies and the men completely tired out fell down on the ground and went to sleep too tired even to wait for something to eat even when half starved.

At midnight orders came to cook three days rations which we did not do. At 3 a.m. we left the capitol of Kentucky and much as we wished <u>not</u> to were forced to continue our cowardly, or rather disgraceful, retreat for we are no cowards and would prove it if the absurd fear of our commanding Generals did not prompt them to urge us forward. At this rate am afraid we will not take 700 men into Louisville.

Sept. 5th 1862 Head Quarters 73rd Reg. I. V.I.. Camp Buell, Ky. (Friday) I have no heart to enter into details of our march from Frankfort to this place. Indeed I was so tired, worn out, distressed and discouraged at the way in which Gen. Jackson treated our Regt. that I did not take any "way-side notes" and events crowd so thick and fast upon each other that I have forgotten many interesting facts in connect-ion with that long weary retreat.

One little circumstance occurs to my mind just now, however, which I must place on record to show that physical suffering had not entirely quenched the spirit of our men, that they are always ready and willing to do the work for which they volunteered. That is to fight.

When within half a mile of Shelbyville a pretty little town and full of good Union people (God bless them) word was passed along the lines that the rebels were in force on the other side of town with the intention of cutting off our retreat. It was simply a piece of strategy on the part of our commanders to get the men through town and it succeeded admirably, hardly a man straggled from the ranks.

If they had not been urged on by the hope of an eng-agement I've no doubt but that they would have fell out by hundreds in spite of the officers and demanded food, drink and rest before proceeding further.

We arrived here and camped in the woods six miles from Louisville at 9 a.m. today. It is a very poor camp and is supposed at these head quarters to be named Buell. The men however are only too glad to get a little rest.

Sept 6th 1862 Camp Buell. (Saturday) Nothing exciting today except falling into line upon a false alarm. Wm. S.

Bartlett from So. Bend paid us a visit today and brought my first letter from home, a perfect Godsend. Water is very poor. The weather delightful. Only order of the day that we have is Reveille at 3 a.m.

Sept. 7th 1862 Head Quarters 73rd Regt. I.V.I. Camp Buell Ky. (Sunday) This is Sunday and yet very unlike our Sabbaths up in Indiana. The same dull routine of military life goes on. Not much routine about it however for the whole Brigade appears to be in extricable confusion. I have an immense amount of business to do but matters are in such a confused state that I cannot make a commencement. Went over to the camp of the 87th Indiana today and had a chat with uncle Shyrock the Col.

Sept. 8th 1862 Louisville Ky. (Monday) Came to the city today in company with the Major and Quarter Master and bought outfit for my mess consisting of Sergt. Major and self. I understand that we have 20,000 troops in and around the city. If so, I hope for God's sake that they will make a stand here and attempt at least to check the rebel advance.

Sept. 9th 1862 Head Quarters 73rd Regiment I.V.I. 1st Brigade 1st Division Army of Ky Camp Buell Ky. (Tuesday) Removed camp today one mile and still I am informed officially that it is Camp Buell. It is a beautiful camping ground. The only objection being the water which is scarce and of poor quality.

Our Brigade consists of the 73rd I.V.!., the 93rd, 94th, and 98th O.V.I. Regts commanded by Brig. Gen. Ward. The Division, as near as I can ascertain, consists of Ward's Brigade, Terrell's Brigade and 2,500 cavalry under the command of Brig. Genl. Jackson.

Sept. 10 1862 Camp Buell Ky Hd Qtrs I.V.I. (Wednesday) We still remain in camp which is wonderful. Reveille is altered to 4 a.m. The Regt. remains under arms till daylight and then Battalion drill till 7 o'clock which is very hard on the men.

Slight rain today. Wrote several letters home. Camp life is somewhat different from a comfortable home.

Sept. 14 1862 Head Quarters 73rd Regt. I. V.I. Camp Buell Ky. (Sunday) Nothing happened since the tenth worth noting, delivered up our arms on the 12th and hope to get better ones.

Orders came yesterday from Gen. Gilbert to prepare to march at a moment's notice, suppose it is only to construct our lines. The 73rd is ready and waiting.

Later. Went into camp about 2 miles from town, miserable camp, and I had a miserable time in laying it out as half a doz different orders were issued in regard to it.

Sept. 16th 1862 Camp Buell. (Tuesday) Superior officers insist that this is still Camp Buell and suppose it must be so. It would be an exception to the rule to allow us to remain in camp three days at a time so last night we received order to move this a.m. at 5 o'clock with two days rations cooked and in haversacks and four days rations in the wagons.

Everybody supposed that a long march was at hand and made preparations accordingly, but no the Division was only marched into the city, drew up in line on Broadway, stood there for two hours, were reviewed and tonight we are in our old camp.

Sept 18 1862 Head Qtrs. 73rd Regt I. V.I. Camp Wilder Ky. (Thursday) Recd. orders last night to march at 5 a.m. today with two days cooked rations. Had a hard blow during the night. The Col.'s tent "going under" and several of the company tents.

The Brigade moved this morning about 6 o'clock. The

73rd in the rear, went into camp ½ mile from the city, pitched tents and commenced fortifying. Our Regt. is on the left wing and is already well protected by a trench and embankment, the work of a detail of 250 men from our own Regt. instead of employing the contrabands.

Sept. 19th, 1862 Head Qtrs. 73rd Reg. IV.I Camp Wilder Ky. (Friday) I have it officially from A. A. Genl. R.J. Wagg-ener that our present encampment is as above but place no dependence upon a name. Our trench looks well today and an assaulting party would be considerably reduced in numb-er before taking it.

By the way I forgot to mention before that the Regt. is supplied with guns but of poor quality. There is great dissat-isfaction among the boys in regard to it.

Gen McClellan has been whipping the rebels finely in the east and I hope we'll soon commence operations in the west.

I have two clerks at present and plenty of work for them. It is surprising how little a person in the army knows of the movements of the army at home. Our friends at home know fully as much if not more of the movements and dispo-sition of our troops as we do.

Sept. 20th, 1862 - Head Quarters 73rd Regt IV. I. Camp Wilder Ky. (Saturday) Formed the Regt. in line of battle at 4 a.m. as per order of the day. Before dismissing orders came to be ready to march at 10 A.M. with one days cooked rat-ions and but 3 tents to a Regt.

We packed up and fell into line ready to march. Wait-ed for orders till after 3 P.M. when they came to the effect that we must up tents and go into camp. We are continually receiving such orders and the consequence is that the Regt. is in a sad state of disorder.

Sept. 22 1862 - Head Quarters 73rd Regt. IV.I. Camp Wilder Ky. (Monday) Yesterday passed off quietly. today everybody is in a state of excitement both in city and camp caused by an order from Maj. Gen. Nelson to the effect that the women and children should prepare to leave Louisville.

Bragg is undoubtedly moving upon us with from 30 to 50,000 well drilled troops. We have here a force probably amounting to 50,000 men perhaps 75 thousand but a great majority of them are the new levies and so far as drill is concerned almost wholly unfit for service. They are brave however, have the advantage on entrenchment and if Bragg is determined upon taking this city there will be a terrible battle.

Since Nelson's order the 73rd have been busy night and day with pick and shovel. We have completed the trenches which will afford the men good protection. The first is directly in front of our encampment, the second from 100 to two hundred yards in advance and runs through the Louisville cemetery a beautiful burial ground and full of costly monuments and beautiful trees which its a pity to cut down and destroy. But it is a necessity and the sleeping place of Kentucky's dead is not thought too sacred a place in which to save the living.

The weather is very warm and a good rain would be welcomed. Water has to be hauled to camp from the city.

The 98th Ohio Regt. was not allowed to slip out as we don't like the Ohio troops any too well.

Sept. 23 1862 - Head Quarters 73rd Regt Indiana V.I. Camp Wilder Ky. (Tuesday) The excitement of yesterday has pretty well cooled down, but active preparations for defense are still going on.

For several days our officers have viewed with some apprehension a hill about 1/3 of a mile in our front. It is thickly wooded and would in case our advance Regts were driven back upon us afford the enemy a fine place for masked batteries. I believe an order has been issued to have it cleared of trees. Terrills Brigade (in our div.) is on our left and has planted a Battery which commands this hill. To-day they fired three shells as experimental shots to obtain the range.

This a.m. I made a detail from our Regt. to cut down all intervening trees and they are now hard at work with the axes.

I understand the 87th Ind. is a short distance to our left. Feel considerable interest in the Regt. as Cil Shryock is my uncle and the Adjutant a distant relation. Cannot learn what Regts are here nor how many.

Gen Nelson commands the army and has issued a short and stirring address to the officers and men. Matters appear to be approaching a crisis and in the words of the army correspondent, "a battle is imminent."

Sept. 24th 1862 - Hd. Quarters 73rd Regt I V.I. (Wednesday) The whole Regt was ordered out on picket duty about 4 P.M. last night. March out and were stationed about a mile and a half from camp, with about a mile front.

I rode half a mile in advance of the picket but saw no signs of the enemy. Slept on the ground with Col. Bailey. and contrary to general expectations were not disturbed by the enemy.

Had a good warm breakfast at a farm house and came into camp early this A.M. to make my morning report.

Rode off to the left and called upon Col Shryock of the 87th.

Gov. Morton called at Head Quarters this A.M. to ascertain the wants of the Indiana troops.

Terrill's batteries have been practicing today and the explosions of shells have become a familiar sound.

Sept. 25th 1862 - Head Quarters 73rd Regt. I.V.I. Camp Wilder Ky. (Thursday) The Regt. was ordered into the trenches this morning at three o'clock. Loaded guns and remained till daylight. Did not expect the enemy but it is well enough to be prepared.

Buell (Maj. Gen.) arrived last night. His veteran army will be here today, and many a heart beats lighter here today.

Bragg has turned off eastward in the direction of Frankfort and Lexington. I believe we will be ordered in pursuit soon.

Our position in the trench last night was a peculiar one. It runs through the Louisville Cemetery part of which is now used as a soldiers burial ground and we were directly in front of hundreds of new made graves of fellow soldiers who have laid down their lives for freedoms sake. And as I looked at the long dark line of motionless figures with the bayonets glistening in the twilight I fancied that we were there to protect the "last sleeping place" from the invaders tread.

Louisville is at last pronounced <u>safe</u> and well it may be, for an army of over one hundred thousand protects. I'm only afraid that we shall not catch Bragg.

Sept. 27th 1862 Head Quarters 73rd Regt. IV.I. Camp Wilder Ky. (Saturday) The Regt. went on picket duty at daylight yesterday morning. As the Adjutant has no particular duty while on picket I concluded to turn about for one day and ascertain if possible how near the enemy we were and whether or not Louisville was safe.

Started about sunrise and rode rapidly forward for about 3 miles and then thinking that perhaps prudence was the better part of valor, I reined down to a walk keeping a sharp lookout for the Rebels. Rode on in this manner until I was eight miles from our lines and yet saw no signs of an enemy. Feeling satisfied that we would not be attacked today at least, I turned my horse's head Louisville wards and came in on the gallop reaching our lines at one o'clock p.m.

Came back to camp about 3 p.m. and found Major Fowler of the 15th who took supper with us. Buell's army of sixty thousand is in at last. The 29th and 9th Indiana are in it. Spent the night with the Regt.

FIELD STAFF & LINE OFFICERS
73rd REGT. INDIANA VOLS.

Name - Rank - Date of Commission

Gilbert Hathaway, Colonel, August 21st, 1862
Oliver H. P. Bailey, Lieut. Col., August 21st, 1862
William Krimbill, Major, August 21st, 1`862
Alfred B. Wade, Adjutant, August 27th, 1862
Robert Spencer, Surgeon, August 21st, 1862
Edward Bacon, Quarter master, August 21st, 1862

NON COMMISSIONED STAFF

John W. Munday, Sergt. Major;
James C. Woodrow, Ord. Sergt.
Charles Zutavern, Qr. Mr. Sergt.
James Spencer, Hospital Steward
Charles Kimball, Com. Sergt.
James Wigmore, Ward Master

COMPANY CAPTAINS

A Richard W. Price
B George C. Gladwyn
C Charles W. Price
D William M. Kendall
E Hiram Green
F Miles H. Tibbetts
G William L. McConnell
H Peter Doyle
I Rollin M. Pratt
K Ivan N. Walker

FIRST LIEUTS.

A Phillip Reed
B Theodoric F. C. Dodd
C John Richley
D John M. Beeber
E Garrett G. Seeger
F Samuel Wolf
G Joseph A. Westlake
H David H. Mull
I Robert W. Graham
K Ithamer D. Phelps

SECOND LIEUTS.

A Alfred Fry
B Joseph Hagenbuck
C John G. Greenawalt
D William T. Grimes
E Henry H. Tillotson
F Matthew Boyd
G Robert J. Connelly
H Andrew M. Callahan
I Emanuel M. Williamson
K John Butterfield

Sept. 28th 1862 Head Quarters 73rd IV.I. Camp Wilder Ky. (Sunday) The dull volume of camp life still goes on, not even a rumor (generally flying so thick and fast) to disturb our quiet.

The boys from the 29th, 15th and 9th have been calling up us yesterday and today quite extensively.

Bragg has not yet made his appearance and I opine will not if we want a fight. We must march out to meet or pursue him and what we are waiting here with an hundred and twenty five thousand fighting men behind the trenches for is a wonder to me.

Gen. Ward refused to permit myself, Capt. McConnell and one or two others to go out on a scouting tour today and are therefore left in glorious uncertainty in regard to the movements of the enemy. I find the office of Adjutant no sinecure. Am worked nearly to death and have to keep a hundred different things in my head at once. Have secured the services of Job Barnard Co K as clerk which relieves me of a good deal of the writing.

Weather pleasant but warm.

September 29th 1862 Head Quarters 73rd Regt. Ind. V.I. In camp near Louisville Kentucky. (Monday) By order of Major Genl.Buell we have been transferred from Ward's Brigade to the 20th Brigade 6th Division Army of the Ohio commanded by Brig. Genl. Wood of Indiana. The officers and men are well pleased with the change for Gen. Jackson (a Kentuckian) was very unpopular.

Our Brigade consists of the 64th and 65th Ohio, the 51st and 73rd Indiana, the 13th Michigan and the 6th Ohio Battery.

We left Camp Wilder and the trenches last night and joined our Brigade in camp just south of Louisville. The Division is under marching orders and will probably leave with the rest of the army tomorrow. The officer's baggage has been cut down very much. We are allowed but one wagon for Head Quarters and all the company officers. I shall have to leave some of my things behind.

The weather is just right for marching and the army is in the best of spirits in anticipation of a speedy pursuit and possible capture of the enemy.

Oct. 1st 1862 Head Quarters 73rd In the Field 8 miles from Louisville. (Wednesday) As per orders we were ready to move at 6 o'clock this morning. After tedious delay of four hours, the natural consequences of moving such a large body of troops, we left Louisville on the Bardstown Pike.

Passed our old camp which looked gloomy and deserted and made eight miles, going into camp after dark with Regiments, Brigades and Divisions on every side of us.

Major Krimbill and Capt. Price of Co. C were left behind on the sick list. Lieut. Connolly Co G was also left for what reason have been unable to ascertain.

Have heard and suppose the figures to be nearly correct that 130,000 troops have left Louisville on different roads in pursuit of Bragg. His fate and the fate of his army is sealed unless he makes double quick time out of Kentucky.

This has been a beautiful day for marching. Hope we shall be favored with as pleasant weather during the entire campaign. The 73rd lost none in stragglers.

Oct. 2nd 1862 Head Quarters 73rd In the field.(Thursday) Reveille this morning at 4 a.m. and breakfast as soon after as it can be prepared at daylight. We got some idea of the thousands and tens of thousands of men who are scattered over the fields in seeming disorder and confusion and yet everything goes on like clockwork with the exception (of) starting - we were ready at daybreak - but so many troops in our rear were marching to the front that the 6th division was unable to move till nearly noon. Marched six or eight miles to Salt River and have gone into camp.

The bridge was burnt by Gen. Jackson at the time of the rebel advance and we shall have to ford the stream. It will not be difficult however as the water is shallow.

Cannonading was heard frequently today. Skirmishing in front. We had a skirmish with the enemy at Fern Creek today, lost one man. Signs of rain. No tents and we will pass a miserable night, rained this afternoon.

Oct. 3rd 1862 On March. (Friday) Rained some last night but passed the night very comfortably with Col. Hathaway under a big tree. Left camp about 7 a.m. Forded Salt River twice. Both bridges being burned. We are now waiting orders from the front. Crittenden's Div. is in line of battle in advance of us. The rebels reported to be in force two miles from here.

Later. The enemy amused themselves for a short time by throwing shells at us from a mountain howitzer and then skedaddled.

We have gone into camp for the night. Hundreds of camp fires on every hill. Beautiful and romantic. Our Division is composed of the 15th, 20th, and 21st Brigades. Col. Harker commands the 20th, Col. Wagner the 21st and I believe Gen. Hascall the 15th. I should judge that we had 10,000 men in the Div. The 15th Ind. is with us, the 29th, 9th and about 30 other Indiana Regts are in the army. The army men and officers are anxious for a fight and the probabilities are much in favor of one taking place before long.

October 4th 1862. (Saturday) Left camp at 6 a.m. No signs of the rebels until we came in sight of Fairfield, a round about way which the 6th Division had taken in order to bag a force of rebel cavalry reported to be in camp at the fairground near Bardstown. 25 of their cavalry were on the march at Fairfield and scattered as soon as we came in sight.

Our advance guard of cavalry came upon the enemy about two miles from B and a severe skirmish ensued resulting in the capture of 40 of our men. Gen. Hascall reports it to be a disgraceful affair on our part.

Arrived at B late in the evening but the rebels had gone leaving quite a number of sick in the hospital and a few stragglers.

Bardstown is a medium sized country town and of not very prepossessing appearance. The rebels had (taken) nearly everything of value from the merchants giving in return their worthless confederate "promises to pay" a large quantity of which is in circulation among the soldiers.

Oct 5th 1862 - Head quarters 73rd Inda. Vols Beach Fork Camp. (Sunday) Left Bardstown at noon or thereabouts and have traveled over a very rough road in the direction of Harrodsburg. Our Regt. captured seven of Bragg's soldiers who had straggled behind. They all give themselves up willingly and expressed the wish to be paroled. Went into camp about 10 P.M.

Oct 6th 1862 - Springfield Ky. (Monday) Start from camp at Beach Fork at an early hour and have made a rapid march of 12 miles in the hot sun. Very wearisome to the boys numbers of whom had to fall behind.

We passed a mill yet smoking which the rebels had burnt together with what provisions they could not carry away.

It is reported that the 87th Indiana had a skirmish with the rebels at this place killing two of them and scattering the balance.

We are camped in the fair ground. A pretty place nicely fitted up. A peculiarity of all Kentucky towns I notice.

Oct. 8th 1862 Head Quarters 73rd Inda. In Camp. (Wednesday) Left Springfield about 11 a.m. yesterday, marched till 4 p.m., laid by and rested a short time, resuming our march through the night, reached this camp at daybreak. Had to march four miles out of our way to get water of which there is abundance here.

Saw one dead union soldier yesterday killed by the rebel cavalry.

The road which we have traveled lately is rocky approaching to mountainous making our march very tedious.

Oct. 8th 1862 4 p.m. On March (Still Wednesday) Stopped in camp till nearly noon killing beef etc. when a message was received from Maj. Gen. Buell to hurry up this Division as the rebels had made a stand at Perrysville and a fight was going on. We left camp and arrived here a short time ago.

Heavy cannonading is going on in the front. Gen. Buell and staff are on our left upon the summit of a high hill. The different Brigades are getting into line.

Oct 9th Daybreak - In line of Battle. (Thursday) Our Brigade first formed line of Battle about 5 o'clock yesterday afternoon at a distance from Perrysville of about two miles.

Very heavy cannonading on our left front and right after forming line. Companies were deployed to the front as skirmishers and we moved forward tearing down fences which delayed us considerable causing frequent halts to dress the line.

Advanced about one mile through trees and cornfield when darkness coming on we came to a halt. Meanwhile the firing on our left increased and as night set in we could plainly see the bright flashes from the batteries of what we supposed to be Mitchells Div. All firing ceased soon after and the men were ordered to lie down in ranks and rest themselves as best they could. No fires to be built.

Rested on arms 'till daylight and are now waiting orders. Firing has not been resumed and suppose the enemy have retired after the most approved southern fashion.

Oct 9th 1862 7 A.M. - Before Perrysville. (LaterThursday) Were ordered forward and have advanced some distance The 51st Ind. is one hundred yards in front of us with skirmishers out. Our batteries have been throwing a few shells to feel the position of the enemy but no response is made. The Boys are hungry but cheerful and are suffering some for water. Its a beautiful day. The Sixth Ohio Battery have just planted a Parrot gun 200 yards in advance of us and the 20th Brigade will soon send her compliments in the shape of a shell.

Oct. 9th 1862, 4 P.M. - Head Qrs. 73rd Ind. Cave Springs near Perrysville. (Still Later Thursday) The Battle of Perryville or Chaplin Hills is over, and nothing to show for it but a ghastly record of thousands killed and wounded.

It was nothing but a drawn fight ended by darkness. The rebels withdrew their forces this morning and are on full retreat.

About 11 or 12 o'clock we found the rebels had skedaddled and march through Perryville. Nearly every house was riddled by cannonballs. I picked up several of the "iron messengers of death." Ugly looking customers which I should "hate to meet" at any time or place. Have go into camp at the Cave Springs just beyond Perryville.

Oct. 10th 1862 - On March. (Friday) I rode over the Battlefield early this morning. That Battlefield which in the history of this great rebellion will rank as one of the bloodiest fought by raw troops for I understand that a great majority of the troops had never been under fire before.

The fight took place on the eighth and yet today I saw twenty four ghastly mangled bodies of rebels still unburied.

Twenty six of their wounded were still on the field attended by our surgeons. Two thousand small arms had been collected besides a great number carried off by soldiers and citizens.

The rebel army in the action was composed of the following divisions. Major Genl. Hardee commanded two Divisions on the left wing. Cheatham, Buckner and Anderson, each one Division. Major Genl. Polk commanding the whole force assisted by Braxton Bragg himself who declined the command however and simply made a "few suggestions" as per his report.

I have been unable to ascertain the number of our troops engaged but Rousseau's Division figured more conspicuously and shows the heaviest loss of any other.

That it was a terrible piece of mismanagement on our [part] is admitted on all hands. Maj. Genl. Buell is blamed for it now and will be blamed for it in the future. If he had pushed us forward on the afternoon of the eighth there is no doubt but that we could have utterly defeated Bragg and in all probability have captured his entire army.

Oct. 10th 1862 10 O'clock A.M. - In line of Battle. (Later Friday) Left camp at Cave Springs about 7 A.M. marched a mile or two, halted, formed line of battle. Sent forward skirmishers. Came by the right of companies to the front and have been marching for an hour or two in this manner. Have wheeled the companies into line and now rest before the prospective battle field of ---------Blank Danville [sic]. Heavy firing on our left at a distance of two or three miles. Later firing ceased went into camp. Signs of rain.

Oct. 11th 8 o'clock a.m. In line of Battle. (Saturday) Slept very comfortable last night in spite of the rain. This morning we received a large mail and I was fortunate enough to get six letters from various friends. I had just finished reading them when a rebel shell came whizzing through Head Quarters about 10 feet over my head. Immediately the camp was in the utmost confusion and with cannonading increasing it was the general belief that an attack was made on our camp but soon order was restored and all the Regts. were ordered forward 200 paces where we remain awaiting orders. The firing has ceased and no enemy in sight.

Oct. 11th 1862 Harrodsburg Ky. (later Saturday) Col. Harker's Brigade was ordered out about 9 0' clock to make a flank movement on Harrodsburg. We left the other Brigades in line of Battle and started through the woods and across the fields over hill and dale. With a line of skirmishers in advance we had a parrot gun in position once or twice but did not fire although once within half a mile of a squad of rebel cavalry. Approached Harrodsburg very cautiously with a strong line of skirmishers out till we were signaled by the waving of flags and white handkerchiefs. We immediately took possession of the town capturing a number of stragglers and all their sick in the hospitals. Have camped in the old rebel camp ground.

Oct. 12th 1862 In Camp. (Sunday) We found our camp full of rebel spies last night and fearing that the rebels would attack us and shell us out silently moved camp to a distance of one mile leaving our camp fires burning to deceive the enemy. It was quite dark and upon reaching the spot selected as a camp ground the order was given to (go) right into line which was executed by the centre on double quick.

This created great confusion and just then a couple of horsemen galloped through the line of company F causing one company (file) to break and run in order to avoid the horses. This caused company A, H, and I to break and run also.

I was in the extreme rear of the Regt. Lieut. Col. Bailey was opposite to Co A with Dr. Brenton. Ward Master Wigmore just in advance of myself. The order had been given not to speak a loud word.

The men all had their guns at a right shoulder shift and in the stampede they naturally clashed together like sabers striking right and left. This together with the half a dozen horsemen coming down on full speed led me to believe that it was a cavalry charge. My horse took fright and ran about 40 yards before I could check him. By this time the men were 100 yards or more in the rear, most of them on the run. I immediately called halt and rally. The first word spoken by any person during the skedaddle. The men immediately stopped and drawing my revolver I threatened to shoot the first man that ran. With some difficulty I got about two companies into line and ordered them to cap guns not doubting but that we should be attacked in a few moments.

Capt. Doyle was the only officer with me. I ordered him to take command of half the men present. Col. Hathaway then rode up and ordered me to bring the men up to the Regt. I was extremely chagrined that I had mistaken a temporary panic for a cavalry charge but do not think I was to blame for I could not see how nearly four companies should break and run in the manner for nothing. I do not think that the simple running proved the men to be cowards It was a dark night and the orders received had put the men in a good condition to be panic stricken at any unusual occurrence. I brought them up into line and are ordered to sleep on arms.

Oct. 13th 1862 In Camp. (Monday) Made a forward movement today in the direction of Camp Dick Robinson. Came in sight of the rebel wagon train and fired a few shells at them which brought the train and its guard to a halt.

We took position about two miles from them and awaited an attack as our Brigade was not strong enough to be the attacking party. None being made we withdrew about dusk and joined our Division.

Our Brigade since starting off for itself has captured a large number of prisoners, probably two hundred. The 73rd numbers now about 700 effective men and 30 commissioned officers present. We are in sight of Danville, a big battle is anticipated in a day or two. Weather for the past few days has been cool.

Oct. 14th 1862 - Noon - On March. (Tuesday) Our Regt. went on picket at a late hour last night. We were called in about 2 a.m. and commenced march. Passed though Danville before daybreak.

When within a mile of Stanford our advance discovered about 2500 rebel cavalry. We opened on them and kept up a slow fire two or three hours, killing a number, among them one Lieut. Col. who was left on the field. Have stopped for dinner. The rebels have retreated.

Evening. Moved about two miles and have camped. The soldiers always use fence rails for fuel and when we have a camp we leave no vestige of fences that were. This is a tolerable good camp.

Oct. 15th 1862 - In Camp. (Wednesday) Left Stanford camp at an early hour and reach Crab Orchard about noon - a forlorn looking place of a few hundred inhabitants. Moved slowly this p.m. and camped about 8 o'clock - cold and dreary, high hills around us - forage scarce.

Oct. 16th 1862 In Camp Rockcastle Co Ky. (Thursday) Started at 8 this a.m. and proceeding about one mile came to a halt on the hillside, remained there all day and were then ordered back into our old camp.

A General Court Martial has been sitting at our Head Quarters today.

Oct. 18th 1862 - On March. (Saturday) Laid in camp all day yesterday. Took up line of march this morn.and made 10 miles over a very rough country. Have fairly entered the mountains of Ky.

We were halted on the mountain side for about two hours and then ordered back half a mile where we've gone into camp. Don't know what these movements mean. This is a good camp but we are crowded. Bought a ten dollar confederate note for 25 cents.

Oct. 21st 1862 - In Camp Rockcastle County Ky. (Tuesday) Have been encamped here 3 days awaiting orders. We have christened it Camp Misereicordia. Don't know the object of waiting here unless it is to allow Bragg to make his escape.

Our provisions gave out entirely yesterday. When coming up this mountain road we were frequently stopped by obstructions placed in the road. Trees cut down in places where we could not "go around" which delayed us considerable.

Bragg by this time is undoubtedly safe out of Kentucky. The blame of this miserable campaign will rest where it belongs upon Maj. Gent. Buell. It is reported that Ohio and Indiana have gone democratic if so matters look gloomy indeed.

This is a great country for walnuts, butternuts, chestnuts, etc. The soldiers relish them. Orders came tonight to take the back trace. We are not sorry for a move in any direction. Will be a relief. I've never passed thru more tedious miserable days than I have here. It is generally understood that we go back to prepare for a winter campaign.

Oct 23rd 1862 - In Camp. (Thursday) Made 25 miles yesterday, tho twas a hard day to march, very windy and dusty.

Marched the same distance today passing through Stanford and Huestonville. Stopped at Stanford to get my horse shod. The whole Div. passed meanwhile. its a long train. Wood's Div. is going to Columbia. The country is much better than in Rockcastle Co. Weather cool.

Oct. 24th 1862 - In Camp. (Friday) Made a hard march of 25 miles today. 300 of our Regt. straggled behind and have not come up yet. We have but 413 men in camps. Passed though Liberty, a small town.

Oct. 26th 1862 - Camp near Columbia Ky. (Sunday) Lieut. Col. Bailey was left back to bring up stragglers. Col. Hathaway took the rear and my humble self led the Regt. all day yesterday. We marched 17 miles very fast as I lost sight of the advance regiments and it took four hours of hard marching to catch them.

We camped in the woods. Slight snow storm last night but our tents protected us pretty well.

Oct. 29th 1862 - In camp near Columbia. (Wednesday) Have been in camp here for three days. Will move tomorrow at 6 a.m. Large mail for the Regt. today including a goodly quantity of newspapers. Quite a treat.

Oct. 30th 1862 - In camp near Edmonton. (Thursday) Made 25 miles today passed through Columbia a small and dilapidated looking town. Have camped on a secesh farm. His (fence) rails suffer.

Oct. 31st 1862 - In camp. (Friday) Made 18 miles. Have camped 5 miles from Glasgow. Was out foraging. Brought in a turkey, sweet potatoes and butter. The Regiment was mustered for pay.

Nov. 1st 1862 - Head Quarters 73rd Ind. Vols. In camp near Glasgow Ky. (Saturday) Started early and made six miles by eleven o'clock. Have camped just south of Glasgow which is rather a pretty camp. We have a splendid camping ground and expect to remain here two or three days. Weather beautiful.

Nov. 4th 1862 - In camp near Glasgow Ky. (Tuesday) Have spent a pleasant three days here and enjoyed the rest highly. Just finished a letter to the Register. Orders have just been issued to start immediately. A hurried striking of tents and packing of wagons and we are off.

Nov. 5th 1862 - Scottsville Ky. (Wednesday) Yesterday made about 5 miles and camped near a mill. Must be secesh property as no orders were giving sparing the fence rails and the consequence is they went like hot cakes. Made 20 miles today. Cold wind and signs of rain. Have camped on a Union farm as no rails so no rails are to be taken.

Nov. 7th 1862 - In camp Tennessee. (Friday) Remained at Scottsville all day yesterday, started this morning enroute for Gallatin Tenn and have made about 18 miles, crossed the line this p.m. Snowed nearly all day but so light and fine that it did not stay on the ground.

Nov. 8th 1862 - Gallatin Tenn. (Saturday) The 20th Brigade was ordered to leave camp this morning at 1 1/2 o'clock. The object being to bag two Regiments of Morgan's cavalry in camp at Gallatin.

We made a forced march and came in sight of G at daybreak, deployed in line of battle on the right of the road and approached the rebel camp cautiously but the bird had flown. Their camp fires were still burning and the condition of the camp showed that they had left but a short time before.

Nov. 9th - In camp near Gallatin. (Sunday) Marched through G yesterday p.m. rather a pretty town but looks deserted. Most of the inhabitants are rebels.

Went into camp on the banks of the Cumberland River which is very low at present being easily fordable. We have a very pretty camp and shall probably remain here a day or two as the teams have gone 25 miles for provision.

Nov. 11th 1862 - Silver Springs camp. (Tuesday) Left camp on the Cumberland River yesterday. Our teams were away after provision and had to leave most of the company baggage in charge of Lieut. Seeger Co. E.

Ten noncommissioned officers and 50 men crossed the river on a foot bridge built by Col. Streight's Regt (or 51st Ind). Arrived at this camp before dusk last night. Morgan's Cavalry were within one mile of us picking up stragglers. As we sent back three wagons for our baggage our loss will be heavy as there is not much doubt expressed but that our Guard and everything is captured.

We have a pleasant camp here having located Head Quarters in the woods. We are 19 miles from Nashville. I like the looks of Tenn. much better than Kentucky - some pretty plantations around here. Saw one field of cotton on our march yesterday.

Capt. Price Company C returned this morning.

Weather pleasant but signs of rain.

November 12th 1862 - Silver Springs camp Tennessee. (Wednesday) Nothing heard as yet from our guard or baggage, undoubtedly they and it is captured.

Col. Bailey and self slept comfortably in his tent last night. Rather muddy and damp today but there is plenty of wood and we keep up a roaring fire making things look cheerful and comfortable. I got the Regt. in line of battle at 5 o'clock this morning. Remained in line till daybreak but no enemy appeared.

Nov. 14th - Silver Springs camp. (Friday) Lieut. Seger came in yesterday with his guard and leaves whereat there was much rejoicing.

The Regt. went out today as guard to forage train. Stringent orders are issued by Genl. Wood in regard to camp guard. No passes are issued.

Everybody pleased with our new General Rosecrans, his orders are sensible. Regiment is required to be in line of battle tomorrow morning at 5 o'clock and remain in line till further orders.

Nov. 15th, 1862 - Lebanon Tennessee. (Saturday) The Sixth Div. started out this morning for this place with the intention of bagging a force of 500 of Morgan's cavalry supposed to be here. Hascall's Brigade moved out on the road south of L [Lebanon. Ed.] and reached the Murfreesboro road about the same time that we entered town. and thought we had them surrounded sure. But it turned out that there was only a squad of twenty or thirty here and they scattered as soon as we approached.

The 15th Ind. was detailed to destroy the contents of a grist mill which had been furnishing the rebels with flour and they made short work of it.

Nov. 16th 1862 - Silver Springs. (Sunday) Made the march to Lebanon and back yesterday in remarkable short time, and yet had no stragglers .... changed the whole camp today and got the tents in order. Suppose we'll move soon as we just got fixed for a stay.

Nov. 18th 1862 - Silver Springs camp. Tuesday) It rained nearly all day yesterday making the camp quite muddy.

Last night had dress parade for the first time since our arrival. It is very sickly here. I report on the sick list 5 com. officers and 133 enlisted men. The water is miserable and we were all glad to receive orders to march in the morning.

Genl. Rosecrans has announced that Major Genl. George H. Thomas commands the center of the army consisting of Rosseau's, Negley's, Dumont's, Fry's and Palmer's Divisions.

Maj. Genl. McCook commands the right wing and Maj. Gen. Crittenden the left wing.

What Divisions constitute the right and left wings are not stated. Woods and Smith's are in the left wing however. We must have a large army here and I have confidence that now we have an able man at the head. Something will be done worthy of ourselves and country.

Nov. 19th 1862 - In camp. (Wednesday) Left Silver Springs at noon and have made about eight miles. Passed the "Hermitage" the former. residence and the last resting place of that man the like of whom is so much needed now, General Andrew Jackson. How I wish that good old Abe had some of his energy and strong iron will. The residence lays on the right of the road and is a beautiful place. A splendid mansion and broad acres. On the left is the residence of Andrew Jackson Donaldson, rather a poor looking place in comparison.

We have made a detour for the purpose of crossing Rock River further up.

Met Will Weber today one of my old friends and new Quarter Master of the 15th. Received letters and papers from home, a rich break -----.The road is bad and the teams find difficulty in coming up. So that we shall get to bed late tonight as tents will have to be pitched after they arrive.

Weather cold.

Nov. 20th 1862 - In camp 7 miles from Nashville Tenn. (Thursday) Left camp this morning at an early hour and had quite a time crossing Rock River. After the Regiments had crossed they stacked arms and lined the bank to assist the teams up the steep hill on this side.

Got into camp here about noon and have a beautiful camping ground tho rocky in some places. I arranged the camp regularly as possible and we have settled down for a stay. Have bot. me a fine horse of Quarter Master Bacon for $100.

Col. Bailey and self get along finely messing together. we have two contrabands as servants, one cook and one hostlier.

Nov. 23rd 1862 In camp 7 miles from Nashville. (Sunday) We still remain here enjoying the resting spell. All but the "Adjutant" who is worked to death. Weather still continues cool but pleasant.

Nov. 25th 1862 - Head Quarters 73rd Regt. Ind. Vols. Camp in the field - 7 miles from Nashville. (Tuesday) Orders have come at last to move. We leave tomorrow at 11 a.m. Have spent a very pleasant time here.

Commenced today to drill the non-commissioned staff.

Major ----- of the 9th Ind. was at our camp today. Was acquainted with him in the three months service. Adjt. ----- of the 15th called on me also. Received a letter from Adjutant Stanfield of the 48th today.

Just finished my monthly report. A great job. Gen. Wood is absent and Gen. Hascall commands the Brigade at present.

Everything appears to have taken new life since Gen. Rosecrans entered upon his command. I do not believe that we shall march far tomorrow but then great are the uncertainties of war.

The weather has been cool for several days, heavy frost every morning. Am sorry to leave our camp but such is the fortunes of war.

Nov. 26th 1862 - Camp in the field 4 miles from Nashville. (Wednesday) Left Spring Place camp about 2 p.m. and after numerous and vexatious delays reached our present camp after dark. We immediately confiscated the rails in the vicinity and after tents were pitched and fires built became satisfied with our camping ground.

Nov 29th - 4 miles from Nashville. (Saturday) I have laid off the camp as near regulation form as practical and we present quite a cozy appearance. We have a good parade ground for drilling purposes, water handy and plenty, tho wood is scarce since the rails gave out. There is a prospect of our remaining here several days longer.

Nov. 30th 1862. (Sunday) The 73rd is ordered tomorrow to guard a forage train. A fight is expected and we are jubilant.

Chapter Three

Dec. 1st 1862 – Mar 23rd 1862 (The Bloody Battle of Stones River)

Dec. 1st 1862 - Camp in the field near Nashville, Tenn. (Monday) Thank fortune and the gods of war the 73rd has at last had a "skirmish" and a lively one. We started about 7 AM in company with companies of the 13th Michigan having about 80 wagons in charge. At 2 miles from camp we came upon our outer picket posts who reported the enemy in sight.

Advancing a quarter of a mile one company of the 13th Mich. was deployed on the right of the road and under direction of the Colonel. I took command of Company G who was deployed on the left as skirmishers. We advanced in this manner till we reached Mill (or Will) Creek. Upon the opposite side of which we found the enemy posted. Five or six rebel cavalry were in plain sight and Company G blood rose to fever heat at the sight, and begged permission to fire but I would not allow it until we had lessened the distance somewhat.

When given the word they blazed away with a will, making the old woods sing. Immediately reloading we gave it to them again which elicited a response in the shape of several rifle bullets which whistled around uncomfortably close. The artillery then opened upon another squad more to our right and we found that we were considerably in advance of the Regt. I ordered them not to cross the creek for fear of getting in range of our own guns.

Firing then commenced on the extreme right and continued for some time. The 73rd getting a shot in now and then as a rebel came in sight. While the artillery continued to play for hours making them scatter at every shot. Our teams meanwhile were confiscating the contents of the mill nearby.

Finally having loaded all that we could find we commenced the march back.

Deeming it not prudent to cross as we had but 250 men. And the bridge having been burnt, it was impossible to get the teams across. About this time another train guarded by the 94th Illinois and a Kentucky Regt. came up and agreed that if we would allow the artillery to go back that they would cross under cover of its fire. We sent the two pieces back and commenced a vigorous cannonading.

When they opened upon us with a rifled cannon Illinois and Kentucky concluded they would not cross and went back with empty wagons, while ours were filled to overflowing.

Since reaching camp have learned that upon hearing the cannonading and its long continuing 2 brigades were sent out to reinforce us and actually proceeded a mile or two on their way.

Dec. 2nd 1862. (Tuesday) The 73rd had a review today at ten o'clock A M, and showed off as usual. This P.M. I took Company C out and practiced the skirmish drill for two hours. An order came tonight that Gen. Rosecrans will review us tomorrow at 8 A.M. So shall have an opportunity to see the commander of the Dept. of the Cumberland.

Dec. 3rd 1862 - Camp in the Field. (Wednesday) The 20th Brigade was not to be cheated out of the review although "Rosey" did not make his appearance. We went in on our own hook and had quite a lively time. Col. Harker complemented the 73rd on its fine marching.

Dec. 4th 1862 - Camp in the field. (Thursday) Today at noon our Grand review came off under the eye of Major General Rosecrans himself. The whole Division was out and made a fine appearance. The General rode through the open ranks of each Division, correcting the faults of each and every man almost.

Upon arriving at the 73rd and viewing the line which I had formed he paid me quite a compliment upon its correctness. The review lasted nearly all day.

Dec. 5th 1862. (Friday) Commenced snowing this morning and the ground is covered with a white mantle. Our boys without shoes are in a suffering condition.

Dec. 8th 1862 - Head Quarters 73rd Regt. Ind. Volunteers, Camp in the field, Nashville (Monday) The whole Brigade went out as forage train guard yesterday on the Wilsonville Pike and near the locality of our former skirmish. We were in such force that the enemy dared not attack although we were in range of their artillery which was posted just across the creek.

Co H however succeeded in firing a shot or two or three at their cavalry who were out scouting and contend that they killed one. We succeeded in filling every wagon.

There are rumors in camp of a speedy departure. If they turn out to be true I shall leave the cozy fireplace which I've built in my tent with much regret. Our Regiment is frightfully reduced, only 283 Privates fit for duty and but 439 present in camp. 24 are absent as prisoners, *35* without leave, 3 in confinement and the rest absent sick. There is a general feeling of despondency amongst officers and men and quite a number have tendered their resignations.

Dec. 14th 1862 - Camp in the field near Nashville (Sunday) The Brigade went out as forage train guard today being accompanied by a Regiment of cavalry. We took the Lebanon Pike and west as far as the Hermitage. It was sad to see how the country was devastated on every hand. Buildings burnt, fences tom down, bridges destroyed and everything appears to be going to ruin.

Dec. 15 1862 - Camp in the field. (Monday) Word came last night that an attack was probable and we formed line of battle at 4 a.m. Remaining in line till daylight but no enemy has yet made his appearance.

Dec. 19th 1862. (Friday) A general order has been issued to the effect that the enemy appears disposed to make a stand at or near Stewart's Creek and that the time which must elapse before we can advance must be improved by constant drilling.

Dec. 24th 1862 - In camp near Nashville. (Wednesday) The Regt. was ordered to move at daylight. We struck tents in a hurry anticipating an advance on the enemy. Waited patiently hour after hour for the order to march, but darkness overtook us and pitched tents not unwilling to spend "Christmas Eve" by our comfortable fire places.

Dec. 25th - In camp near Nashville. (Thursday) Christmas morn dawned clear and cold and our task for the day was soon understood to be the guarding of a forage train. The whole Brigade started out on the Nashville Pike till we reached Sheridan's old camping ground (about 2 miles) where we were joined by what appeared to be a whole Division. Then taking a by road which turns to the right, proceeded about ten miles encountering a large body of the rebel cavalry who showed fight and retreated slowly.

The other troops drove them back until we had arrived at our foraging ground, when we were sent to the front and immediately commenced a lively skirmish with the enemy who were posted in a piece of heavy woodland which commanded a range of open space about 1/2 a mile wide.

Our boys posted themselves in the edge of the timber and opened a heavy fire upon them which was vigorously returned. Each party was in plain sight of the other as well as hearing and the compliments sent to each other as they dodged behind the trees to escape the deadly bullets were numerous as well as sarcastic.

The firing was kept up by both sides until our wagons were all loaded. But the range was so great and our men so well protected that not a man of the 73rd was injured tho some of our other regts. were not so fortunate, the 51st Ind. having some casualties, the 13th Mich.1 killed and 1 or 2 wounded.

When we started on our return trip the rebels followed us closely annoying us by their long range rifles considerably. We arrived in camp about 9:00 clock safe and sound but extremely tired.

It is rumored that the grand advance takes place tomorrow. The whole army will move and drive the enemy from Stewart Creek, Murfreesboro or wherever they make a stand or perish in the attempt. We'll trust to Rosecrans, he'll never be whipped.

Dec. 26th 1862 – Camp near Lavergne Tenn. (Friday) The Left wing took up the line of march Dixie-ward this A.M. and have made about 10 miles from Nashville driving the enemy before us, but do not know the particulars of what has been done at the fronts, unfortunately we were elected as train guard and were dispersed throughout the whole train in detachments of two companies I kept with the front of the train and was a listener to the skirmishes but could see none of the results.

It rained during the morning making the march rather disagreeable.

Dec. 27,1862 - Camp near Stewarts Creek Tenn. (Saturday) Advanced on Lavergne this AM. and found the enemy in some force The 26th Ohio was in the extreme advance and went at them with a will sending the rebels flying back in a hurry, not however until after a sharp skirmish in which the 26th lost a member.

We occupied the town with colors flying but did not stop long. Our Regt. was sent to the left of the road as flankers and sending forward a strong line of skirmishers of which I took command.

Moved forward through the cedar thickets regulating our movements by the column which moved on the pike. We marched in this manner nearly all day through a drenching rain.

About 4 P.M came insight of the rebel camp on Stewarts Creek. Col Harker ordered my line of skirmishers forward and soon stirred up the enemy who immediately broke and ran followed by a few federal bullets. There was some little skirmishing done on our right when about dusk the enemy having entirely disappeared we took possession of their camp and prepared for a nights rest. But were doomed to disappointment as the whole Regt was ordered on picket.

Dec. 28th, 1862 - Camp on Stewarts Creek Tenn. (Sunday) We made no movement today as former indications gave rise to the belief that the enemy would make a determined stand at this point. Their pickets have been in sight all day and more or less firing has been going on.

There are half a doz or more rebel camps in the immediate vicinity at one of which a company from our Regt. and one from the 51st captured one hundred cavalry sabers, shot guns, etc. etc. valued at $1500. There are half a doz. cotton bales laying in a cotton field directly in front of our camp. The cotton is only about half picked, And the "product" looks strange to my eye.

December 29th 1862 - Camp on Stones River 2 1/2 miles from Murfreesboro Tenn. (Monday) The right wing under McCook has driven Kirby Smith out of Franklin, he [Smith] retreating to Murfreesboro

The Left Wing crossed Stewarts Creek the AM. and

taking position (our Brigade on the left and in front) moved forward, the only enemy in sight being cavalry who fell back as we advanced. Our batteries throwing a few shells now and then. We moved forward by the right of companies to the front till we reached Stone's River at a point distant from Murfreesboro about 2 miles.

Here we found the whole force of the enemy whose right wing was posted in advantageous positions upon the opposite bank and directly in our front.

A fine large residence just on the right of the Murfreesboro Pike had been fired by the rebels just before we came up undoubtedly to prevent it from becoming a shelter for our skirmishers. [and] the bright lurid flames as they shot up into the air was a grand spectacle.

We sent a line of skirmishers forward who advanced under cover of the woods to the river bank and engaged with the rebel line which was posted in a cornfield just across.

The firing was kept up briskly until dusk when the order was given to our Brigade alone "Forward to Murfreesboro." (Note - Col. Hunt with 3 Regts. from Hansins Brigade and Cobb's battery were then..........- on crossing Stone River and driven back on...........line, see his reports)

We received it with a cheer and immediately advanceed to the ford. The bed of the river is very rocky and full of holes so that the men went in at times waist deep.

The enemy's skirmishers of which they had a very strong line opened fire upon us (The 51st Ind. and the 73rd were abreast) but we dashed across and with the 51st claim the honor of being the first Regts. of the whole army to cross the river.

The enemy still continued their fire upon us until we formed the left wing which was first over and moving forward drove them back until we were near enough to the whole command of the rebel General Breckenridge to hear his officers rally their men and implore them to advance and drive us back.

By this time the whole Brigade was safely over and as we numbered only about 2000 very prudently took position and awaited the attack which we confidently expected would be made.

The rebels had force enough within 800 yards of our position to have cut us all to pieces if they had the pluck to have attacked us or sense to turn it. But it seems that the very boldness of our attack confounded and intimidated them.

Our position was perfectly untenable against a force even the same as ours and to have successfully retreated back across the river was an impossibility. The officers appeared to comprehend this at a glance and yet all were determined, if fight we must, to win victory out of all these unfavorable circumstances or die in the attempt.

The skirmishers kept up a slow fire for an hour or two and as stray bullets were whistling through the ranks the men were ordered to lie down and remain in that position until the enemy should advance within 10 paces. Bayonets were fixed and when that moment should arrive they were ordered to rise up fire one volly [sic] and then charge. We lay in this position for some time when the firing having ceased and some apprehension existing that we would be flanked on the right I sent out Co B as skirmishers in that direction. Shortly after fearing that they had not gone out far enough I tied my horse and went out afoot to advance the line. When I returned I found the Regt. and my horse gone.

Somewhat puzzled at this I went along the line we had occupied to the center where I found the 51st still in position and learned that the Brigade was being quietly withdrawn. Was ordered to leave the skirmishers out. I forded the stream on foot and found the Regt. evacuated for the night. Our loss was but one man supposed to be killed. The 51st lost 1 killed and 1 or 2 wounded.

December 30th 1862 - Camp on Stones River 2 miles from Murfreesboro Tenn. (Tuesday) Passed a miserable night as we had to lay on the damp muddy ground and scarcely anything to protect us from the drizzling rain with which we were favored. My hat got half full of water which causes the brain to be quite cold this morning. But then a hard cracker and a little fat pork was all that was necessary to bring me out all right.

Unfortunately we pitched our camp directly in range of the enemies guns and they opened on us with round shot this morning early, causing a rapid "change of base" to about 100 yards in the rear where we were somewhat protected by the crest of a ridge in front. The rebel balls came most uncomfortably close but did no damage to our brigade.

A battery quite a distance in our rear however was not so fortunate as one of their shells struck a gun carriage killing 4 men.

The 6th Ohio (our Battery) took position and such a chorus of shot and shell was poured into them that they soon withdrew.

Heavy musketry firing and cannonading has been going on on our right nearly all day. But no decisive results. We have retained our position doing nothing but skirmishing.

December 31st 1862 - bivouac on Stone River 2 ½ miles from Murfreesboro Tenn. (Wednesday) Last night by making a hut of corn stalks the "Field and Staff" including Col. Hathaway, Major Krimbill and myself managed to sleep quite comfortably though everything is damp underneath and overhead.

Our fighting on the right yesterday does not appear to have been very favorable and the general feeling this morning was that something desperate would be done today.

The balance of the rations were distributed and the teams sent to Nashville. 60 rounds of cartridges were ordered to be carried, 40 in the boxes and 20 in the pockets.

Breakfast was eaten and strange as it appears the inexorable "regulations" must be followed and we mustered for pay.

I ordered a morning report which showed 309 men present about 10 of these were on sick list and remained behind when the Regt. moved.

The Ball opened on the right at an early hour and the firing had been kept up quite lively for about half an hour or more. We were making preparations to cross the river when a messenger from Gen. Rosecrans rode up in hot haste and ordered us on the double quick to the extreme right a distance even then (after it had been driven far in towards our center) of about a mile and a half. We had accomplished about half the distance when we were halted for some moments in an open space of ground and directly in range of the enemy's cannon who commenced pouring in the shot and shell with a vengeance.

Gen. Rosecrans and Staff was here personally directing the movements of the troops who appeared huddled together in extreme confusion. But he soon brought them into order sending them principally to the center and right center.

Our Brigade he ordered again to the extreme right and we started on the double quick. Just as we were leaving I involuntarily "ducked" as a rebel shell came whizzing through the air within 3 feet of my head cutting off the limb of a tree a few steps beyond. It was a close call but was saved to take part in the deadly fray which even unionized the 31st of Dec. 1862 [sic].

By the time we arrived at our position several had given out through fatigue so that we had but about 290 men in ranks. We were to take post in a piece of heavy woodland about 200 yards from the Pike and were marching up when a soldier addressed me and requested to be allowed to join our ranks as he had lost his Regt. I ordered him into Co E (I mention this circumstance as the brave fellow stuck to us during the fight but disappeared immediately afterward. He fought nobly. Never could ascertain his name.)

About this time a rebel Regt. came in sight and opened fire upon an Indiana Regt. stationed on our left but belonging to another Brigade. We had a good chance to see a brilliant little fight but not to participate as they did not fire at us although at easy range and in plain sight.

The Rebels poured in volly after volly [sic] and the charge so near that we almost outflanked them and I wondered that no order was given for us to advance & take the whole of them prisoners but it seems Col. Harker did not consider it a free fight and held us to our position.

The Indiana Regt. rallied, charged, and in turn drove the rebels helter-skelter back until the thick woods hid them from our view.

It was ascertained that a Div. supposed to be Claytons was moving on us from a direction almost in our rear. We made a hasty change of front and moved forward to meet them. In a short time we emerged from the woods coming out on a plantation, the mansion of which had just been fired by the rebels. We first discovered a rebel battery in the cornfield to the right (see diagram mightily executed by the best my genius can afford) We exchanged a few shots [with] them. Their balls fell short but bouncing as they struck the ground were dangerous things to men.

Against one large ten pounder I noticed in particular it struck the ploughed ground in the cornfield made a tremensdous bounce of 30 or 40 feet struck the ground and finally jammed square through one of the Ohio Regts who were marching 4 deep and yet strange to say I could not see that it injured anyone.

About this time a Brigade belonging to Van Cleves Division, I believe, was sent across the uncultivated field to the left of the piece of woods jutting out from the main thick woods as perdiagram. The (Regt.) entered the woods at the point marked "rebels in force" and instantly became engage-ed. In a few moments stragglers and rider-less horses were flying back in confusion.

We immediately advanced by the route indicated and took position in the woods. The 65th Ohio in advance as laid down in the map. They had hardly reached that point before they were engaged with the rebel in front (The prisoners taken at this time say that this brigade was composed entirely of South Carolinians)

As we could do nothing in the rear we were ordered to lie down to escape the bullets which were beginning to fly thick and fast.

Our Battery (which was moved to the right then laid down) now opened on the four lines of the enemy with good effect. The 65th fought well for ten or 15 minutes but finally overpowered by numbers gave way and ran directly over us.

This was extremely trying to a new Regt. Already, although we had not fired a shot, one Capt. was killed and half a doz. men wounded. Some of the men got up and took a step backward but a single caution from myself and some other officers and every man kept his place.

In reality an order had just been given to fall back. The 13th Mich. was gone. The Battery and the 51st Ind. was withdrawing, but the order had never reached us.

When the last man of the 65th had passed over we rose up and poured a deadly volly [sic] into the ranks of the pursuing enemy who had approached within very close range. They returned the fire vigorously. Their battery opened upon us with shell, grape, and canister and for a while the scene was terrific, beyond description.

Our men fought bravely, nobly, heroically. Vollv after volly was poured into the rebel ranks. After ten or twelve rounds had been fired we charged and the rebels gave way contesting the ground between stubbornly. We pressed them back however until we occupied the ground marked TREES [see map] in advance of the 65th former position.

In the meantime the 64th Ohio, which like us had not

received the order to fall back, had come up on our right throwing that wing into some confusion but doing well in the fight.

At this juncture I discovered 4 Rebel Regts coming up on our left flank The left wing of the first Regt. was not more than 100 feet from our left wing. It was wheeling around to take position where it could pour in a murderous enfilading fire.

I immediately rode up to Col. Hathaway and informed him of the dangerous position in which we could be placed in less than 3 minutes but he turned and paid no attention to me whatever. (He says now that he understood me to say that we were being reinforced on our left. If he had understood the military term of outflanking he certainly could not have misunderstood me. But I can't blame him for he showed himself to be brave, at least)

But what was to be done? I had no authority to order the Regt. back and now it was almost too late anyhow. The time taken in informing him was improved by the rebels. Their right wing was in position behind the fence scarce 50 feet from our left. And already their terrible cross fire was mowing us down. I was in direct range, could not leave my post. But yet did not want to be murdered in this manner.

So I dismounted and covered my left flank by a friendly tree leaving the range in front however open.

Somehow I felt if I must be shot. I would rather it would be from the force we were fighting rather than by a force whose fire we could not return.

All this time my attention had been directed to the extreme left of our Regt. When looking toward the right I saw the 64th Ohio and our right on the full retreat. Immediately thereafter the left gave way, unable to stand the terrible fire.

My horse had given a plunge a moment before and supposing him to be shot I had let him go so that I was left to get out of that scrape as best I could on foot.

The major had been injured somewhat by his horse

throwing him before the fight commenced and had gone to the rear. The Cols. horse had been shot before the fight fairly commenced so that the 73rds Field and Staff were in a sorry predicament. My sword and fixeus [?] bothered me considerable in the double quick but I finally got back to the reserve safe and sound, but could hear nothing from the Regt. except that it had gone farther to the rear.

I went back to the pike and met some of Co G's men taking the wounded to hospital but could not find or hear anything of the Regt. I went back to the Brigade and found the 51st Ind. the 13th Mich. and the Battery in position on the edge of the cedar thicket .

I reported to Col. Harker for duty at which he seemed pleased and promised to give me something to do. Shortly after the Regt or what was left of it came up. Scarcely one hundred men were left in rank. But of these I was proud in spite of the disorder in which they had been compelled to fall back. They had rallied near the rail road and now came to the front stout hearted and determined to breast another leader storm if need be.

Our loss shows the deadliness of the conflict. The proportion between killed and wounded being far less than usual (The enemy held the battle ground for three days after the fight so that it is almost impossible to obtain an accurate list of the killed and wounded. But after the enemy had retired we found 25 bodies including two Capts. (Tibbets and Doyle) belonging to our regt. and we know of 42 wounded

The balance of our loss which has been ascertained to be 25 cannot be accounted for. Some perhaps were killed and buried by the rebels. Others are undoubtedly wounded and in the hands of the enemy. We went into the fight 290 strong. We were actually engaged about 25 minutes and in that time lost 92 killed, wounded, and missing. Can anyone say that the 73rd does not present a glorious and yet sad record.

I regret much that we fell back in disorder but we

immediately rallied and came to the front again READY if not eager to engage the overwhelming force of the enemy. Our proud old banner still waved over us pierced by 8 bullets. Our color guard, every man of them were either killed or wounded, but a hundred brave hearts were gathered around that noble flag who would spill their last drop of blood before it should be trailed in the dust by the rebel hands.

We held our position in the cedar thicket till dark. The enemy had been so severely punished that he dared not make another attack. Our brigade had saved the right wing. Gen. Rosecrans himself indicated it in a short complimentary speech to the Regt. a few days after.

About 9 o'clock P.M. we moved back to the position previously occupied and bivouacked for the night. It was cold and raw but no fires were allowed to be built and we had to do the best we could.

January 1st 1863 - Camp on Stone River 2 ½ miles from Murfreesboro. (Thursday) The new year opens gloomy enough. Many an anxious heart throbs painfully today for [our] position is desperate, and yet stern determination to fight to the bitter end is the prevalent feeling. We trust to our noble and brave General to wrest victory out of the very jaws of defeat.

Our lines have been driven in at every point except the left and now form a semicircle. Nearly every Regt. in the army has been engaged and the slaughter on both sides is appalling. Yet how soon one gets accustomed to scenes of carnage and destruction. Dead bodies lie in every direction but no attention is paid to them. There is no time now for funerals as it is almost impossible to attend to half of the many thousands of wounded.

About 4 o'clock this morning our Brigade fell back a quarter of a mile to a better position in the edge of a piece of woods. About 8 A .M. the enemy advanced with shout and yells upon this position but the 6th Ohio Battery opened upon them with such a storm of shot and shell that they fell back, making no further attack until about 3 P.M. when their Batterys opened up having obtained accurate range. The shells burst over and around us continually but fortunately our Regt was protected by a thicket of large trees and we sustained no loss.

January 2nd 1863 - Same Position. (Friday) Expected to be shelled last night as we built our camp fires in plain view of the enemy. But I guess they concluded that it would be as bad for them as for us and so we rested in peace.

Early this morning however they opened a terrific fire upon us. The 6th Ohio answered and for half an hour the scene was grand beyond description. The Rebels had obtained accurate range and the famous Washington battery from New Orleans played upon us with round shot and shell until the air was perfectly alive with death dealing missiles.

Soon a caisson with six frightened horses attached dashed back to the rear, all the riders having been disabled Then another rider-less officer' s horse from the different Regts. supporting the Battery dashed here and there and the wildest confusion reigned.

To crown all, the Chicago Board of Trade Battery opposing the enemy had charged (This Battery was located in the rear) opened upon our own men with grape shot. One of our own men detailed [designated] for the time being as [an] artillery man was killed and another wounded by this fire.

The 13th Michigan was on our right and directly in [the] rear of our Battery. It had been cut up considerably by the enemy's fire and when our own Battery opened on us it was more than they could stand. They broke and ran, re-forming again, however, and taking position in the rear of us who were protected somewhat from the enemy's fire by the trees. The Battery boys took their guns to the rear by hand, lustily cheered by us for their brave work.

An hour or less afterwards our Regt changed position to the open ground on the right. Here we have been annoyed all day by the Rebel sharp shooters 2 or 300 in number who are posted in a strip of woods about half a mile to the front (Some places the distance is less.) They have excellent guns and as soon as a person rises up he is greeted with that siren song which is peculiar to a minie ball after it is most spent.

About half an hour since we advanced a strong line of skirmishers numbering 120, twenty of whom were from our Regt [advanced] and drove [the sharp shooters] back handsomely killing quite a number. As soon however as our men entered the woods they were greeted by a storm of grape and canister for the rebel battery was posted but a short distance off. And were compelled to fall back with a loss of 5.

Evening January 3rd 1863 - Across Stone River on the extreme left. Saturday) About 4 P.M. yesterday we gained a decided success on the left wing. Our position at that time had become about the center and when the fighting commenced on the left we could distinctly hear the cheers of our men.

Soon it became apparent that we were driving them. The enemy, enraged at this [and] to prevent us from sending reinforcements, opened their whole line of batteries upon us.

We replied with every battery that was in position and the sight and sound was one never to be forgotten. My position for viewing the grand artillery duel was excellent. The rebel line of batteries was about a mile long, poured forth a continued stream of fire while we replied as vigorously.

The old 6th Ohio in spite of the hand fight in the morning soon succeeded in silencing the battery opposite to us and in the course of half an hour both sides appeared to be satisfied and the firing died away with the exception of an occasional shot now and then.

Shortly after dark were ordered across the river to hold the ground gained by our success. We took position in front and had barely arrived before we could hear the reinforcements of the enemy advancing on our lines. The skirmishers became engaged and kept up a vigorous fire for some time. But they made no attack in force.

During the night we built a temporary barricade of rails which will afford our troops much protection It rained all night and my bed was a puddle of water.

This morning we were allowed to go 1/4 of a mile to the rear for a few hours to make coffee and get a little rest.

With this exception we have been in the front since the 29th inst. We eat what provisions we had among hundreds of dead bodies both rebels and union. The sight was sickening.

We resumed position in front again the P.M. There was a short sharp fight in the center just after dusk and I learned that we charged their entrenchments driving them out at the point of the bayonet. Have heard that my horse was not injured much and that one of our wounded men had taken him to Nashville. Meantime am riding one belonging to Col. Harker our Brigade commander.

January 4th 1863 – Battlefield. (Sunday) We were relieved from the front about 12 o'clock last night and I think was time. To keep a brigade constantly marching and fighting in the front for five days is rather tough.

It was discovered this morning however that enemy were on the full retreat having evacuated last night so that we were in front during the entire battle. Bragg is whipped out completely in spite of his first success. The victory is in a great measure due to the indomitable perseverance of our beloved General Rosecrans. The regiment went over in a body this afternoon to the battle ground where our desperate fight of the 31st took place. They resumed the same position which we had then occupied and gave three cheers for the victory. Gen. Rosecrans met us on the return and made us a short and highly complementary speech. He said that matters looked rather squalby [?] on .the 31st when he had ordered us up to the right. And that he could not say how much he did give to our little Brigade for checking the enemy's advance.

I visited the Div. Hospital today and find our wounded boys all in good spirits and cheerful. But it was a wretched sight to see the thousands of brave fellows suffering from every conceivable sort of a wound. The wounded die off so fast that a long line of bodies constantly lie on the burial ground awaiting the last act which (we) can do for him.

We have a pleasant camp and the weather is clearing up.

January 6th 1863 - Battle field of Stone River. Tuesday) Have laid here all day yesterday and today The rest has done us good.

We number now about 208 men. I sent a list of the killed and wounded to the Indianapolis Journal yesterday The 9th, 29th, and 15th Regts all suffered severely in the fight

John Richley, Capt. Co.C, came up today or yesterday. The Major went on duty also. The Sutler came up and brought relief to the boys by his tobacco. We have suffered somewhat for provisions and hard crackers and pork never tasted so good before as they have for the last few days But in spite of the privations we feel glorious over the victory and the news from other points

The rebel communication has been cut at Knoxville Tennessee and it is reported that Vicksburg is taken. This last however is not confirmed, [Note - Vicksburg did not fall to Union forces until July 4th, 1863, Ed.] but without that we have glory enough for one day

Jany 7th 1863 - Camp near Murfreesboro Tennessee. (Wednesday) We crossed the river this morning [Stones River] passing through Murfreesboro on our way to camp. It is a pretty town though looking desolate and gloomy now. Secesh camps were scattered in every direction around town and the substantial brick chimneys which were built to almost every tent show plainly that they intended to winter here. But we spoilt their calculations.

We went into camp but before pitching tents were ordered out and moved a mile farther east where we have a beautiful camping ground.

Wrote to the Register today. Have built me a nice fire place.

Jany 9th 1863. (Friday) Were ordered to move camp again and are now on the east or north east side of town in a bad location if it should happen to rain hard. The weather is cool and raw and am not feeling very well.

Jany 11th 1863 - Camp near M. (Sunday) We commenced building fortifications yesterday and have almost finished them. They are quite strong being proof against cannon and well as rifle balls. Am quite unwell today. The first time I've been so since entering the service in August last.

Jany 17th 1863 - Same Camp. (Saturday) The weather is miserable having been raining almost continually for several days. The whole camp except Hd.Qrs. is under water and the company tents have been moved to the little strips of high ground around Hd. Qrs.

I have been too unwell to do anything since the weather. 1st Lt. Phelphs Co K is acting Adjt. but he makes sad work of the reports from inexperience.

The Regt went out on the .... in search of some cavalry. They were gone three days and came back in a miserable condition, it having rained most of the time. Hope I shall improve some for its misery to lay here in this kind of weather.

Jany 23rd 1863 - Camp near Murfreesboro. (Friday) Moved camp this morning to get out of the mud. We are ¼ of a mile farther out and in a much better place. Am heartily glad of the exchange and hope it will help us to get well. Am improving slowly.

Col. Hathaway has gone home and Capt. Walker is in command of the Regt. Weather is pleasant and drying up fast.

Jany. 29th 1863 - Same Camp. (Thursday) The Regt. went foraging today. Was not well enough to go with it. Have finished my December report. Have a great deal of writing to do but am really to unfit for duty to do it and yet my ability to keep the Regimental affairs straight keeps me at work.

Was elected delegate to the meeting of officers of the Ind. Regts held at Murfreesboro Tenn a few days ago. Attended and took part in the proceedings which were harmonious. Strong feeling were manifested against home traitors etc etc

Feby 12th 1863 - Camp near Murfreesboro Tennessee (Thursday) The Regt went to Nashville on the 5th as train guard returning on the 8th. Was not able to go with them. Are still in the same camp and the routine is dull beyond measure. no drill. nothing for the men to do but lay in camp and work. now and then there [is] a little as its needed.

Feby 17th 1863 - Head Quarters 73rd Ind. Vols Camp near Murfreesboro. (Tuesday) Matters civil and military are in status quo. Everything moves on in the same dull way that has characterized everything since the battle.

Was over to the Head Qrs. of my fellow townsman John F. Miller who has just received the appointment of

Brigadier General an honor well deserved I guess.

General Paluins Division is stuck in the mud on our right. Generals Reynolds and Uegley come next.

The monotony of camp was somewhat relieved the other morning by the order to "fall in" at 4 o'clock in the morning. A Division of Rebel cavalry had been discovered making demonstrations on our left and an attack was apprehended. but nothing came of it. Our advance consisting of "my old" Regt. the 9th Ind. and other troops are at Readyville 12 miles in advance.

Col. Hathaway is expected home today. Weather still rainy with an abundance of mud. I have applied for a leave of absence for 20 days. Don't know whether "Kind Rosey" will grant it or not.

Feby 20th 1863 - Camp within the fortifications near Murfreesboro, Tenn. (Tuesday) Moved camp today and are now located within the entrenchments north of town and near the Nashville Pike and rail road. Found Stone River high but fordable. Weather is pleasant and am feeling much better than usual. The Rail Road bridge is just completed and trains now run into M. daily.

\

Feby 22nd 1863 - Murfreesboro Tenn. (Sunday) The birthday of Washington. That name so dear to every American patriot's heart could not pass by without some respect being paid to his memory Even tho were in the midst of great and trying troubles, a stirring and patriotic order was issued by General Rosecrans and read at the head of each company at sunset. A salute from each/our battery in each division made the hills tremble with their deep ....thunder.

March 1st 1863 Camp 5 miles from Murfreesboro. (Sunday) Our whole Div. started this morning on a foraging expedition. We had an enormous train to guard estimated at over 700 wagons. Reaching this point, some time was spent in building a pontoon bridge which our Regt. has been detailed to guard. The rest of the troops and train have passed over. 3 pieces of artillery are left with us. Am feeling quite unwell.

March 9th 1863 - Murfreesboro. Tenn. (Monday) Orders came this morning to strike tents and pack wagons. Supposing an advance of the army was contemplated we did so with alacrity but after waiting patiently all day for orders to move we finally received instead an order to unpack and pitch tents.

March 11th 1863. (Wednesday) Major Osborn our Pay Master was "around" today and made the boys hearts light with 2 months earnings of "Green Backs."

March 23rd 1863 – Murfreesboro. (Monday) Have been so unwell lately that I take no interest in keeping up my journal or anything else.

We are still at work on the fortifications which approach completion.

The fine weather puts all the "well ones" in good spirits.

Rumor has it that Vicksburg is being evacuated. If so we will hardly leave Murfreesboro for some time. A raid will undoubtedly be made into Ky soon by the rebels. But guess "our folks" are prepared for them.

My Bro. officers for an Adjutant is out of the line of promotion and all the officers especially the Capts were entitled to it in preference to myself and it is a self denial on their part to give way in my favor.

It is rumored that our Regt. is to be sent on expedition soon and hope it will prove true. As a hard march would cure me up.

Chapter Four

April 9th, 1863 – May 4th, 1863
(The Raid of Streight's Brigade)

Note: As we've seen in Chapter Three, following the Battle of Stones River the 73rd was allowed some rest for about three months near the small southern town of Murfreesboro, Tennessee.

It was during this time that the Regiment became part of the "Independent Provisional Brigade" composed of the 73rd and 51st Indiana, the 3rd Ohio, the 80th Illinois and two companies of the 1st Middle Tennessee Cavalry and led by Colonel Abel D. Streight.

As we shall see in Chapter Four, the Brigade's mission was to carry out a mounted raid across northern Alabama to Rome, Georgia where they planned to destroy the railroad that went through that city and any manufacturing concerns they found.

The raid got off to a shaky start when Colonel Streight found there was a shortage of horses and that the soldiers would have to break and ride mules. This situation led to several entries in Colonel Wade's journal in which he described Indiana farm boys trying to break wild mules and attempting to learn how to fight like a cavalry regiment.

The raiders left Eastport, Mississippi on April 24, 1863 and almost immediately were in trouble. The mules were still a major problem and some of the men still did not have animals to ride.

Famed Confederate Cavalry General Nathan Bedford Forrest picked up their trail and soon involved them in heavy fighting that led to the death of Colonel Hathaway, Commanding Officer of the 73rd Regiment at that time.

After a week of almost continuous running battles the "Provisional Brigade" was forced to surrender on May 3rd,

1863 near Rome, Georgia, just short of their goal.

The captured enlisted men were paroled within a month and released, but the Brigade's officers were sent to infamous Libby Prison in Richmond, Virginia. Most remained there for the rest of the Civil War…though, Col. Abel D. Streight and a few others escaped in the largest POW breakout of the War and returned safely to Union lines

Colonel Wade was held prisoner for over eleven months, in Libby Prison for nine and a half. Schuyler Colfax, then Speaker of the House, arranged for Wade's exchange. Released from prison, Wade traveled the 100 miles north to Washington where he stayed with his good friend Colfax.

There he was introduced to several National leaders such as President Abraham Lincoln and General Ulysses S. Grant.

Finally on March 13, 1864 the Colonel returned to South Bend for a thirty day leave before returning to his regiment.

And so, Col. Wade's Diary continues…

Michael P. Downs

Apr. 9, 1863 - Nashville Tennessee. (Thursday) The 73rd has been taken from Harker's Brigade and came down from Murfreesboro today (I mean day before yesterday)

It is now attached to the "Independent Provisional Brigade" composed of four picked regts viz the 51st and 73rd Indiana, the 3rd Ohio, the 80th Illinois and two companies of the 1st Middle Tennessee Cavalry. All commanded by Col A. D. Streight who is an able man. The whole brigade is to be mounted and it is intended to make a …….through northern Alabama and into Georgia and cut the enemy's communication besides accomplishing other objects. I have just procured a discharge from the Hospital and shall go with the expedition of course. I would not miss it for almost anything and besides am confident that hard riding will cure me up.

Apr 10th 1863 - Nashville Tenn. (Friday) We received orders to get aboard a fleet of steamers which are lying in the river today. And after turning over heavy Regimental property to be put in safe keeping until our return we marched through town down to the levee and shipped aboard the Henry Fitz Hugh and will probably leave for down the river during the night. We have a fleet of eight or nine steamers among which I have noticed the Izelta, Cottage, Luminary, Imperial, Aurora, Nashville and others. All officers and men are in good spirits.

Apr 11th 63 - Palmyra Tennessee. (Saturday) Left Nashville this morning at daybreak. Stopped a short time at Clarksville arriving here at 5 PM. We have brought down about 500 mules and shall have to break them in here.

Commenced unloading them this evening. Our regiment was sent on picket.

Major Walker and self have established Head Quarters in a comfortable farm house whose former occupants have skedaddled. We built a roaring fire and find it quite comfortable as our clothes were soaked through while posting the Regt.

Palmyra a few weeks since was a pretty little place of a dozen or two houses but now nothing is left of it but a few blackened chimneys, a deserving punishment for the cowardly guerrillas who made it their quarters and fired upon passing steamers. Signs of a stormy night.

Has been drizzling for some time.

Apr. 12, 1863 - Palmyra Tenn. (Sunday) The Regt. was called in from picket at noon. And having mounted those of our companies on good mules and horses we started out with a Company of Cavalry and troops from other Regts. on a foraging expedition. It was exciting work. Every available horse or mule we found was confiscated and we returned at night with a large number of animals.

Many laughable scenes occurred amongst the "Mounted Infantry." A mule would stumble and his rider pitch over his head, etc. etc but fortunately nobody was hurt. Companies B, I and H are to go around by Paducah in the steamers while the balance of the Regt. go to Fort Henry and Donaldson by land.

Our men are about half mounted and will have to march on foot. We have two Mountain Howitzers with us. The boys call it the Jackass Battery.

Apr. 13, 1863 - In Camp. (Monday) I don't think I have seen so many ridiculous things, or laughed as I have today. The Regt has been engaged in breaking mules at Palmyra and the obstinate brutes appeared to have made up their minds not to "break in" but to break everybody's head if possible. I got about a hundred men mounted and tried to form line of battle. But one mule wouldn't come up to the front and another would go far beyond and so it went. Many were the hair breath escape that occurred from their victims heels. I think the start was one of the richest things I've ever seen in the way of the ridiculous A rider was off over a mules head or under his heels every five minutes and every stream we came to half the mules would lie down in the water. We have picked up quite a number of animals on our march today.

April 14th, 1863 – Cumberland Iron Works Tennessee. (Tuesday) Arrived here at four o'clock PM during a heavy rain. It has been raining for some time and am soaking wet.

The 73rd has taken possession of four houses and we are now comfortably quartered. Head Qrs is established in a deserted residence, the furniture of which has been mostly left behind. A roaring fire has been built in the huge fire place and things look very comfortable and pleasant. We are going to have a splendid supper of ham and eggs.

Picked up a few horses and mules on our march to-day and had many laughable scenes.

The men broke into a store kept by the proprietor of the works and destroyed some things before the officers could prevent them. But as he (the proprietor) is somewhat disloyal, not much sympathy is expressed for him.

Apr. 15, 1863 - Fort Donaldson (Donelson) (Wednesday) Arrived here and passed through the town at noon. Our appearance and especially the jackass battery amused the good people in the vicinity amazingly.

We rode silently by the Fort. The scene of one of our first and most signal victories over the rebel hordes and where so many of our brave soldiers poured out their blood for the Union.

Apr 15th 1864 [1863, Ed] - Fort Henry. (Still Wednesday) After leaving Donaldson we struck across the country for the Tennessee River, arriving here late in the afternoon.

This fort is almost deserted having a garrison of but one company and no pickets out. Fortifications are being built upon the other side of the river which is high ground and better calculated for a fort.

The fleet has not yet arrived. We are tired and hungry, having made 19 miles today.

April 17th, 1863 - On board Steamer Baldwin Tenn. River. (Friday) Camped near Fort Henry on the night of the 15th inst. The fleet of boats came in from Paducah the same night Yesterday we loaded up with our animals and put the Regt aboard.

Major Walker and self with the right wing on board the Baldwin and Capt. Kendall with the left wing aboard the Aurora. We have 303 men being the smallest Regt. in the

Brigade. We left the fort this mom. and are steaming up the river. Col Ellets Marine fleet accompanies us as our escort.

Our destination probably is Tuscumbia where we shall be in the rear of Braggs army. (it being at Tullahoma)

We had one little adventure today. Supposing we had found a nest of guerrillas we sent a cannon ball across the bow of a small boat containing a family of refugees. They hove to after a short chase and explained the matter.

Apr. 19th - Eastport Mississippi. (Sunday) Steamed up the river all day long yesterday but nothing occurred of interest. The banks of the Tennessee look dreary and inhospitable on both sides.

The Baldwin was the fastest boat in the fleet but poorly conducted. It was a fine sight to see the long string of boats winding along this crooked river.

Passed Pittsburgh landing where the bloody battle of Shiloh was fought about 9 o'clock this A.M. Saw the positions which our forces held and the spot where our Gunboats held the enemy at bay until reinforcements arrived. Arrived here the P.M. and all the troops have disembarked.

Col. Streight took an escort and went over to Iuka to see Gen. Dodge tonight. Col Lawson of the 3rd Ohio is in command. A stampede of mules occurred and we lost over 300 It will take two or three days to replace them. Weather pleasant but signs of rain.

Apr. 20th 1863 - Eastport Mip [sic]. (Monday) The 73rd was ordered aboard the steamboat Nashville to go on a foraging expedition. We went down the river ten miles landing on the Mip. side. Captured thirty mules and returned this evening. We shelled the shore before landing.

April 22nd 1863 - Chickasaw Station Alabama. (Friday) Yesterday P.M. the 3rd Ohio and the 73rd boarded the Delaware and other boats and steamed up the river two miles where we landed, bidding good bye to water transportation and started for Chickasaw Station. The other two Regts took a different route under Streight while we were under Col Lawson. My horse had become so lame from an injury received while on the boat that he could not travel. I therefore got an order from the Brigade Qr. Ms. to exchange him for a fine animal that we captured yesterday.

We plodded along on our journey (Half the men being on foot yet) until night over took us and then commenced one of the most miserable times that our men ever experienced. It was perfectly dark and the road was a wild lonely by path full of rocks, logs, streams, deep holes, thick underbrush and everything that would delay and annoy us.

I was at the head of the column and we pushed on through this infernal road until midnight and then concluded to halt for the night. We attempted to communicate with the rear but could find no rear as the column was strung out for ten miles. Every man laid down and slept as best he could while a cold drizzly rain soaked us through and through. In the morn we found the rebel pickets but a short distance off. We joined Gen. Dodges forces about 9 o'clock (see next volume.)

April 22nd 1863 - Chickasaw Station Alabama. (Still Friday) Col. A. D. Streight issued an order to the "Independent Brigade" telling them of the perilous nature of the undertaking upon which we had engaged. That we would have to penetrate hundreds of miles into the enemy's country where we would always be surrounded by a wily and unscrupulous foe. That for at least six weeks, if successful, we would have to subsist entirely upon the country not being able to take provisions with us. But the hardships and privations before us seems only to give the men an unusual flow of spirits and everybody is busily preparing for the coming march and the inevitable fighting which must take place more or less, although we hope to avoid any large forces of the enemy which may be in our way. Especially if they be infantry.

Apr. 24, 1863 - Tuscumbia Ala. (Friday) We left Chickasaw Station on the 23rd accompanied by Dodges Division encamping in the evening near a small stream (Bear Creek I believe)

Here our Regt was placed in a rather peculiar position viz faced to the rear as small parties of the rebels had been observed to pass our flanks in that direction during the day and an attack might have been made.

Early in the morning Col Hathaway joined us having followed the expedition from Nashville. Lt. Williams Co. K came with him. We moved forward to this place today. Dodges troops preceding us and driving the Rebel General Roddy with two Regts of cavalry out to Tuscumbia which is a beautifully located town on the Tennessee river. This country is noted especially for its fine large springs of pure water one of which is at the foot of the hill upon which we are camped.

Apr 26th 1863 - Tuscumbia Ala. (Sunday) Yesterday and today have been busily engaged in mounting the men. Gen Dodge loaned us over 200 saddles and some horses. All of our Regt are now tolerably well mounted except Comp F who will have to march on foot for the first day until we can pickup stock enough for them.

It is circulated at Hd Qrs. that we start tonight at midnight. Gen Dodges troops took possession of Florence on the north side of the river yesterday. Roddy with 2000 Rebel cavalry is hovering around this place and we have to send out several companies on every foraging expedition. Drs Myers and Spencer who joined the Regt just before starting on the raid are with us. Dr. Pottinger is detached with the two companies of cavalry. Archie one of our colored servants whom we captured from Bragg when he was in Kentucky is so sick that we shall have to leave him here when we start.

Apr 27th 1863 - Mount Hope Ala. (Monday) Left Tuscumbia at 12 o'clock midnight taking a due south course over a very mountainous road until day light when the road although still very rough improved somewhat.

We passed through Russellville Franklin County during the day where we captured a rebel Major. Brought him along with us as far as this place and then sent him back to Dodge under an escort.

Arrived at this little dilapidated town during the afternoon and have encamped to await the arrival of our train and the dismounted men. We picked up a few horses today and shall remain here sending out foraging parties until the whole command is mounted.

We saw a few of the enemy's cavalry today but they got out of the way as soon as possible. The 73rd is in excellent spirit and delighted with the idea of "riding a raid" through the enemy's country.

Rained a little today.

Apr 28th 1863 - Moulton Ala. (Tuesday) About 9 o'clock this AM while lying at Mt. Hope Col Hathaway gave me command of Co. "G" to make a scout and pick up provisions and animals. Taking an intelligent contraband as a guide we rode off gaily and after a three mile wade through a swamp came upon the fine plantation of Dr. Napers who is now in the rebel army. We discovered here a large smoke house filled with hams and I loaded two on each horse. Although it was disagreeable work as three handsome young ladies who were occupying the house begged of me not to take anything from them but stern necessity demanded it and I had to turn a deaf ear to all the entreaties of the fair ones. I had received orders to burn all forage but refrained from doing it here as it would endanger the house. We also paid a visit to Dr. Jacksons and pressed a horse or two. Returned to camp well loaded with supplies.

Apr. 28 1863 - Moulton Alabama. (Also Tuesday) The "Independent Provisional Brigade" moved out of Mt. Hope 1500 strong about noon today and by a rapid march reached this secession hole shortly before dusk. Scattered a company of rebels out of town on the double quick and took possession.

We captured a mail and this week's issue of the Moulton Newspaper a little sheet about 6 by 8 inches and full of secesh brag and bluster. One paragraph stating that the "cowardly yanks" would not dare to come as far as Moulton.

The 73rd took possession of a fine yard full of shrubbery and went into camp. Roddy's force has been skirmishing with Dodge today 16 miles north of here. It is rumored the Genl. Forrest with 3000 cavalry is with him. If Dodge does his work however and attracts their attention until we get two days start we need have no fears of him.

I posted Co "I" on picket myself tonight on the road leading north. As there is no telling but what the rebs may conclude to come this way.

Apr. 29th 1863 - In Camp Alabama. (Wednesday) As our position at Moulton was anything but agreeable being in such close proximity to a superior force of the enemy and in the event of a fight taking place before we had fairly started upon our long expedition our plans would probably all be disarranged. Col. Streight concluded to place as great a distance between him and Roddy as possible before the rebel Genl. should divine the purposes of the expedition.

Accordingly orders were issued to leave at midnight as quietly as possible. I rode out and called the picket Co. in and by the time I got back to town the Regt had changed position and did not find it till near morning. The roads have been very rough and although we traveled till after dark today our train troubled us so much that we .have not traveled a great distance. We have encamped by the road side and am tired and sleepy.

Apr 30th 1863 - Days Gap. (Thursday) We arose early and were just falling in to start when the crack , crack of a volley of musketry told us that out pickets were attacked.

The enemy had followed us all day yesterday camping at night only a few miles in the rear and had sent on a body of cavalry to hold us until they could come up with their whole force.

We were nothing both to accommodate them but as our camping ground was a poor battle field we pushed on some distance to what is termed Days Gap. Although the country does not present much of the appearance of a gap. It being what a Hoosier would term an oak opening, the ground being considerably rolling. Here Col. Streight determined to make a stand.

The Brigade was soon dismounted and in line while the horses were sent to the rear. One man out of four was detailed to take care of horses which left the 73rd only about 200 strong and the fighting force of the Brigade about 1000.

The 80th Ill. was placed upon the right flank. The 3rd Ohio next on the left. The 51st Ind. next and the 73rd on the extreme left. The two mountain Howitzers were placed in position in the center of the Brigade.

A hospital was established a short distance in the rear. Men detailed from each Regt to carry off the wounded and every preparation made for a severe fight .

Skirmishers were sent to the front. The two companies of cavalry watched the flanks and we lay quietly on our arses awaiting the enemy's.attack. The woods were so thick that we could not see more than 75 yards in advance.

Soon a few scattering shots and then a brisk volley from the right flank proved that the Rebs were jealous of our position. This died away shortly and almost immediately after the left flank was attacked and the skirmishers in front of the 73rd and 51st were driven in. But these two regiments did not fire a shot. We were waiting for them to charge when we would give them a specimen of Hoosier fighting that would astonish them.

But they maneuvered very cautiously and appeared disinclined to charge our position. However as we did not open on them paying no attention whatever to the fire of their skirmishers they became bolder and advancing their line somewhat we could see that they outnumbered us for it extended far to the left of our left flank. And there was great danger that when they charged they would flank us and get in our rear.

To remedy this companies G and H of the 73rd were thrown to the rear and left to act as skirmishers If attacked from that side and to hold the enemy in check until we could change position.

But as it turned out there was no attack made upon that flank and those two companies did not participate in the fight. The enemy by this time had brought into position his artillery and opened upon us with round shot shell and canister. At the short distance of 150 yards our two little howitzers replied nobly and for half an hour a storm of cannon shot and rifle bullets was rained upon our devoted band. We did not return the fire generally along the line. Our regiment reserved its fire for the decisive moment but as we were suffering severely under their heavy fire it was deter-mined to charge and either make them run or fight at close quarters..

Just as the order was issued we observed the rebel line move forward. They had anticipated us and their splendid cavalry rushed towards us on the gallop and it seemed for an instant that our 1500 were doomed. On came the troopers but not a man of the Regt flinched. When within from 20 to 50 yards we poured into their ranks three or four quick withering volleys and then with a shout that I shall ever remember charged on the full run. Scattering them before us like sheep and killing and wounding scores who attempted to stand and stem the living torrent that swept down upon them.

It was a happy moment for men when breathless from our hard run I looked around upon the field where a few moments before a rebel host had defied us and who were now scattered to the four winds. So impetuous had been our charge that they did not have time to save a single gun or limber of their artillery and two fine pieces fell into our hands.

I shook the hands of brave officers and with them sent forth a shout of victory after those of the enemy who had succeeded in escaping. We placed the captured artillery in position and forming line awaited further developments.

For much to our surprise we found amongst our prisoners some of Forrest's men. They say that the force we have so badly whipped was Roddy's command and one regiment of Forrest's. That Forrest is coming up rapidly with his whole force and that we shall have to fight him in an hour or two. As Forrest has double our numbers of the flower of the Southern Cavalry this looks bad.

Our loss today is about fifty killed and wounded. The Rebels about 75 as near as we can ascertain. We have sent our train on and have been laying here some time expecting Forrest to make his appearance. But if he don't come soon I guess we will leave on the double quick and avoid him if possible. For if we fight his fierce men and whip him even it will cripple us so much that we shall not be able to accomplish the main object of our expedition.

Just after, Col. Hathaway gave me command of the Regt. this was quite an honor for an Adjutant to be placed over all the Captains. Major Walker was present but the exertion incident to the fight had used him up. Captain Garley of Co E shot through the leg severely and Lt Booher Co I in the face, comprise the list of casualties amongst the officers of the 73rd.

One poor fellow of company F saved my life by a sacrifice of his own. I was directly behind him when he was shot and instantly killed. Had he not been there the bullet would have struck me fairly.

One rebel trooper seemed determined to capture our flag, both he and his horse was shot within a few feet of the colors. I captured his gun and gave it to the Chaplain (who by the way is a fighting man) reserving the gun strap as a memento of the fight. Several of our animals and one or two men were injured by shells although in a deep hollow in rear of our line. A Captain in the 51st was killed.

Apr 30th 1863 - Hog Mountain Ala (called by some Crooked Creek). (Later Thursday) We left the Battlefield of Days Gap about noon. Up to that time the enemy had made no demonstration on our lines although he was in strong force.

We traveled as fast as possible in the hopes of gaining time and doing the work assigned us before being compelled to fight again. But fate had decided otherwise and before we had traveled far the cavalry of the enemy were on our heels and harassing our rear terribly. This they can do with impunity for it is impossible for newly mounted infantry to turn and fight regular cavalry without dismounting.

We managed to keep them at a respectful distance however until about sun down. When in crossing a stream as everyone stopped to water the animals the Brigade became strung out for two or three miles. The Rebs seeing this pressed the rear regiment (3rd Ohio) so hard that they sent on word for us (who were next) to help them. We immediately sent a courier to Col Streight who was at the head of the column and upon receipt of the news came back on the gallop. He was in favor of dismounting and forming line there but at the suggestion of Col Hathaway concluded to go back to where the 3rd Ohio was still skirmishing.

Col Streight directed me to have the 73rd posted on the extreme right flank at a certain point but Col Hathaway through mistaken zeal led the Regt directly under fire before dismounting. This disconcerted both men and animals and it was several minutes before we could get the men in line and the horses taken to the rear. Our Regt. then advanced slowly loading and firing as fast as possible and soon cleared the rebels from our immediate front. Our position here was upon a perfectly level and open piece of ground.

Meantime the other Regts. took position upon our left and a general engagement commenced all along the line. The enemy however fired almost invariably too high and our loss considering the heavy firing which we were under until after dark was astonishingly low. Not more than 50 were killed or wounded out of the Brigade. The loss of the 73rd was 11 men out of 150.

Our Mountain howitzers and the two pieces captured at Days Gap did good execution and poured the shot and shell into them until the ammunition was about exhausted. We repelled every assault that was made upon our lines but owing to their position did not attempt to charge them.

After dark the firing almost entirely ceased on both sides and we fell back about a mile to where our animals were taken. Our Regt. acting as rear guard and showing a full Regimental front with skirmishers. Arriving at this place the 73rd was ordered to hold the enemy in check while-the balance of the Brigade mounted and on the road. This was a difficult thing to do with our small force but we disposed them in a good position behind some fallen trees sending Company G well to the front as skirmishers.

We had hardly taken this position before the rebel skirmishers were halted by our men all along the line. It was very dark and they came right upon us before we could see them. They answered the halt by discharging their carbines and we returned the volley with buck and ball. This checked them and they remained quiet until they got their artillery to bear on us.

When they commenced a furious cannonade, meantime, all the brigade except the 73rd had mounted and put off, leaving our Regt. to get out of the scrape as best they could. Col. Hathaway had ordered me to find Streight and get the two companies of cavalry to remain with us until we mounted. But owing to the darkness and confusion was unable to find him.

The 73rd after holding the position as long as it had been ordered to, gave the rebels one volley which we ascertained afterwards killed and wounded a large number and then mounting as quick as possible left Hog Mountain and the scene of our second fight.

We had punished the enemy so severely that he was afraid to follow us with his whole force and only sent a small party to ascertain where we went to during the night. We whipped 2900 of the best cavalry in the rebel service in two separate engagements. But the nature of our expedition did not allow us to delay and this accounts for our leaving the battle fields which we had fairly won in the hands of the enemy. It must be remembered that all this time we were going southeast penetrating farther and farther into the enemy's country. This is conclusive proof that we were not fleeing from them.

May 1st 1863 - Blountsville Ala. (Friday) After withdrawing from Hog Mountain battle field last evening we traveled at a pretty good pace all night long and reached this little town about 8 o'clock this morning. And have stopped to feed and rest both men and animals. Are very much fatigued by our hard marching.

As our train has delayed us a great deal we've concluded to do without and except one fast team. And a huge bonfire is now burning consisting of 12 wagons and some of the superfluous baggage. All the Negroes in the county appear to have determined to follow the fortunes of the Yankees and Col. Streight was compelled to issue a general order driving all the poor contraband away from us.

The indefatigable enemy has caught us again and brisk skirmishing is going on. On the other side of town.

May 1, 1863 - In Camp Ala - 12 o'c midnight. (Later Friday) I left Blountsville about one hour after the main part of the Brigade did. Capts. Smith and McQuiddy's cavalry was holding the enemy in check that long. We then had to leave at a rapid gait for fear of being captured. It was Smith lost some ten men out of his company who could not get away.

The Rebels kept close on our heel in such force that on coming to a small river during the afternoon we had to dismount the whole brigade and drive him back with the bayonet before we could cross. He did not trouble us after that and we pursued the even tenor of our way until midnight when exhausted nature could stand no more and we dismounted in the woods to bait our animals and get a little rest.

The officers are confident that we will not be able to get back to our lines safe. But all hope to accomplish our object first.

May 2nd 1863 - Gadsden Alabama. (Saturday) Left our camping ground early this morning and pushed on. Our regiment in advance, shortly before noon we came upon the town of Gadsden a quiet village on the Coosa River. And pushed in at a hard gallop capturing several rebel officers before they were aware of our coming.

I took a corporal and file of men and took possession of the Post Office. The postmaster was very polite and handed me the different keys belonging to his office. And in a short time I had confiscated the whole concern. A mail was found already made up and ready to go out. I took the mail bag (which had one of Uncle Sams locks on it) and stuffed about a thousand letters, a full file of Southern papers and two or three hundred Confederate postage stamps into it and then slung it across my saddle. Bid a polite good day with the P.M. and was after the Regt.

May 2 1863 - Crumps Farm (by some Blounts Farm) Later Saturday) We had a merry time this afternoon riding slowly down the beautiful Coosa valley. This part of the country is by far the finest that we have yet seen and the Rebels kept a good distance to the rear. Not a shot being fired since we left Gadsden. This gave Col. Hathaway, Maj. Walker and myself a good opportunity to dissect the mail which I had captured.

We were compelled to ride slow and every once and I [sic] while I would thrust my hand down into the mail bag and bring forth a bunch of rebel letters. These often, being read, were thrown in the road for the edification of our friends who followed us so closely in the rear. It must have been aggravating to the Rebs to see these letters on love, marriage, business and every kindred subject thus rifled of their contents. And forming subject of amusement to the "Yankee vandals" which they are please to term us.

About 4 oclock PM we stopped in a small valley called Crumps Farm to feed. Plenty of forage was found here and we expected a good time but just as the rear guard came up and before Company G which had been detailed as videttes had taken their spot they were attacked by the enemy's advance guard. Of course the 73rd was ordered to support Co G and we double quicked to the front and formed line across the road just in time to save our company from being driven in or captured.

The enemy was very bold and active attacking as first in front them of the left flank and finally on the right. But although our ammunition was nearly spoiled by dampness yet we poured in the buck and ball so fast that he could make no impression on our line nor compel us to yield an inch. Col. Streight formed the balance of the Brigade far to our right and rear leaving us to hold our position alone He sent one howitzer up to us however which materially assisted us in repelling the attack from our front.

The firing was very brisk for about half an hour and then gradually died away. The enemy contenting themselves with annoying us by their advance line of sharpshooters. We were well protected however by the woods and underbrush and lost but very few men killed or wounded.

We have to morn [sic] however the loss of our gallant Colonel Gilbert Hathaway who was shot through the heart and almost instantly killed while cheering on his men during the fight. Col H. a short time before his death placed me in command of the Right wing (which.was on the right of the road) and went over to see how Major Walker was getting along with the left. That was the last order he ever gave me and the last time that I ever saw him. He was carried to the rear and taken to a farm house. But the Brigade left before they could bury him. When the Col left me I had the three companies at the front and two companies bent back on the right and deployed as skirmishers to protect that flank.

We remained in position about an hour with only a few scattering shots fired now and then. I was laying down reading some rebel letters when suddenly Company D fell back because as they stated the left wing had gone. This puzzled me a good deal. I had not heard a word from Major Walker and was left there alone without orders. I determined however to hold the position until I was ordered in and forming a new line posted the men behind logs and ordered them not to fire a gun without orders. I staid [sic] in this position some time when I saw that officers were much dissatisfied. My position was a peculiar one. I had been put in command by the Col. but still my rank was only 1st Lt. and Adjt. and here were three or four Captains any of which were my superior and according to the army regulation could command me.

I therefore decided to leave it to them whether we should remain or go in. They decided on the latter course. I therefore mounted my horse and ordered the line to fall back without changing position until we reached a point one hundred yards to the rear when as the enemy had not attempted to molest us I formed in the road and marched back at quick time. We found the left wing all mounted a mile or more in the rear. By this time it was dark. When I fell back from our advanced position the enemy advanced and just as we reached our horses we were again ordered to the front to repel an attack. I collected all of the 73rd that could be found and taking command marched back but no attack was made.

We set fire to two large bams in our immediate front in order to light up the battlefield. We lay upon the ground for sometime awaiting an assault but Forrest had tried our mettle thru several times and did not appear anxious to press matters although he had more than double our force. We possessed this advantage over him however that we fought as infantry and he as cavalry.

About 8 o'clock we commenced preparation to leave. Fifty good men and the best horses were selected from each Regt. (making 200 in all) who were instructed to march upon Rome with the utmost expedition and destroy the iron works there and also the Round Mountain Iron works. This precaution was taken in case that we should have to surrender tomorrow for it is believed now that it will be utterly impossible to continue against the enemy any longer as our ammunition is nearly exhausted and what remains is in a damaged condition. The men are greatly exhausted and our horses can scarcely travel.

We left Grumps (Blounts) Farm about eight o'clock last night and did not stop till eight o'clock this mom. Such another night march I never want to experience again. Nature had been outraged too long. The men had to sleep and the Brigade was strung out for ten miles. Nine out of every 10 being fast asleep although the animals were traveling as rapidly as they could go. I was asleep myself half the night but found no difficulty in keeping the saddle.

Arriving at this place we found it was impossible to

proceed further without rest and something to eat. We dismounted therefore and Col. (Maj) Walker and myself had just set down to a breakfast which had been obtained by extraordinary exertions when a volley from the pickets only a short distance off started us to our feet and an order to getting the Regt. in line.

The men were completely exhausted and could scarcely drag one foot after another. The ammunition would not carry a ball half the usual distance and matters looked very discouraging. But still the <u>will to do</u> was there and every man would have stood up till shot down if nothing more. Our howitzers fired the last round of shell and then ceased with an ominous silence. Gen Forrest sent in a flag of truce and we agreed to surrender on the following written conditions.

That we should be permitted to retain our <u>Colors</u>, our side arms and all private property, to be paroled and sent north immediately. As soon as the negotiations commenced I was glad of a moments respite and laying down on the ground immediately fell asleep with instructions to wake me as soon as the fight commenced. When I awoke we were prisoners of war.

Forrest's men treated us with a great deal of consideration, no cheering or insulting language. They had fought four times and had learned to respect us. The Brigade stacked arms and were addressed by Col. Streight upon the necessity of the surrender and then the officers and men were separated.

In spite of the honorable conditions given us, I never saw so much disappointment exhibited by men as ours did at the termination of the raid.

May 3rd 1864 (1863.Ed) - Rome Ga. (Sunday) Genl. Forrest escorted (us) into Rome this evening. Our advance guard of two hundred men had waked up the citizens of this little town by their impudence and audacity, in judging their houses in sight of the city and a large crowd was on hand to see the Yankee raiders. The citizens were exultant and insolent while Forrest's troopers were respectful and considerate showing the difference between people who do the talking and those who do the fighting.

The officers were quartered in the Etowah house. Had to pay $1.50 for supper of corn bread and my coffee. This is pretty good on prisoners of war. Am quartered in room 24. Rome is rather a pretty little village of one or two thousand inhabitants and would have been a hard place to take as the bridge was all prepared to burn at a moment's notice.

May 4th 1863 - Rome Georgia. (Monday) Rome is at the terminus of the Rome Railroad which connects at Kingston with the Western and Atlantic running from Atlanta to Chattanooga. It is the county seat of Floyd County and the center of a rich farming country.

I heartily wish that the advance guard had taken a mountain howitzer with them and battered the infernal secesh hole to the ground. We were joined this morning by Genl. Forrest, and have changed quarters to the crust house. And in spite of our parole, a guard is placed around us.

The rebel papers today are jubilant over our surrender and among other things published the outrages [sic] lie that our Brigade of 1400 surrendered to 800. When we have abundant evidence otherwise. Then the admission of Forrest that his force was nearly double ours. His Quartermaster (with my personal knowledge) made a requisition immediately after the surrender for forage for 4000 horses for one day. This included our 1400 and showed that his force then up was 2600 and our men who were captured assert positively that after the surrender a portion of his force went back and did not come to Rome.

We tell the citizens here who want to know what "genius wanted with we'ens" that we were only the advance guard of an army that sooner or later would make this country a howling wilderness.

Today our rations consist of a small piece of meat and corn bread which hardly deserves the name. But the officers are in good spirits and crack lively jokes over this novel position. I bought some rebel currency in Kentucky some time since at the rate of 5 cents on the dollar and am using the worthless stuff to good advantage here, although prices are very high.

Colonel Gilbert Hathaway

Chapter Five

May 5th, 1863 – February 26th, 1864
(Libby Prison in Richmond)

May 5th, 1863 - Atlanta, Ga. (Tuesday) After a good night's sleep on the "bench" in (the) Court House at Rome, we left in the morning for this place via Rome and Atlantic and Western R.R. a distance of 79 miles where we arrived this p.m. and have been quartered in the Court House.

There are about 100 officers in the Brig including Surgeons and Chaplains. The authorities here seem to have some humanity about them and have fed us pretty well tonight, although did not get supper til about 11 o'clock.

The citizens are terribly alarmed at our audacity in penetrating 300 miles within their lines and fear that there is a larger force behind.

Atlanta is a thriving city and a great deal of business is done here especially for the so called Confederate Govt.

Have been invariably treated well by the soldiers but insultingly by the citizens.

May 7th. 1863 - Atlanta. Ga. (Thursday) Yesterday passed off quietly. We have but one or two guards over us but are not allowed to leave the enclosure.

The men were sent to Richmond Va. today, but there are no signs of our following them.

A number of bouquets have been sent to the officers by Union ladies. Recd. one from Mrs. Schofield. Am going to preserve it as a memento of the union sentiment here which the rebs in spite of their cruelty cannot always keep down.

I bot a quart of strawberries yesterday paying $3 in confd. for them. I took a lot of money at Rome in change for bills which can't be given away in Atlanta.

We just began to hear rumors of a hard fight on the Rappahannock river. Our forces have won the day but the rebs. claim a victory and am afraid that it is another of those drawn battles which the army of the Potomac is noted for.

May 10th, 1863 - Military Prison Atlanta. Ga. (Sunday) We were removed to this prison on the 8th.

The Rebels have concluded that they have won a great victory in the East [the Battle of Chancellorsville. Ed.] and are disposed to be a little bolder and treat us harshly.

This is the same prison where Genl. Willich, Col. Ducan and numerous other officers were confined. The hours come and go and bring nothing to relieve the monotony of prison life. This in comparison with our truly exciting raid is almost insufferable.

We have divided off into measures getting nothing to eat except com bread and beef. This is Sunday and we have had divine services three times: in the morning by Chaplain of the 80th Ill., p.m. by the 3rd Ohio, and this evening Chaplain Frazer (who by the way is a much better soldier than preacher) gave us a sermon. Lt. Hunnicut is Commander of this Prison and is something of a gentleman. We hear rumors of leaving and hope that they are true.

May 12th, 1863 - Augusta, Ga. (Tuesday) We were glad enough to leave that miserable prison and Atlanta behind us at 7 p.m. last night. After a ride of 171 miles arrived here at 8 a.m. and found a large crowd of the "chivalry" waiting to see the "raiders."

Augusta is a lively town situated on the Savannah river and the terminus of several railroads. We stop here only to await transportation east.

May 13th, 1863 - Columbia South Carolina. (Wednesday) Left Augusta late yesterday p.m. on the S.C. Railway,

Reached Brandville during the night distant 70 miles. Then taking the northern branch after a run of 67 miles reach Columbia after daylight. Were marched through the city by a red haired drunken confed. Lt. to the Charlotte & S.C. RR Depot. Columbia is decidedly a handsome place but as pris. of war we were not allowed to view it at our leisure.

May 13th, 1863 - Charlotte North Carolina. (Later Wednesday) I've made a mistake of dates somehow and for a day or two have been 24 hours behind the time. But our journey to the Confederate Capitol over Confederate Railroads all broken down and used up is terribly tedious and we are only too anxious to reach our destination, be exchanged and breathe the fresh air of the north once more.

South Carolina is a poor state. We have traveled today on this C. & S.C. R.R. for 109 miles and a more desolate looking country I never saw.

Arrived at C- about 3 o'clock this p.m., have no rations and there is nothing in town to sell in the eatable line. I shall remember this place for we've sat for a long time leaning against a warehouse filled with rations but as hungry and surly a looking set as we could well be. Our clothes are nearly gone and nothing to purchase more with.

Apr. 14th, 1863 - Raleigh N.C. (Thursday) Our one hundred officers together with the officers and crew of the Gun Boat Indianolia were crowded upon open cars with cross ties for seats at Charlotte and shipped over this North Carolina Railway, a distance of 175 miles, on very slow time.

We stopped at the company shops halfway for dinner and got a mouthful apiece for $2.00. Arrived here about 9 o'clock this p.m. and are waiting hungry and tired for the train to start north.

Have not been able to see much of the capitol of North Carolina as it was dark when we came in. A few hard crackers and a little spoilt meat has just been issued to us by our inhuman keepers and we are glad enough to get anything to eat. For a wonder they intend to give us a passenger train tonight.

May 15th, 1863 - Weldon N.C. (Friday) Left Raleigh last night on the Raleigh and Gaston Railway at 11 0' clock arriving here this a.m. This place is within 30 or 40 miles of our lines. How I long to be there once more. Distance from here to Raleigh 97 miles.

May 15th 1863 - Petersburg Va. (Later Friday) Reached this city over the Petersburg Railway a distance of 64 miles late this p.m.

We were kept waiting in the street for several hours and then tumbled into the 2nd story of a brick building to pass the night as best we could. Southern Chivalry indeed. We at the north would treat our hogs better than this. The room is packed full and it will be all we can do to find sleeping room on the floor.

Petersburg has a population I believe of about 20,000 and appears to be a flourishing city but the people all look reckless and concerned Its some consolation to know that they will look and feel more so before this war is over.

May 16th, 1863 - Richmond Va. (Saturday) Arrived at the famed capitol of the so called Confederate states this a.m.

Richmond is situated on the north bank of James River and is noted for the beauty of its environs but as yet have not been able to see it. A guard has been placed around us at the depot and we are the cause of many prying eyes.

I succeeded in buying a slice of bread and a mouthful of fish for a dollar. It was delicious.

The distance from Petersburg here is 22 miles. The whole distance traveled by R.R. from Rome, Ga. is 787 miles which took nearly six days. This added to the distance from Murfreesboro, Tenn. to Rome by the route we came which was accomplished by stamina and march about 500 miles makes the long distance of 1287 miles which Streight's raiders have made in a little over a month.

May 16th 1863 - Libby Prison Richmond Virginia. (Later Saturday) After much delay at the depot we were finally marched though the city to this noted place and the first operation to be gone though was a minute search of each officer. They took from me my pencil (which looks ominous), a memorandum book, all writing paper and envelopes, canteen, etc. etc. and then guided me up through many rooms and more stairways to the third or fourth story east room. Here I found Col. Streight the only one of our party yet admitted. About 50 officers were here from the Potomac Army who were taken in the late fight at Chancellorsville. They greeted us cordially but most of them appeared to be deeply engaged in a 25 cent game of poker. I took a seat on the floor and commenced ruminating on the situation.

May 30th 1863 - Libby Prison Richmond Va. (Saturday) Two weeks in this miserable prison and no sign yet of an exchange. All the Captains were at first placed in the lower middle room. The Colonel, Lt. Cols., Majors and Lieuts. in the upper east room. On the 22nd inst. we were notified to be in readiness to leave for the north as flag of truce had been signaled but our disappointment was great when we discovered that none but the Army of the Potomac officers could go.

On the 24th we were again disappointed when the officers and crew of the Gunboat Indianolia were released and we were left behind. Capt. Brown of the Gunboat is a big gentlemanly officer. Have got a piece of his flag which was flying at the time he was compelled to surrender.

June 1, 1863 - Libby Prison Richmond Va. (Monday) Day after day, hour after hour comes and goes and still nothing to relieve this dreary prison life. The confinement to me is almost insufferable and if I thought we were going to spend many more weeks here I shall become sick or make desperate efforts to escape but we live in hope that a exchange will soon be effected.

None but our Brigade officers are here now with the exception Julian H. Brown and another N. Y. Tribune correspondent captured at Vicksburg and one or two other officers.

We have divided off into measures of from 4 to 8. Lts. Mundock, Van Ness and Connolly and self constitute no. II. The Captains have all been brought up in our room making the numbers in one room 40 ft. wide by 75 long. 115. Here we eat, drink, sleep and exercise. Am not allowed to leave the room for any purpose.

June 13th, 1863 - Libby Prison. (Saturday) "Cooper" a jolly fellow and clk.to Capt. Brown of the Indianolia was sent north today. We envy him. Three squads of officers were brought in lately making 135 now here. The room is crowded so as to be uncomfortable.

Recd. a letter from Hon. Schuyler Colfax M. C. informing me of my promotion from Adjt. to Major of the 73rd. This is very gratifying and creates some surprise amongst the officers here outside of our Regt. who wonder how all the Captains of the 73rd could exercise so much self denial as to give up their claims and allow a Lt. to be promoted over them.

Haven't received any letters from home yet and judge that in spite of the privilege granted to write and receive letters that not one in a doz are allowed to and come.

June 30th, 1863 - Libby Prison. (Tuesday) We have received such additions to our numbers lately that we are uncomfortably crowded, there being in one room half the large number of 300 officers. Among them are 108 of Genl. Milroy's command lately captured at Winchester.

Our rations are miserable in quality and very scant in quantity, actually not being sufficient for a person's health. If it were not that some of us have a little money and are allowed to buy vegetables, we would be in a state of semi-starvation all the time. In fact, with all that we get outside of the rations that the Confed. Govt. issues, we are perfectly ravenous at every meal. We have to buy our own cooking utensils etc. and cook our own victuals besides scrub our rooms, a species of menial labor which the officials delight to see us do. The more shame for them.

July 4th, 1863 - Libby Prison Richmond Va. (Saturday)
Hail blessed day tho we see your light through grated windows yet our hearts are glad to know that our friends, the loyal people of the free north are this day celebrating the birthday of our independence. We had made preparations to have a little celebration of our own in Libby. By stealth a few of the officers have procured some red, white and blue cloth and secretly manufactured a goodly sized American flag. This we hung from one of the rafters and electing Col. Streight Chairman proceeded with several patriotic speeches which created so much enthusiasm and clapping of hands that rebels suspecting what we were at came up and ordered the room to be quiet, tore down our flag and threatened to do something serious if any loud talking was heard. The officers became very excited and some were in favor of carrying it through at all hazards. but better counsel prevailed and knowing that we were completely in their power concluded to do nothing rash. But talk of the "good day" in little knots of 4 or 5...

I may as well put our rations down here for the benefit of history. It consists of Bread ½ loaf (enough for two meals if we had other provisions plenty) Fresh beef ¼ lb., rice or beans as much as one man would eat, salt and vinegar in very small quantities. This is all and is about 1/3 of the U.S. Govt. ration.

There is a good deal of excitement in Richmond just at present in regard to the raid of Genl. Dix. He can come into the city and release us just as well as not but am afraid that he won't do it. Weather pleasant.

July 5th 1863 - Richmond Va. (Sunday) There is interest felt among the prisoners in regard to the Rebel General Lee's invasion of Pennsylvania. [the Battle of Gettysburg, Ed.] It is a bold move of his. But I cannot see how he ever expects to make a foothold in the north. He will do well to get back safe with his army which I do not anticipate.

There is also much interest felt in Vicksburg and Port Hudson. Our gallant General Grant has done well so far but the Rebels are confident of holding the place. It is rumored today the Genl. Rosecrans (our Rosy) is advancing on Gen. Bragg and I hope it is so. For all we want is the assurance that he is moving and a victory can be accounted on as pretty certain.

Greenbacks sell here 4 for 1 of the currency. By paying 25 cts we get the daily Richmond papers. Miserable little half sheets full of traitorous intentions.

July 6th 1863 - Libby Prison. (Monday) Genl. Burnside commanding in Kentucky has lately hung two Confederate captains who were found recruiting within the Federal lines. This was perfectly right and according to the laws of war, but the Confederate Government having great hopes of succeed -ing in Penn. and Mississippi and inflated with the idea of having us soon whipped has concluded to retaliate.

Accordingly an order came today to Capt. Thomas Turner Commandant of the Prison to select two captains by lot to be executed. There are about 75 captains here who were collected together in one room.

It was a very affecting ceremony. Their names were all written down on separate slips of paper and then put into a box. At the request of the officers one of the old gray headed captains was selected to draw. The first two names drawn to be the unfortunate ones. Amidst a breathless silence two slips were drawn out and the names announced by Capt. Turner. They were Capt. Henry W. Sawyer of the 1st New Jersey Cavalry and Capt. Flynn of the 51st Indiana. A slight change of countenance by these two, a sigh of relief from the others and the assemblage separated. The two unfortunate captains being taken to cells. As Captain Flynn is from our Brigade we are all feeling very melancholy over his fate and not knowing when our turn may come.

I amused myself today in finding out the different officers here and their ranks. There are six Colonels, six Lt. Cols., eight Majors, 14 Surgs., seven Chaplains and three newspaper correspondents. All of rest of the 300 are Capts. and Lts.

We are hoping to be exchanged almost any day but have no good grounds to base a hope upon.

July 11th 1863 - Libby Prison. (Saturday) Vicksburg is taken!! The tardy news of its surrender on the fourth of July has come at last. The Rebs in Richmond are despondent. The prisoners jubilant. The papers think matters in the Confederacy look gloomy although they claim a victory and 40,000 prisoners at Gettysburg which <u>we</u> don't believe.

General Neal Dow, the Maine law celebrity, and new Brigadier arrived today and was initiated into the mysteries of Libby. He is a small man and does not look as if he has much military talent but as he sports a star. I suppose we will have to pay all due deference to rank. His sleeping bunk is next to mine and have a good chance to examine his character. As yet have seen no striking points except a penchant for driving nails in the floor.

July 31st, 1863 - Libby Prison. (Friday) Many and stirring events have happened since last I wrote but my imprisonment is so irksome and depressing that I have no heart to keep a diary.

Port Hudson has surrendered to our armies with 5000 prisoners. This with the 31,000 taken at Vicksburg gives us a very large overplus but unfortunately Genl. Grant committed the fatal blunder of paroling the whole of them including one Lt. Genl. (Pemberton) and half a doz Maj. Genls. without saying anything about Brigadiers.

The papers this morning announced that the Rebel raider Genl. Morgan and his whole force are captured after running through Indiana and Ohio.

Genl. Lee has been driven from Penn. and the prospect looks cheery for the Union cause on all sides.

Brig. Gen. Graham and a number of other prisoners captured at Gettysburg have arrived and now share our imprisonment.

August 3rd 1863 - Richmond Va. (Monday) It is just 3 months today since the Provisional Brigade surrendered to the enemy. For twelve long weeks have we been surrounded by the four gloomy walls of Libby Prison. Meantime our numbers have been increasing almost daily with now instead of the original 100 there are 566 Federal officers confined here. Two more rooms have been allotted us making <u>four</u> for the accommodation of that large number. The fact of it is that our immediate prison officials have never been in jail and don't know how to treat prisoners. We have but 5 cook stoves, something over a hundred officers to a stove. The exchange of officers, the one all absorbing topic of which we never tire, is still a mooted question between "Uncle Sam" and the spurious "Cousin Sallie."

The weather is becoming very warm and owing to our crowded state we suffer much from the heat. If it were not that we have access to plenty of water there would be much sickness.

Aug. 5th 1863 - Richmond Va. (Wednesday) We can get greenbacks changed now at the rate of 5 for 1. The Confederate currency is going downhill fast. Gold is quoted at 11 for 1.

We are allowed to buy a few things in the city, but prices are enormously high. Potatoes 10$ per bushel.

There has been much excitement lately in rooms no. 1 and 2. The difficulty arose between the large mess party and the small messes. As I belong to a small mess am happy to say that they have finally come off victorious.

There is one "institution" that if I had pretended to keep a diary of prison life I should have mentioned before (have not done so so far for the want of paper) and that is "Ben" a good humored darkie who "sells de papers." Every morning we are awakened by his clarion voice "Heres de morning papers." "All four copies of de morning papers." "Great graphic news from de sout west" and he sells a good many of news. Enquirer, Dispatch, Whig and Sentinel at 20c apiece.

August 12th 1863 - Richmond Va. (Wednesday) Quite warm for several days past. Thermometer ranged at 98 in the shade.

In room no 4 of Gettysburg officers a lyceum has been established. Room no 2 proposes to start a grammar school. In our room (no 2) called Streight's room or the "upper West" (By the way have removed from the upper east) we have a horizontal pole consisting of a hickory broom handle for gymnastic exercises.

There are plenty of rumors afloat in regard to the exchange but nothing reliable.

Papers have advanced 5 cts. Gold quoted today at 1200 pr ct discount. It does one good to see it go up here. At the north I believe it is only 30 pr ct discount.

We have heard at last from the 73rd. It took part in the capture of the Rebel Genl. Morgan who raided through the Hoosier and Buckeye states and is now at Indianapolis guarding the prisoners captured. Capt. Williamson is in command.

Aug. 15th 1863 - Richmond Va. (Saturday) By an order from the Confederate Genl. Winder all our money is confiscated that was sent to us from the north. They had expressly arranged to deliver it to us if we sent for money. But I was not surprised at this perfidy. It is nothing more than we could expect from the southern chivalry.

Major Morris 6th Penn. cavalry (Grand son of Robt. Morris of revolutionary fame) died of scurvy a day or two since. The natural effect of the nation supplying us. He was a fine officer.

For week I have been earnestly engaged in forming plans for an escape from this miserable hole. And have examined every chance that I could possibly see but am forced to acknowledge that it appears almost impossible. Not a prisoner has escaped from here since the war commenced. If I had plenty of money might possible bribe the guards.

Aug 26th 1863 - Richmond Va. (Wednesday) Time wears wearily on. Everything has become so terribly monotonous that I haven't the energy or heart to write details of our prison life.

Money (since all in the hands of the Confederate authorities has been confiscated) is becoming scarce and most of us including mess II are reduced to Govt. rations and miserably small. They are hardly enough to sustain life.

There are two or three Naval officers captured in the night attempt to take Fort Sumter who have just come in.

Major Henry gave us a lecture yesterday on mesmerism his favorite theme.

No news from Charleston lately. I do hope they will

take the infernal city soon.

There are signs of activity in the Dept. of the Cumberland. Wish I was there.

Have been carving a paper knife and full blown rose out of bone to pass away the time.

The Exchange Commissions have met but the results have not transpired.

Sept 3 1863 - Richmond Va. (Thursday) 4 months in Libby! and no signs of an exchange yet. It certainly looks discouraging.

Recd. a letter from Hon. Schuyler Colfax a day or two since. He gives news from home. Yesterday the citizens (Mr. Buckley, Herald Cor. Julius H. Brown and A.D. Richardson Tribune Corp. and Mr. Thompson) were transferred from Libby to Castle Thunder.

There are some ladies confined in the Castle a short time since (which is distant one block from here) with whom we used to signal by the waving of handkerchiefs, etc. The same kind of communication is kept up with Union ladies who frequently pass along on Cary street. It is aggravating to see "calico" so friendly and yet so far off.

Rosecrans will undoubtedly occupy east Tennessee soon.

We all have strong hopes that Charleston is doomed to fall soon.

Sept. 13th 1863 - Richmond Va. (Sunday) The Rebels evidently have some great movement on foot. Heretofore it has been extremely quiet in the vicinity of the city, but today I saw from 75 to 100 pieces of artillery cross James River Bridge going west. A good many troops on cars and on foot have also passed. Am afraid that this force is going to reinforce Bragg in which case Rosecrans will have a very large army to continue against but still I have great faith in his ability to ship the enemy and gain east Tennessee and only hope that he may be able to penetrate to Atlanta.

Morris Island with its Forts have been taken by our troops which is good so far but Charleston certainly ought to be taken as soon as possible. It would have a great moral effect.

Sept. 26th 1863 - Richmond Va. (Saturday) For some time past great indignation has been expressed by nine tenths of the officers against Lt. Col. Sanderson C.S. of one of the Army of the Potomac Corps who has taken sides with the Prison officials in the ration question and did all he could to nullify our protest against the insufficiency.

Spencer Kellogg an alleged spy was hung at Camp Lee. Some officers are of the opinion that our Govt. will retaliate.

The news from "Chickamauga" the late battle in Georgia comes in slowly in spite of the rebel boasts. Enough is known to prove that the object (Chattanooga) for which the battle was fought is gained and there is no likelyhood of our being driven from it. Yet we cannot deny that <u>some</u> of our hopes were blasted. Great confidence was felt that Rosecrans would penetrate to Atlanta. This is his first not exactly defeat but driven back.

November 1st 1863 - Richmond Va. (Sunday) More than a month has rolled away since I've dotted a line of "experience." This "pris. of war" life is becoming so indefinitely extended that I've settled down into a sort of apathy and am ready for anything that future has in store for me.

Our condition has slightly improved, for now boxes of eatables from our friends in the north are allowed to be sent to us and no II has its share of good things. The Sanitary and Christian societies have also bestirred themselves in our behalf and now every Truce boat that comes up is loaded with comforts for the prisoners.

This is one of the most extraordinary spectacles

witnessed now that the history of any war has ever shown. [sic] The United States Govt. has lately sent 40,000 rations to its starving solders now confined as prisoners in Richmond. The Confederate Govt. has received it thereby tacitly acknowledging their inability to feed them. What a community!

Nov. 10th 1863 - Libby Prison. (Tuesday) So many additions have been made to our numbers lately that the six upper rooms of Libby accommodate over a thousand officers now.

Lt. Col. Lapelle of the 9th Ind. is here and has joined no. II. He was captured at Chickamauga. Some of the officers of a lively turn have organized a Minstrel troop and their concerts are excellent and help pass away the time pleasantly.

The Libby Histrionics gave an exhibition last week and performed very well. For some time past there has been a steady determination on the part of the officers here to terminate our imprisonment in some way before the winter settles in. "After this civil war is over" I may say something about this but while it lasts I must not commit anything to paper or talk to family. Weather is becoming uncomfortably cold.

Nov. 24th 1863 - Richmond Va. (Tuesday) There is some signs that humanity and common sense has returned to the two August Comon. of Exchange. All the surgeons here numbering nearly 100 are to be sent north today.

The Confederate Congress is in session at Richmond and I can see from my window the hated southern flag raised over the Capitol every morning. Am reading their proceedings in the daily papers with interest. The Virginia Legislature is also in session now but is such a weak body that it doesn't appear capable of doing much mischief.

December 10th 1863. (Thursday) The authorities here have lately allowed us to draw from 25 to 50$ per month in Confed. currency of our money on deposit with the A. Q. M. but today an order was issued confiscating the whole. Simply a repetition of what has occurred once before.

January 1st 1864 - Richmond Va. (Friday) Little did I imagine when we surrendered on the 3rd of May last that the new year would find me languishing in this southern bastile. I cannot begin to describe my feeling now. No one but those who have experienced a similar imprisonment can know the longing with which we await our release.

Col. Streight smuggled through some Greenbacks lately and I believe is going to attempt to bribe the Guards!

We made a general subscription of Confederate money lately in order to send one man out if possible but you can't bribe southern soldiers with southern money. They know its value too well, in fact it is perfectly worthless. A soldier's pay here would hardly buy his tobacco. Last fall it took just one month's pay of a private soldier to buy a watermelon.

Feb. 1st 1864 - Richmond Va. (Monday) Today the first escape from Libby Prison proper that has occurred since the war broke out was successfully executed. Major Bates 80th ILL., Capt. Porter 14th N. Y, Lt. King 3rd Ohio, Lt. Cupp 11th Mass. and Lt. Canithis of a Virginia Regt. all dressed in citizens clothes coolly walked out of the prison, one by one passed the guards and off into the city. Bates, Cupp and King have been caught and brought back. It was a rich thing to see them walk off so coolly. If I had a citizen's suit I should have followed them. The escape of these men has given that miserable wretch Major Turner an opportunity to annoy us by roll calls all day long and by every other means in his power.

Col. Streight the other night gave one of the guards 100$ Greenback and two watches to let him escape but the guard betrayed him and he was caught immediately after getting outside of the Guard line and he and Capt. Reed who attempted the same thing are now in a cell and in irons.

We look with hope to the approaching spring campaign as our only chance for release. Four officers including Col. Powell 2nd Va Cav. to whom I gave a letter of introduction to Hon. Schulyer Colfax were released lately and sent north on special exchange.

Feb. 7th 1864 - Richmond Va. (Sunday) Butler is reported to be at Bottoms Bridge in force. Richmond is alive with excitement. Bells ringing and the militia and department clerks assembling. I sincerely hope that the "malicious" may be gobbled, but do not anticipate that Butler is coming in here. Capts. Ives and Reed and Maj. Sterling were sent to Salisbury Penitentiary today for 15 years. Before this month is out I hope to see them released by our Federal Army.

February 10th 1864 - Libby Prison Richmond Va. (Thursday) I have to record today one of the remarkable events of this war and one which interests us as prisoners of war very much.

For nearly two months a number of officers who have deemed it feasible to tunnel out of Libby have been busily at work. After studying and devising numerous plans it was finally decided that the east cellar was the only place that offered any chance of success whatever but as the prisoners are all confined in the second and third stories it was a difficult problem to solve how we should get down.

This difficulty was finally overcome by a little quiet work each night at the fire place in the dining room. A hole was dug though this fire place in an oblique direction which opened into the cellar mentioned. Men were now sent down every night who worked with a will using an old hinge and sugar scoop.

After digging through the massive cellar wall the work

progressed slowly but surely. The object being to reach the sewer and escape by that outlet but upon reaching the sewer they found to their chagrin that this was impassable for various reasons.

Determined not to be discouraged however they boldly struck out to tunnel across the street a distance of about 60 feet. This was accomplished in a little over a month's work.

During the time it was being dug Capt. Johnson of a Kentucky Regt. was left in the cellar by mistake and in the morning roll call was missing. The confederates were greatly puzzled to know how he escaped but didn't find out till recently.

During this time the matter had been kept by the working party with wonderful secrecy, not more than 30 out of the 1000 officers knowing anything about it. This was necessary as the rebels had spies amongst us.

The absence of Capt. Johnson awakened my suspicions and soon by staying down in the dining room all night I discovered the plot and determined to avail myself of this opportunity to escape after the working parties got out.

About seven o'clock yesterday evening the workers commenced going out emerging at the other end of the tunnel in an open shed and then quietly walking off down street although within sight of the guard.

Soon it became noticed abroad that there was a chance to escape and hundreds came crowding down into the dining room anxious for the chance. I waited while I thought the original party had had time to get safely off and then made a bold push for the hole. After an hour's work I had succeeded in squeezing my way through the crowd and was right in front of the fire place. Only two .were to go down ahead of me when the alarm was given that the guards were coming in. A general stampede took place, each one to his own bed. This alarmed the guards and they came up to see what the matter was but the hole had been closed up and we quieted them by saying that it was one of our raids. I had been up all the night before watching and was so sleepy that when I laid down before I knew it I was fast asleep and did not wake till morning. Meantime the hole was reopened and 109 officers escaped.

Feb. 21st 1864 - Richmond Va. (Sunday) I was most agreeably surprised to be called downstairs today to meet Major James S. Gholson 16th Georgia Vol. Rebel Army who came down on the last Flag of Truce steamer direct from Johnson's Island. He was captured at the battle of Gettysburg and has been a prisoner of war ever since. His home is Athens Ga. He is now here on 30 days parole instructed by the U.S. Govt. to effect my release if possible to be considered a special exchange if successful.

This was something extremely unexpected. I had never asked anybody to use their influence to effect my exchange and is the more gratifying on that account. The mere prospect of being free once more and perhaps in a day or two nearly blinds me. It is almost too good to be true.

Feb 25th 1864 - Richmond Va. (Thursday) I've been in sweetly painful suspense since the 21st in regard to my release. The order has not been issued yet and the thought sickens me that possibly the Rebs will refuse to exchange one of Streight's command.

Nearly one-half of the officers who escaped through the tunnel have been recaptured and most of them are in those damp dungeons under the prison. Some of them were out over a week but it is almost impossible to get through their lines even after getting out of the prison. Col. Streight, however, has not been recaptured yet and I do hope that he will get through safely. Col. Walker and Capt. Phelps of our regiment were taken. Capt. Boyd, Lts. Reynolds and Williams will possibly get through safe.

Chapter Six

February 26th, 1864 – March 23rd 1864 (Meet President Abraham Lincoln)

February 26th 1864 - Rebel Steamer Shultz River Rocketts. (Friday) This morning was ordered up into the city to the office of the Rebel Commission of Exchange and had an interview with Judge Ould who is an austere and non committal personage. He was very particular to inquire if I was a son of Senator Wade of Ohio and whether old Ben was executing his influence on my behalf but could not get him to say whether I would be released or not.

At four o'clock this p.m. the prison clerk (Ross) came up and notified me that I was exchanged. My heart gave one great bound then fearful that something even yet might prevent it. I took things more calmly and proceeded to "pack up" amid the congratulations of all the officers.

Bidding them all an affectionate farewell I took one last look at that building which in future will appear to me like a huge nightmare and wended my way down to the Shultz.

Feb. 26th 1864 - Rebel Steamer Shultz - James River off City Point. (Later Friday) After waiting at the wharf at Rocketts for a short time, Col. Ould and Cpt. Hatch of the exchange bureau arrived and we steamed slowly down the river.

I forgot to mention that Lt. Doughty 51st Ind. who has become perfectly deaf was released with me. Arriving at the boat I also found Col. Delaney of Pierpont's staff and Buckley of the N. Y. Herald formerly in Libby but just released from Castle Thunder with a few citizens repatriates.

Capt. Hill of the Shultz ordered us below deck until we passed Drewry's Bluff so that we would not be able to see the river defenses but by looking out of a side window I discovered all that was to be seen viz. 2 boat obstructions and 3 lines of torpedoes and one unknown probably of stone.

We arrived (at) City Point at 9 o'clock p.m. and laid alongside the US. Steamer N.Y. with a flag of Truce forward and the glorious stars and stripes aft but I didn't feel perfectly safe yet.

Feb. 27th 1864 - U.S. Flag of Truce Steamer New York off City Point Va. (Saturday) I've been laying up on the hurricane deck for hours looking at the dear old flag which floats so defiantly at the mast head and came very near shedding tears for my joy. it is impossible to describe my feelings. My cup of happiness is full and overflowing.

Last night we were transferred from that insignificant little craft, the Shultz, to this magnificent steamer which is no more to be compared to that than a palace is to a hovel.

Maj. John Mulford 3rd N. Y. Infty. Comdg. the boat welcomed us warmly and immediately ordered refreshments which were partaken of with zest in the after cabin. What a grand glorious thought it is to realize that you are free. How little that treasure is appreciated until once lost. The Major has lent me money and am making myself at home on the boat.

Feb. 28th 1864 - U.S. Flag of Truce Steamer New York off City Point Va. (Sunday) The little Rebel boat went back to Richmond yesterday and we are waiting to return with dispatch. Am enjoying myself quietly but hugely. Major Mulford has his wife on board who is a pleasant woman. City Point looks dreary and desolate. We are anchored in the middle of the stream. I smuggled through from Libby a large number of letters from officers to their friends. I ran the risk of being detained on this account but could not resist their appeals. The Rebs. did not search me very closely when I left and I had them concealed so well that it would have bothered them to find some of them. One was concealed in a military button sewed on my overcoat, six in the lining of my boots and a great many in the thick lining of my overcoat while I carried two or three openly as a blind. These I gave up.

Feb. 29th 1864 - Flag of Truce Boat New York off Fortress Monroe. (Monday) Got up steam today and was not sorry to leave City Point at one p.m. at a pretty fast rate. The trip down was delightful but nothing to see until we got within a few miles of the fort and then first an iron clad picket boat and then a long line of ships: monitors, iron clads, schooners and any known craft among which were the 3 turreted Roanoke, a line of battle ship cut down and heavily plated (her compliment of men is 800), the Atlanta (lately captured from the rebels), the Minnesota, a Russian Frigate, an English man of war and many others. It was a lively scene. We rounded to at old point comfort about dusk and now lying under the gray walls and black cannon mouths of Fort Monroe. I feel perfectly safe and know that before the rebs get me in Libby again somebody will be badly hurt.

March 1st 1864 - Fortress Monroe Va. (Tuesday) At 9 a.m. a tug conveyed us from the steamer to the Fort where we reported in person to Major Genl. B. F. Butler Comdg. this Dept and after an interview with him were ordered to report at Washington to the Commissary Genl. of Prisoners. The boat will not leave for Baltimore till 5 p.m. and in the meantime we are inspecting this noted Fortress.

The 3rd Penn. Infty. are doing garrison duty here now. I have forgotten to mention a young lady named Molly Johnson who was released from Richmond and came down on the same boat as myself. She told me her history which was in substance that she was with the 6th Ky. Infty. a year before being captured. After capture she remained with our boys on Belle Isle two or three months before being discovered to be of the opposite sex but an unfortunate slip precipitated matters and when found out was taken to Castle Thunder and soon released.

Mar. 2nd 1864 - Baltimore Md. (Wednesday) Arrived in B. this morning at 6 a.m. Our trip across Chesapeake was a stormy one, a gale blowing all night long. Stopped during the night at Point Lookout, Md. where a large number of Confederate soldiers are confined.

Lt. Doughty and self have stopped at the Eulow house. Col Dulaney under whose charge we are has become so much under the influence of newborn liberty and conduct that I have concluded to go on to Washington alone and report.

Baltimore looked cold and bleak this morning as we steamed up the bay in the fine boat Adelaide. Snows half an inch deep covers the ground but the sun has come out warm and we shall have a fine trip to Washington. The city of Monuments has not fairly woke up yet but judge it must be a busy place.

March 2nd 1864 – Washington D.C. (Wednesday) Arrived here about 11 o'clock a.m. and put up at the Willard Hotel on Penn. Av. Found Col. A.D. Streight here and was heartily glad to see him. He stayed in Richmond a week after escaping from prison concealed by the union people and then came through safely with Capt. Scorce 51st Ind., Lt. Sterling and Maj. McDonald.

Streight informed me that I was expected to dine with him and the Hon. Schuyler Colfax but was dressed in the same clothes in which I entered Libby 10 months before and had to decline. He gave me a hundred dollar bill however to "rig up" with and said I must come. I bought some new clothes in time to go up and spend the evening and found that he had collected all the South Benders in Washington at his house to welcome me among whom were Mrs. and Carrie Mathews, C.M. Heaton, Ed. E. Ames, James Sample and Capt. Sanders.

Schuyler, the Speaker of the House of Representatives and the third in power in the United States seemed as though he could not do me enough honor. He very kindly insisted upon my making his house my home while in Washington and after that was settled proposed to go up and call on the President which we did stopping on the way to settle accounts with the Willard but we found that the President and his wife had gone to the theater to witness one of the old "Abe's" favorite plays. As the next best thing we called at the War Dept. to see Secretary Stanton and Chase (the greatest financier of the age) and from him (Stanton) closeted with Genl. Halleck to both of whom I was introduced and conversed with for a short time and so ended my first day in Washington.

March 3rd 1864 - Washington D.C. (Thursday) I find that my surmises are correct in regard to the person who procured my release. Schuyler was the one who brought the influence to bear on the Govt. and succeeded in getting a rebel Major sent down with instructions to effect my release.

He has been trying to effect it for a long time but both powers are so much opposed to exchanges at present that it was only by great influence and persistent application that it was finally effected. I owe a debt of gratitude to him which I fear can never be repaid especially as he has done all this of his own accord without my asking the favor.

Senator Wade is stopping at his house and of course had to relate to him (and) his son (who is Lt. Col. in a colored Cavalry Rgt) how I was taken at Richmond to be one of the family.

Speaker Colfax awoke me from a deep slumber in my downy bed (which I could not but help compare with Libby's own board floor) and after breakfast went with one to Col. Hoffman's (Com. Genl. Of Pris. and made arrangements as Genl. Halleck promised me I could last night to delay reporting a week in order to extend my furlough and from then to Adjt. Genl. Vincent's on business regarding my commission.

Telegraphs to Adjt. Genl. Noble of Indiana to send it immediately. Schuyler is anxious to have me stay till Dr. Dayton and Sister Mariane arrive in about a week.

This evening attended a "hop" at the National in company with Schuyler who introduced me to Maj. Genl. Sickles who lost a leg at Gettysburg. Met Miss Ann Stephens the authoress, Miss Clay of Kentucky and number of gay girls. This p.m. carried Col. Streight's report to the House Military Committee in regard to our treatment in Richmond.

March 4th 1864 - No. 41/2 8th St. Washington D.C. (Friday) Arose early and wrote a number of letters to friends of officers in Libby. Schuyler franked them and then gave me a card to see him at any time while Congress is in session. This will admit me to the floor of the House a great honor by the way.

Went down to Willard's and played billiards with Capt. Barton and then in company with Col. Streight took the street car to the Capitol and were admitted through a side door near the speakers desk and for the first time saw Congress in session and was introduced to a great many of the members.

I listened to the debates with much interest and was proud of the way which the speaker fulfilled his duties. It is admitted on all hands that he makes the most efficient and popular speaker that the House has ever had. Tonight the Speaker's reception took place and although somewhat unwilling I became an "object of interest" amongst the assembly. All that I remember about it now is that my old Col. now Maj. Genl. Milroy was there and that I met Genl. Starkweather, the Editor of the Globe, Col. Hoffman, etc. etc. and escorted Miss Coon of Lancaster, Penn. to refreshments. Washington is a gay place but I feel disappointed in seeing so much that glitters which is really of no worth. The ladies even I am sorry to say are not beautiful according to nature or if so spoil it all by a superfluity of the artificial. This gaiety will do to pass away an hour or two but to be in the whirl for a life time would be worse than solitary confinement in "Libby."

March 5 1864 - Washington D.C. (Saturday) Went to the Capitol today and was admitted to the floor where I sat for some time studying the mysteries of Congress and then went with the Speaker to his private room which all speakers occupy. It is splendidly furnished and from these to his work room.

We then took the Penn. Ave. cars and went up to the White House to attend the Presidents' Matinee. The Speaker introduced me to the President and Mrs. Lincoln and had the honor of a few moments conversation with a man who will figure in history as one of the most remarkable of the age. Mrs. L. did not advise much. They receive visitors in the Green room who after the customary greetings pass on into the Blue room and from there to the magnificent East room where a fine band was discoursing sweet music.

Was introduced to General whose name I've forgotten now, also to Miss Harlan, daughter of Senator Harlan and another young lady whose name strange to say I've forgotten although I escorted her through the Conservatory for half an hour. She was from New York City and just like all the other ladies in Washington. From the President's, Schuyler went back to his duties in the House and I no. 41/2 8th St.

Mar. 6th 1864 - Washington D.C. (Sunday) Attended the 2nd Presbyterian Church this morning with Schuyler and Mr. and Mrs. Mathews. Coming out was introduced to Admiral Dalghren or Dalgren who has been hammering away at Charleston for so long.

Took a long walk in the afternoon and examined the Capitol carefully. Was much struck with its solid massive appearance. From there went to the Washington Monument which is still uncompleted. It will make a grand monument when completed and will last for ages. In the evening attended church with Carrie Mathews.

Mar 8th 1864 - Washington D.C. (Tuesday) Yesterday reported to Col. Hoffman, Com. Genl. Of Pris. and then to Col. Ed Townsend, A. Adjt. Genl. where I was ordered to report to my regt. and leave, to delay reporting 30 days, given.

This morning Col. Streight, Schuyler and myself went out to breakfast (a strange custom) with Mr. Robison, Register of Wills. The family insisted on having two or three of my autographs.

In the afternoon draw from the U.S. Treasury $1,363.50 pay for 4 months as Adjt. and six months as Major.

In the evening escorted Carrie Mathews to the President's levee and enjoyed myself much better than I expected. After shaking hands with Mr. Lincoln, I paid my respects to Mrs. Lincoln by a bow and was passing on when she called me back and insisted upon shaking hands and was very talkative.

About eight o'clock then a buzz ran through the crowded room and Lt. General Grant was announced. He had just arrived from the west and came to pay his respects to the President upon entering the East room. The people forgetting where they were gave him their hearty cheers. I had the honor of shaking hands with my chief and was proud of it. He is a very quiet unassuming man and to be made a show off annoys him very much. He promenaded with Mrs. Lincoln and afterwards saw him in private consultation with the President and Secretary Stanton, Wm. H Stewart, Genl. Sickles, General Birney and half a doz. Brigadiers were present. Returned home well satisfied with a sight of the great men of America. This p.m. met Maj. Genl. Meade at

Willards Hotel. The city is full of officers and soldiers. I am longing to be home and shall start tomorrow.

Mar 9th 1864 - Baltimore Md. (Wednesday) Procured Transportation to Nashville Tenn. and left Washington at 3 o'clock this P.M. Have established myself at the Eutaw House for a day or two while I am engaged putting up provisions for the officers of the 73rd in Libby for which purpose I brought a letter of introduction from Colfax to the Editor of the Baltimore American.

Mar. 10th 1864 – Baltimore. (Thursday) The morning papers state that a number of prisoners including some officers have just arrived from Richmond and will postpone sending provisions till I hear whether a general exchange will take place or not.

Mar. 11th 1864. (Friday) Missed the train last night and have lain over till tonight. Called on Col Eleys friend at 98 North St. and met Agnes who is a charming girl. Shall leave for Pittsburg tonight.

March 12th 1864 – Pittsburg Pa. (Saturday) Left Baltimore over the Penn Central R.R. at 9:30 P.M. and reached Harrisburg about 2 AM. Changing cars we proceeded to "Smoky Hollers" as this place is called. General Grant came down on the same train but he kept very quiet and but few knew of it.

At Altoona we stopped to breakfast. He went in and sat down to the table. There next to him having no suspicion that they were thrusting their elbows into the face of the greatest Military hero the war has produced. but it was soon whisking around that he was there and a large crowd gathered to charm and welcome him. He is my ideal of a soldier, gent and …….. - and yet with a determination on his face that vodes a victor.

March 13th 1864 - Plymouth Indiana. (Sunday) Left Pittsburg at 1:45 yesterday P.M. reaching Crestline 10 P.M. where I changed cars and paid my fare to Plymouth, where arrived at 8 this AM. Called on Mrs. Haltin Kendall wife of Capt K. also Capt Boyd and our old Lt. Col. O.H.P Bailey.

.

Mar 13th 1864 - South Bend Ind. (Later Sunday) It seems good to be at "home" once more after being tossed on the stormy billows of war for twenty months. Left Plymouth in a carriage at noon and after a tedious ride over the worst of roads reached "good old South Bend" about 5 P.M..

Attended Presbyterian Church this evening and saw a few old friends. Including L__ who __ but as I don't know who may read this journal I won't say anything about it__.

Mar 23rd 1864 - South Bend Ind. (Wednesday) have been enjoying the comforts of liberty, home and friends for a week and now although I have 30 days leave I think my duty calls me to my regt. Have recd. several letters urging and begging me to come.

Recd. invitations from several different towns to lecture on Libby but declined them all.

Attended funeral of A. Andersons child today and could not but notice what a difference there is between death at home amongst friends and death on the battle field.

Have attended a few gatherings and enjoyed myself very much amongst old friends.

Sent 135 dollars worth of eatables to Libby Prison to the officers of my Regt. If the rebels don't steal it. It will cheer them up and enable them to get along much better than formerly.

Congressman Schuyler Colfax
Speaker of the House of Representatives
Vice President of the United States

Chapter Seven

March 25, 1864 through August 31st 1864. (Return to the 73rd Regiment)

Note: Near the end of March of.1864 Colonel Wade decided to cut short his leave and return to active duty with the 73rd Indiana.

He arrived in Nashville, Tennessee on the 26th and almost immediately began to pull together the companies of the 73rd from their scattered duty stations. By mid April of 1864 he was in LaVergne, Tennessee but had only managed to unite about 300 men of the regiment.

On June 9th he moved his men to Stevenson, Alabama, a sleepy little town near the Tennessee River. It was in this area of northern Alabama from Stevenson, Scottsboro, Huntsville, Decatur and Athens that Colonel Wade and the 73rd was assigned to protect the numerous military outposts from roving rebel cavalry, local saboteurs, and deserters.

Also during this time period General Hood and his army led an invasion of Tennessee and while searching for a safe crossing of the Tennessee River the 73rd was once again confronted by Gen. Nathan Bedford Forrest and his cavalry.

However, with Hood's disastrous defeats at Franklin and Nashville life soon returned to quiet garrison duty for the Union soldiers. As the war drew to a conclusion Wade discussed in his journal what should be done with the South, especially after the assassination of President Lincoln.

With the surrender of General Lee and the Army of Northern Virginia the 73rd was ordered to Nashville where the regiment was mustered out on July 4, 1865.

After returning to South Bend Colonel Wade married Jennie Y. Bond of Niles, Michigan on September 5, 1865 and then enrolled in the law school at Michigan State. After becoming a lawyer he once again returned to South Bend and opened an office.

While his good friend Schuyler Colfax was Vice-president, Wade was also appointed Post Master in South Bend. However, while on a nearby hunting trip in 1877 the Colonel died of an apparent heart attack.

Michael P. Downs

Mar 25, 1864 - Indianapolis Indiana. (Friday) Left So. Bend yesterday P.M. Laid over at Salem Crossing till 1 AM Took charge of Miss Armstrong as far as the battle ground. The cars frightfully crowed.

Arrived here at 9 AM and have stopped at the Balis(?). Had an interview with Col Streight. Saw Capt Scorce and Anderson. Sent telegram to Alex Wilson that I couldn't meet him. Called on Adjt. General Noble and Genl. somebody at the capital in relation to the War Dept. order, authorizing the appointment of 2nd Lt. in the 73rd Ind.

Mar. 26th - Galt House Louisville Ky. (Saturday) Came in at 4 this A.M. a tedious ride from Indianapolis here.

Mar. 26th - St. Cloud House - Nashville Tenn. (Later Saturday) Reached here at six this P.M. The Regt is somewhere in the vicinity and must hunt it up tomorrow. Nashville looks natural.

March 28th 1864 - Hd. Qrs 73rd Indiana Vols. Nashville. (Monday) Found Hd. Qrs. Of the Regt. yesterday without any trouble. but finding the Regt. is a different affair. I assumed command this morning of 48 men. Camp is located on the comer of Broad and Vine streets. Matters here need reform sadly. They are in a terribly disorganized condition.

Capt. Williamson who has been in command is totally incompetent and not fit to hold the position of corporal.

Had an interview with Genl. Granger Comdy. Post

today and he promises to do all he can in getting the Regt. together.

As near as I can find out the men are distributed as follows: 141 men at Fort Negly, 150 men on N.W.R.R., 60 men Cheatham Mills, 12 men on siege guns, 48 men at Hq. Qrs., a security party out and numbers of men detached singly.

Great preparations are making here for the spring campaign.

Hd. Qrs. 73rd Ind. 1st Brig. 3rd Div. 12th A.C. I find that we are brigaded as above. Sent up a statement today of the condition of the Regt. and hope soon to have my 500 brave boys together. Dr. Meyers and wife are here. We are boarding at Mr. Hughes on Spencer street, an old original union man.

April I, 1864 - Hd. Qrs. 73rd Ind. (Friday) Today the order was issued returning any man on the North Western Rail Road and shall then have two hundred to commence drilling with.

Have had a great deal of trouble with Capt. White who attempts to control the Regt. Have flatly refused to obey his orders and referred the matter to Genl. Granger.

Had scout mounting this morning the first time in many months. Succeeded in getting Dr. Spencer relieved from detached duty and he came to Regt. today with his wife. Who by the way is a very homely woman.

April 3rd 1864 - hd. Qrs. 73rd Ind. Vols - Camp near Nashville. (Sunday) Moved camp today one mile from the city in the rear for Fort Gillian. It is an excellent location and we now only await the coming of our men.

Yesterday Lt. Williams reported. Sent Charles M. Heaton $10 to help make up a $500 silver tea set as a testimonial to Hon. Schuyler Colfax. Should not like to have any esteem for the speaker be measured by this sum.

April 7th 1864. (Friday) The detachment of 150 men came in today and now have 235 in camp. Genl. Granger has not fully lived up to his promises for the Fort Negley men are not relieved yet. The boys look tough and hearty and even glad to see me but expect that I shall be very unpopular soon as they need discipline. Made a mistake in the date above. It should be Apr. 8th.

Apr. 12th 1864 Camp near Nashville. (Tuesday) Have commenced dress parades and for the first time in our Regt. I make the troops pay the customary honors to the colors. It makes the men respect their flag and shall keep it up.

Yesterday we were drilling as a Brigade with the 13th and 18th Wis. and 18th Mich. Did as well as any Regt. in the different movements but can learn a great deal yet.

This afternoon had a fine battalion drill. The boys are learning fast. They see the reason for it and go at it with a will but having but one line officer here and he is worthless (Capt. Williamson) makes it bad but will succeed in spite of that if our Generals will only give us a chance.

Weather very changeable, generally cool and often rain. Have 252 men in camp. Tents are very poor. Hope the Fort Negley detachment will be here soon.

April 15th 1864 - Camp near Nashville. (Friday) Just before Brigade drill today a detail for 50 men to do guard duty in the city came and I was left with about 60 for drill. After the representations I had made and the promises to one to the effect that I might keep the men here and drill them. Made one somewhat angry and I went out without any colors, band, or sword. Expected that the General would put me under arrest sure but he simply sent an officer to me ordering me to draw my sword which order I couldn't obey and so thought it best to leave the men (who had been consolidated with another Regt.) and dismounted until the drill was ended and then led my men back to camp with all the dignity imagineable. It had some effect however for the Genl. immediately ordered all the men at Negley to report to me except Co. D. This will give me 100 more men.

Apr. 16th 1864 - La Vergne Tennessee. (Saturday) Yesterday Col. Doolittle 18th Mich commanding the Brigade in the absence of Genl. Granger, ordered one to detail two hundred men to guard the N. & C. R. R. I immediately ordered my horse and galloped down to Genl. Rosecrans and upon my earnest request he changed the order so as to let all the men I now have in camp (343) and myself go to LaVergne and the different stockades between Nashville and Murfreesboro.

Left camp this morning. The Regt. looking something like it used to in size and, with 5 well loaded teams, filed through the city to the sound of music and out on the Murfreesboro pike.

As I came along left 30 men at Mill Creek No. 1, 30 at Mill Creek No.2, 30 at Mill Creek No.3, and 20 at Hurricane Creek No.4. Reached LaVergne distant 15 miles and went into camp in sight of our future Head Quarters.

Apr. 17th 1864 - Head Quarters 73rd Ind. La Vergne. (Sunday) Sent Lt. and acting Adjt. this morn with a detachment of 90 men to relieve the troops at Posts 5, 6 and 7. Reported to Col. Baird Commanding Post and relieved him. His Regt. 85th Ind and the 33rd Ind who have been here for a month or two number over a thousand men. I relieved him with a little over 300 but the 73rd is good in that proportion.

There is a Fort here but my little squad of 83 fighting men could hardly man it. Have made application for Company D & K and then shall have sufficient force to resist almost any attack. I like the place very much. The quarters are very comfortable consisting of good log cabins and only hope that Col. Baird will move soon and let me into them. Have issued Gen. Order No. 7 establishing a ...... line and shall get men for the patrols as soon as possible.

Weather windy and cold.

Apr. 19th 1864 - Head Quarters 73rd Ind. La Vergne. (Tuesday) This morning Capt. Boyd and I took a trip to posts 5, 6 & 7. A ride the way we went of about 25 miles. Posts 5 and 6 are very good stockades. No. 7 stockade is not yet completed. A force of 30 men in each could hold a larger force at bay easily. The situation of the Regiment is as follows:

Company A, Lt. Clark Comdj., Mill Creek Post 2
Company B, Sergt. Kiersted Comdj., Mill Creek Post 1
Company C, Sergt. Slick Comdj., Hd. Qrs. La Vergne
Company D, Lt. Grimes Comdj., Fort Negley, Tenn.
Company E, Sergt. Cole Comdj., Overalls Creek No. 7
Company F, Capt. Matt Boyd Comdj., Stewart's Creek No. 7
Company G, Sergt. McBane Comdj., Mill Creek Post No. 3
Company H., Sergt. Dailey Comdj., Hurricane Creek Post 3
Company I, Sergt. Arnold Comdj., Sugara Post No.5
Company K, Sergt. Reynolds Comdj., Cheatham Mills Tenn.

Each of the above Posts on the N. & C. R. R. are pleasant locations and comfortable quarters. The boys are very well satisfied with this kind of soldiering.

Apr. 20th 1864 - Head Quarters U.S. Force La Vergne. (Sunday) Col. Baird, Lt. Col. Crane and all the troops here moved to the front today and I remain in undisputed possession of this Post. Have established my quarters in a roomy building and after a general house cleaning am at last fixed up quite "nicely."

A citizen came in 7 miles today to report a gang of guerrillas who are roaming about Davidson Co. 6 or 7 miles west. In order to try my immortal 83 I had the long roll sounded this evening and it did me good to have them tumble out anxious for a fight.

Capt. Williamson has been dismissed from the service by the President and he richly deserves it. He and the Chaplain begged me to recommend him for reinstatement but I wouldn't give him position of Corporal.

Reports came in from various directions of a good many guerrillas in this vicinity and only wish I had Co. D & K here.

Apr. 26th 1864 - Head Quarters U.S. Forces - La Vergne. (Tuesday) Dr. Spencer has been promoted to Surgeon of the 10th Tenn. He is welcome to go if he hasn't got more state pride than that.

Made a requisition for 12 horses for scouting purposes. They came in today.

Yesterday I disarmed a fellow who was brought in by the pickets. He was a rebel deserter which is the case with 1/3 of the people around here.

Also stopped a Negro today who was traveling without a pass and confiscated his horse.

9/10 tenths of the people here are intensely secession in their sentiments and yet they have all taken the oath. I expect I shall be the most unpopular commander that they have had here for a long time as I shall not grant many favors to southern men who have taken the oath intending to switch it the first chance that occurs.

Weather pleasant today but has been very windy.

Apr. 28th 1864 - Head Quarters 73rd Ind. La Vergne. (Thursday) Took seven mounted men this morning and made a rapid scout through Rutherford, Davidson and Williamson counties after Green Hall, Bob Battle and Everett Patterson particularly and all guerrillas generally.

Took a Union man by the name of Noe and skirmished through several cedar thickets under his guidance but the birds had flown. We then dashed into Nolensville, on the gallop surprising that little secession hole out of its prosperity but didn't find anything suspicious.

On our way back the Surg. and I stopped and called upon Mrs. Buford a very handsome woman and young too. She has a husband who is an officer in the rebel army but as she has taken the oath... .. its her duty to support the Govt. by giving all the information in her power and promising to keep us posted. She is a beauty.

Apr. 30, 1864 - Hd. Qrs. U. S. Forces LaVergne. (Monday)
Have appointed Lt. Hagenbuck Provost Marshal of LaVergne and Lt. Hubbard Post Commissary and the "Post" is now in running order.

Reduced Chief Musician Fryer to the ranks for drunkenness and then made him walk 5 hours carrying a rail and gave him 3 buckets full of water all over him for making a disturbance.

Dr. Myers & self find a good deal of amusement in chess now as there is not work enough to occupy all the time.

My trip yesterday after guerillas makes me stiff today. We rode 30 miles in 6 hours. Can't get the picture of Mrs. Buford out of my mind. If she was single I might be foolish enough to turn my horses head that way again.Especially as L ......has not written since I left S.B.

A strong wind blew our garrison flag pole down and a magnificent flag 30 feet by 20 is lying idle.

May 3, 64 - Hd. Qrs. U.S. Forces LaVergne. (Tuesday)
This is the anniversary of our surrender at Days Gap Ala and twenty of our brave officers still languish in Libby Prison.

I sent out Willson Dailey and 7 mounted men today to Wilson County to hunt guerrillas they have just come bringing one man a son of Mose Buchannon who has been in Douglas's battalion in the rebel army and who has not taken the oath. He agreed to take it here and I let him go.

Lt. Sheets of Brig Genl. VanCleves staff at Murfreesboro came down today having visited the Posts at Overalls Creek, Stewarts Creek, and Smyrna to hurry up the completion.

It is rumored that our army is on the march in Georgia and hope that it is so. I hope for stirring times soon.

Tho General Forrest's movement south indicates that they know where we were going to move as soon or sooner that our army and doubters are well prepared to resist our advance.

.**May 9th - Hd. Qrs. 73rd Ind. Vols La Vergne. (Monday)** This has been an exciting day in LaVergne. Genl. Rousseau telegraphs our post this morning that the Rebel Genl. Roddy has crossed the Tennessee with 5000 cavalry and was aiming to strike the Nashville and Alabama road at Tunnel Hill and commanding me to keep on the alert. I then [sent] out my infantry pickets farther from camp and stationed mounted vedette on the principal roads. Gave orders to have the men ready to fall in at a moment's warning.

In about an hour another telegram came from Brig. Genl. Van Cleve at Murfreesboro warning me to have my men in hand for any emergency and giving the same news in regard to Roddy. I began to think that we would be attacked sure and exercised unusual vigilance. Had the colors planted in the fort and issued an address to the Regiment ordering a surrender to be thought of under no circumstances whatever

This evening recd. another telegram from Genl. Van Cleve ordering 200 rounds of ammunition to be distributed. Detail Lt. Eaton to proceed to Nashville on the first train to procure it.

A Federal Lt. was sent in from Post 7. He is either crazy or a spy. I forwarded him to the Provost Marshall at Nashville.

I enlisted two new recruits yesterday who came in from Wilson County. They are young but will make good soldiers. Have ordered the Regt. to assemble quietly half an hour before day break tomorrow and if Roddy pays us a visit shall welcome him with bloody hands to hospitable graves. I believe that our little band of 75 men can whip anything less than 500 that may attack us.

Mrs. Meyers is in a strange predicament. She doesn't know whether to go or stay.

May 10, 64 - Hd. Qrs U.S. Forces La Vergne. (Tuesday) Have heard nothing from Roddy today except that a small party dashed in and cut the road below Nashville. Am exercising great vigilance and if he pays La Vergne a visit will give him a warm reception.

May 11, 64 - Hd Qrs. U.S. Forces La Vergne. (Wednesday) The excitement in regard to Roddys raid has nearly died away and although I keep up my usual picket force yet do not fear an attack.

According to reports from the East Grant is having his own way around the rebel capital. If he succeeds in taking Richmond and bagging most of Lee's army the war will be virtually ended. I sincerely hope he will.

Today has been the coldest I've seen this spring. The spring is very backward in Tennessee. Mrs. S. called on me yesterday.

May 14, 64 - Hd Qrs U.S. Forces LaVergne. (Saturday) Matters have settled down to their usual quietness today and no fears are entertained that Roddy will pay this place a visit.

The news from the East is glorious. Grant has whipped Lee and is pressing him back to Richmond. Butler has landed from James river and has fortified Bermuda Hundred cutting the Rail Road between Richmond and Petersburg.

The papers state that Lt Col Ivan N. Walker [73rd Indiana Regt. Ed.] has been released. The bal. of the 73rd officers undoubtedly are rejoicing at the near prospect of the capture of Richmond and their release.

The news from Georgia is cheering. The Army of the Cumberland is advancing slowly but surely, fighting as it goes. The wounded already begin to arrive at Nashville by the hundreds. Our losses in the East are heavy----

May 22 1864 - Hd, Qrs 73rd Ind. Vols. La Vergne Tenn. (Sunday) My application for two pieces of artillery has been granted and have mounted in the fort one James rifled six pounder and one twelve pound howitzer.

Companies D and K have arrived and we can whip any brigade of rebels that may attack us.

I issue rations now to nearly one hundred refugees. Amongst is one case in which I have become somewhat interested. A Mrs. Earp whose husband L.W. Earp is a prisoner of war in Indianapolis. Shall use my influence to have him released as he is undoubtedly loyal. Weather is warm.

Was out the other evening & called upon Mrs. Davis and Mrs. Copple and Berl whose husbands are in the rebel army, also Mrs. Mason & Miss Bennett. On the road home was fired at but no damage done.

I find considerable difficulty in governing the Regt. on account of the longtime it has been without discipline. But guess a steady hand will bring them out all right. Have heard that Col. Walker was released and suppose he will soon join the Regt. and relieve me. Shall lose whatever credit may be given to getting the Regt. together. But suppose I shall have to submit like a soldier. Shall try to do my duty in all positions whatever occurs.

Lts Reynolds and Williams brought their wives with them and we now have three ladies in camp.

Is a great burden to have a county of 20 miles in extent to govern and it takes up my time pretty well.

Took a night ride to Post 6 this or rather last evening and rode into camp with six troopers without being challenged. Reprimanded them for it.

May 23rd 64 - Hd. Qrs. 73rd Ind. Vols. La Vergne Tenn. (Monday) Took ten mounted men last night and started west on a scout. Stopped at Mr. Noes a good union man who volunteered to act as guide. About four miles west we stopped at Mrs. Battles, Hd. Qrs of a gang of guerrillas, reconnoitered the house and posted pickets.

One of the scoundrels approached the house (and) was halted by the picket who sent a bullet after him when he started to move. Couldn't ascertain whether he was shot or not. We changed position then on the other side of the house and watched the roads all night. At daybreak I searched the premises thoroughly, captured a rifle and shot gun, and arrested one man. They all admitted that the bushwhackers made that place their rendezvous. Took a trip around on the Nolensville pike. Captured a gun or two and returned to camp.

May 25, 1864 - Hd. Qrs. U.S. Forces La Vergne. (Wednesday) Have just received orders to march as soon as troops arrive to relieve us. My orders and instructions are rather indefinite - simply telling me to march by the most expeditious route to the Tennessee river, establish Hq. Qrs. of six companies at Triana, and 4 companies at Piney Creek, build block houses and picket the river. I've never marched over this route before and it will require some ability to pilot the Regiment through a country filled with rebels and guerrillas.

Shall take my horse (22) and the two pieces of artillery that I have with me. The Regt numbers about 450 for duty. I have not had the Regiment all together yet and expect they will be hard to manage. But believe that by the time we've marched our 150 miles I shall have control of them.

May 30, 64 - Hd. Qrs. U.S. Forces Lavergne Tenn. (Monday) Am waiting very patiently for the 100 day men to come and relieve us. As soon as they do so shall commence my 150 mile march. The Regt. is in good spirits and morale.

Have Battalion drill every day and the four companies here (C, D, H and K) are learning the drill fast. Also have recitation in tactics of the commissioned officers in tactics every day. Guard mounting and dress parade.

Arrested a man for murder today but the evidence was not sufficient to detain him. Arrested two deserters from the 2nd Mos. Vol. and sent them to the Pro. Mar. at Nashville.

Mrs. Siwney called on me today & presented me with six pies. Get together frequently from the ladies in the vicinity. Called on Miss Ella Harris. She's intensely rebel.

Reports confirm the existence of a band of guerrillas 16 in number 5 miles from here but it is hard to catch them.

June 3 – Hd. Quarters U.S. Forces LaVergne. (Friday) My reign in Lavergne and vicinity is drawing to a close. Even if we don't march soon Lt. Col. Walker, who has been exchanged, will supersede me and I must come down to second in command.

Well it is some consolation to know that that state of things will relieve me of a great many concerns and troubles always incident to the position of Post Commander.

Although I believe that men who have once held power are last to give it up for such reasons.

And indeed it was a pleasure to me to have control of the 585 brave fellows of the 73rd Ind. and hope that I have been able to do them some good. Have the satisfaction of knowing at least that I've had to do my duty towards them and my Government.

Lt. Col. Walker was here today but has returned to Nashville until his furlough is out.

June 3, 1864 - Hd. Qrs. 73rd Ind Vols. LaVergne Tenn. (Later Friday) Today is rainy and gloomy and pregnant with bulic devils. Nothing to stir the dreary monotony of life at Lavergne. Not much prospect of leaving for several days and as the Col. will take command in a day or two all my plans for improvement, the march etc have vanished in air.

Called on Mrs. Birdwell tonight. atmosphere of the house decidedly secesh.

The Col. sent word from Nashville that I could not take the two pieces of artillery which are here. Guess I shall ask permission to do so however tomorrow. Arrested one deserter today and turned him over to the Provost Marshall here for disposal.

The news from Grant and Sherman is cheering. Grant is within five miles of Richmond.

June 5, 1864 - Hd. Qrs 73rd Ind. Vols. LaVergne Tenn. (Sunday) It is more in sorrow than anger today that I record the determination to night that whether it takes one month or six I shall dismiss Capt. Boyd of Company F from the service. Perhaps there is a little anger mixed up with this. Indeed there is plenty of cause for but I hope that my sense of right and justice will curb my passions, that I may do nothing more than the interests of the service and my duty demands.

The companies are separating one by one and shall probably start for the south day after tomorrow morning.

Col. Walker will be here tomorrow I suppose and assume command. Shall write a recommendation tonight to Genl. Thomas for the dismissal of Capt. Boyd but don't suppose it will accomplish the object.

June 7, 1864 - Nashville Tenn. (Tuesday) Lt. Col. Walker came to the Regt. and took command last night. I obtained permission to come down here on business.

Transportation has been furnished the Regt. by rail road and we shall leave for the south in a day or two.

Met Capt. Eaton formerly Lt. on Col. Harkers staff. He is promoted to Lt. Col. in a new regiment.

Have succeeded in having seven or eight new officers appointed in the Regt. and we now have one to each company. I recommended and Gov. Morton commissioned Capt. J.E. Woodrow Capt. Co. B, John W. Munday and James Kiersted Lts. Co.B, John Y. Slick Co. C, Horace Gamble and Otto H. Sollan Lts. Co. F, Capt. Wm. C. Eaton, Adolphus Booher and Charles Arnold Lts. Co. I , and Joseph Hagenbuck Adjt. of the Regt.

June 8th 1864 - LaVergne Tenn. (Wednesday) I went up to Nashville early this morning and brought down two trains. On which Lt. Col. Walker with seven companies embarked leaving me here with K. G. and B. to procure transportation as best I could. The Regt numbers 530 present and am proud of it.

June 9, 1864 - Stevenson Ala. (Thursday) Took forcible possession of the three o'clock train this morning and my three companies are now sheltering themselves from a drenching rain under the eves of the passenger house at Stevenson.

Took dinner this noon at War Trace. Passed through historical Tullahoma but didn't admire it much. Am much disappointed also in Stevenson. It is a wild desolate looking country around and a miserable muddy little town.

June 11th 1864 - Junction Ala. (Saturday) Left Stevenson last night at 10 o'clock. Stopped one hour in Huntsville but as it was dark and rainy did not see Adjt Stansfield of the 48th who is stationed there. Arrived here at 5 o'clock this A.M. and found a messenger from Walker who is with the bal. of the Regt. at Decatur to remain here until he came up as we have to march to Mooresville.

June 14th 64 - Mooresville Ala. (Tuesday) Have been here two days awaiting on train which has arrived at last. I am placed in command of four (A. B. C. and G.) and will make Hd. Qrs at the mouth of Limestone Creek.

We have had dress parade once or twice for the first time (with the whole Regt.) in nearly a year and I can see that the boys are very deficient in drill. I shall labor for the good of the detachment in this respect.

Have made the acquaintance of Mrs. Ray and her daughter who reside here and are intensely rebel. We marched here from the junction distant about four miles. My instructions from Brigade Hd. Qrs. are to erect fortifications and Block houses at every ford, ferry, or crossing between Limestone Creek and Butlers Ferry a distance of ten miles.

June 14, 1864 - Tennessee River. (Late Tuesday) I march my command of 200 men & four teams down the west side of Limestone & found we could not ford it. Sent the teams 10 miles around and spent the afternoon in ferrying the men across 8 at a time on a raft which I made. Have gone into camp to await daylight.

June 15, 1864 - Limestone Point Ala. (Wednesday) At daylight this morning I explored the bank for five miles and concluded to locate right at the mouth of the creek, which is a commanding and very pleasant point. Marched the troops here and in three hours threw up field fortifications which our invincible "200" can hold against a thousand men. They consist of a redoubt, a ditch and embankment thrown up against a log wall and an excellent abatis of sharpened rails driven into the ground on the two most dangerous sides .It will be impossible for the Rebs to charge up against these rails if the men show any fight at all. Shall proceed to erect a Block House as soon as possible and have placed the work of getting out timber under charge of Lt. Kiersted.

June 18th 1864 - Limestone Point. (Saturday) Am getting "fixed up" very comfortably here. My tent is within five yards of the river and under the protecting branches of two trees. The boys have built comfortable quarters and we all enjoy ourselves fully as well as at LaVergne.

I keep out 12 men as pickets and do not intend to be surprised. We have reveille at daybreak and turnout under arms, roll call and then squad or company drill until breakfast time. Guard Mount at 8 ½. Recitation in tactics at 9 when all the commissioned officers and Sergts assemble at my quarters to recite. There is room for them to learn a great deal and am surprised to find that they have been in the service so long and know so little of the theory or practice. The drill time and patience however will improve them greatly. Battalion drill at 5 1/2 and dress Parade at 6 1/2 o'clock P.M. Tattoo 8 ½. Taps 9.

Am boarding with Mrs. Griffith a widow lady living just across the creek We have established a ferry so that it is not inconvenient at all. She has a charming daughter of sweet sixteen and there is also another lady visiting at the house who is good looking and an exile, having been banished from Decatur on account of rebel proclivities. Of course I find female society rather pleasant.

I patrol the river with mounted men once in day time and once at night between this point and Butlers Ferry, Connecting them with patrols to Hd. Qrs. Also have a courier line between here and Hd. Qrs. who carries the mail and official documents. Have captured two or three boats.

June 20th 1864 - Hd. Qrs. Detachment 73rd Ind. Limestone Pt. (Monday) I communicated with the enemy under flag of truce day before yesterday. Rather uncertainly however as I did not know their character until they were gone. Three of them (A Lt. and two privates of Roddys command) appeared on the other side and waved a flag of truce. Supposing it was some refugees or confederate deserters I sent over a man to bring them over. They inquired of him the number we had here and said they had lain on the bank of the River all day watching us but were afraid to show themselves for fear we would shoot. They kept him a prisoner a short time then allowed him to return I could have captured them easy if I had a small force across the river.

I am getting along very pleasantlywith Mrs. Griffith over the way and her daughter Rebecca who is a perfect angel and never expresses rebel sentiments.

Shall commence putting in the timber of our Block House tomorrow and shall have it finished in a few days.

There are rumors afloat that 300 of the enemy are trying to cross a short distance above me but our boys would rather relish a fight with that number. and it does not give us much uneasiness. Although have sent Co. A to Mooresville leaving about 130 fighting men here.

June 22nd 1864 - Hd Qrs Det. 73rd Ind. Vols. Limestone Pt. (Wednesday) Miss Laurine Ray a girl of very lively disposition and decided rebel tendencies has been stopping at Mrs. Griffiths for a few days and also Miss Rogers and another who with charming Becky and stately cousin Sue have kept the house full of sunbeams. Am fearful that I shall lose my heart with some of these Rebel beauties Their society however has not rendered me invisible to the beauties of unionism as witness my preference for Becky (sweet sixteen, but every inch a woman) who never expressed rebels sentiments in my hearing. They all discourse most beautifully on the piano.

Two rebel cavalry men appeared upon the opposite bank today in plain sight but I do not wish to get in the habit of firing at or being fired at by everybody who makes their appearance there, and did not allow any powder or ball to be wasted. They soon disappeared in the woods and suppose they were only reconnoitering our position. I hope they will not bring up any cannon until we get our stockade completed.

Am of the opinion that an attack will be made on this post soon and trust we shall be prepared for them.

Weather warm but not uncomfortable as we get all the benefit of the water breeze here. News from Sherman and Grant cautiously encouraging.

June 24th 1864 - Hd. Qrs. Det 73rd Ind. Vols Limestone Pt. (Friday) Weather is terribly warm today and is likely to continue so all summer.

I sent a squad of four men under a reliable Sergt. (Moss of Co. G) across the river today and hope when they come back they will bring the Rebel patrols which we have seen nearly every day. If a force too large for them should attack we will cover their retreat by firing from this side.

Have got in a slight difficulty with the Griffith family in regard to "fair Becky" but upon mutual explanation it was settled satisfactorily.

Am using unusual precautions with my pickets as there are rumors of an attack.

June 26, 1864 - Hd. Qrs. Det 73rd Ind. Vols Limestone Pt. (Sunday) Well well!! Staid soldier that I am. I awaken this morning to a realization of the strange fact that I'm half in love with fair Becky Griffith of Limestone Pt. heiress to 3,000 acres and some score of negroes. Perhaps the latter "stern realities" have their due weight, perhaps not. At all events if I were anxious to encumber myself with a wife here is a good opening (for) an enterprising young man. Beautiful, accomplished, wealthy and "sweet sixteen" what more could mortal man ask. Every meal that I've taken "... the creek" has consumed two mortal hours. But have come to the conclusion that I'm making a fool of myself and with a sigh and the following crowning act of folly I admonish thoughts of domestic bliss.

Double Acrostic

Rebecca, fair one, 'tis the privilege of rhyme
Alf, musing, tenderly links his name with thine
Ever charmed by thy beauty and grace of the form,
Loving thee truly, for thy dear self alive
Be lenient, forgive him, perhaps you're to blame
Few men could resist it "0 a beautiful name
E're now as I gaze on that tiny gold ring
which you "sent," perhaps gave one (tis a beautiful thing)
Comes to me bright thoughts which I must not express
And only in silence the circlet I press
Close to my lips, only wishing twese you
Doubting some, hoping much "will" it be true?
And yet perhaps discords of this cruel war
Enter protest 'gainst these words to "Becky the fair."
'Alf

I think that is a "prima facie" evidence that the author is not fit to perform the onerous duties pertaining to Major Cmdj. Det.and shall for the future abandon love and return to ambition.

June 26, 1864 - Hd. Qrs. Detachment 73rd Ind. Vols. Limestone Pt. Ala. (Later Sunday) We had a little bit of "excitement" which (is) well do to record. Today about ten o'clock I noticed a party of three or four of Roddy's cavalry on the opposite bank and detailed Sergeant Cole of Co. C and Privates Fetzer, Miller and Ledwick to cross in the "dug out" we have and capture them if possible. They did so some distance above the party entirely unobserved, landed and were proceeding down the river when they observed two rebel cavalry men approaching and immediately concealed themselves until the unsuspicious rebels reached the bank.

Then by a flank movement got in their rear and ordered them to surrender. The Rebs immediately took to their heels but a bullet from Sergt. Cole's rifle brought one of them to the ground. The others succeeded in making their escape.

The firing startled the party lower down and they mounted and galloped towards our little squad who fearing for the result and not knowing how many might be there, jumped into the canoe and paddled back bringing with them the wounded Reb.

They had scarcely reached this bank when the enemy appeared in considerable number on the opposite bank and it turned out to be a narrow escape from capture.

The wounded man turned out to be Private William Bailey Company L 5th Alabama (a resident of this county four miles west of Athens). He was wounded through the groin rather severely. I had his wound dressed as well as I could and sent him to Post Hospital Decatur. He says that Capt. Patterson Comdj. his Co. has sixty men in camp four miles from here.

I have asked permission of Lt. Col. Walker to take one company and go over and give them a Irish.

He [Confederate soldier Bailey, Ed.] says also that Capt. Griffin has one company opposite Triana and Capt. Garner one company between Triana and Decatur. Hd. Qrs. Of the 5th Ala is near Decatur. His Co. is on Flint Creek. The Lts. of the Company are Hart and Singleton. I hope permission will be granted me to go over and give them a drubbing.

June 28th 1864 - Hd. Qrs.73rd Ind. Vols. Limestone Pt. Ala. (Thursday) Weather excessively warm and nothing particular to record. One wing of the Block House is completed and am pushing the whole as rapidly as possible.

Lt. Hart of Patterson's Company 5th Ala. with two of his men came to the river bank today at 9 a.m. and waved a white flag. I sent over Sergts. Morgan and Romig of Co. "C" to communicate with him. His object was simply to inquire whether the man belonging to his company was shot or now (whom we captured the other day). The Rebs were being friendly and shook hands with our boys and were anxious to know the news as in that benighted country over there few papers circulate. He says that Roddy's command is near Decatur and we may expect stirring news soon.

Lt. Colonel Walker's resignation has not been accepted yet. Sincerely hope it will be as I should then have full control of the Regt. and shall devote my time and what little talent I have to its interests. Am getting along with my three companies very well although am strict, yet I think the boys like me better on that account. They complain a good deal however on account of the hard work to do here.

June 30th 1864 - Hd. Qrs. 73rd Indiana Vols. Triana Ala. (Thursday) At 6 a.m. this day I mustered the three companies of my detachment, eat breakfast and then started with one mounted orderly for the Memphis and Charleston R.R.

By 9 o'clock a.m. had mustered companies A, E and I who are stationed in Block Houses guarding banks and bridges across Big and Little Piney and Big and Little Limestone Creeks.

After a hot ride of 10 miles reached Triana at one p.m. and "Auntie" gave me a fine dinner.

Hd. Qrs. is established in a good cool place and they appear to be enjoying themselves here. Mustered the four companies here and shall start back tomorrow.

July 2nd 1864 - Hd. Qrs. Det. 73rd Ind. Vols. Limestone Pt Ala. (Saturday) The Rebs are evidently building rafts to cross the river as a great pounding and chopping has been kept up for four or five nights.

I sent a detachment of ten men to Gillsport to establish a post at that place.

Has been raining nearly all day and the atmosphere is quite cool and refreshing.

Have two wings of my Stockade completed and shall soon commence a well in the center and be prepared for an emergency.

Have had great apprehensions lately that the Rebs would open fire from the opposite side of the river. In which case my tent presents the best object for a target.

July 4th 1864 - Hd, Qrs Det. 73rd Ind. Vols. Limestone Pt. Ala. (Monday) I've celebrated this glorious day of our nation's birth by a little extra work on the fortification whereat the boys grumbled greatly.

Becky has returned from a short visit to some friends and looks as bright and beautiful as "herself' which is saying a great deal.

One of our patrols was fired upon 2 miles from camp this morning and returned on the double quick. I sent out two more with him but they failed to find the guerrilla.

The boys captured a pontoon boat on the other side of the river this morning but were carried nearly to Decatur in recrossing.

July 6th 1864 - Hd. Qrds. Detachment 73rd Ind. Vol Limestone Pt. Ala. (Wednesday) Time drags slowly along. Not much of interest to chronicle wither in or outside of our lines.

"Fair Becky" left this morning on a visit to some friends and that makes it gloomier than ever

The boys are baking and intend to have soft bread instead of hard tack.

Sam (the Sutler) was down this morning and dispersed some extras to the boys.

Night before last we had an alarm and the boys tumbled out into the fortifications in a hurry.

Weather hot and river misty which is a strange phenomena.

Am changing the quarters to prevent sickness.

No answer to Col. Walkers resignation yet and am getting impatient to get control of the Regt. and commence righting abuses.

July 8th 1864 - Hd. Qrs. Detachment 73rd Ind. Vols. Limestone Pt. Ala. (Friday) I am nearly bored to death with ennui. The command of this little detachment does not give one half enough do and I pass my time miserably. Nothing to read and almost nothing to do.

Weather terribly hot and flies troublesome. Sergt. Sheeder of the Gillsport Detachment reports the enemy building rafts at that point preparatory to crossing and hope it is true, and that we'll have a little excitement to vary the monotony.

Mrs. Taggart is stopping with Mrs. Griffith now. I wish Becky was back from her visit.

July 10th 1864 - Limestone Pt Ala. (Sunday) Sunday and a quiet lonely day. Took a ride to Decatur this afternoon - a sorry looking place it is. The entrenchments wind through and though the streets, yards and houses in many instances completely ruining handsome and palatial residences for all time to come. The river is crossed by means of a long pontoon bridge.

Saw General Rousseau who is down this way on an inspection tour I suppose.

On my return to camp found a special courier from Hd. Qrs. announcing the acceptance of the Col.'s resignation and that I was needed there to take command of the Regt. Shall start tomorrow.

July 12th 1864 - Head Quarters 73rd Ind. Infty Triana Ala. (Tuesday) Am fairly installed as commander of Post Triana and the Regt. Left Limestone yestermorn with King of Co. "C" for mounted orderly. Found the squad at Gillsport busily erecting a Block House. At Butler's ferry one is already completed and one ordered to be commenced 1 mile above Gillsport. Another 1 mile below Butler's ferry. Arrived safe at Hd. Qrs. about 9 a.m. and found Ethan S. Reynolds from South Bend, Paymaster U.S.A. paying off the Regt.

Walker left soon after I came. Hd. Qrs. is established in the parlor of Mr. Dillon one of the first families of Triana. The front yard, which is filled with beautiful shade trees, is principally occupied by the tents of Company Commanders. The parlor which the Surgeon Adjt. and self occupy contains two fine bureaus, two large mirrors, a piano, chairs, table etc. and is a very pleasant room.

Have not become acquainted with the lady of the house yet as she keeps herself pretty close. The men have built themselves good quarters on an open common on the opposite side of the street. Companies D. F, H, and K are here, the first three being the largest in the Regt. The officers (Qr. Mr. Surg for hospital) occupy different houses in town. Many of them being deserted by their inhabitants. It is said that some time before the war Triana did a larger business than any town on the river.

July 13 1864 - Hd. Qrs. 73rd Ind. Triana Ala. (Wednesday) Have commenced my plans for the improvement of the Regt. Drill twice a day, recitation in tactics, and a regular order of the day. Have applied for two pieces of artillery and can find use for them if attacked. Have appointed a Post Commissary and Provost Marshall. Have asked permission to tear down an occupied house in order to build a new fort and on my own responsibility have ordered Co. C and G from Limestone Pt. to this place as there is no earthly use for them there and plenty of need for them here.

The Rebs are trying to communicate with us today from the opposite bank but I refuse to send anybody over unless they show a flag.

July 16th 1864 - Hd. Qrs. 73rd Ind. Infantry Triana Ala. (Saturday) Weather hot and sultry. Am making good progress in the drill especially battalion.

Have an interesting class composed of the commissioned officers and 1st and second Sergeants. If we are allowed to remain here long shall soon perfect ourselves in the drill.

Capt. Boyd has tendered his resignation assigning as a cause incompetency. This is the second step in the work which I commenced two months ago. I did not expect however that he would stultify himself to such an extent as to acknowledge his incompetency.

Shall send out tomorrow a scouting party of 20 men under Lt. Williams to explore the country.

July 19th 1864 - Head Quarters 73rd Ind. Infantry Triana Ala. (Tuesday) Lt. Williams reported today from his mounted scout. Lt. Grimes Co D sent in his resignation assigning as a reason incompetency. As I knew this to be the case I had no hesitation in approving and forwarding it "for the good of the service". The poor officers are being weeded out of the 73rd pretty fast.

Called on Mrs. McIntosh today, her husband is in the rebel service and appeared upon the opposite bank of the river a day or two since but was afraid to cross over.

Have received permission to press in fifty negroes to clear the bank of the river. They are pressing them in at Huntsville also so that this country is getting cleared of the "main cause of the war."

July 20, 64 - Hd. Qrs. U.S. Forces Triana Ala. (Wednesday) Lt. Williams commanding patrols found a raft this morning and believing that some of the enemy has crossed on a thieving excursion is now after them.

Three Rebel soldiers, Jesse J. Dunn Corpl, Patterson's Co. L. 5th Ala Cavalry, Peter B. Dunn, Riches Co. D 4th Ala. Cavalry, and White Lt., Caiuel Private Co. G 5th Ala. Cav., together with one citizen crossed the river and surrendered themselves this morning. After getting all the information I could out of them I forwarded all except citizen to Brigade Hd. Qrs at Decatur.

Sent Lt. Sollan on a scouting party day before yesterday. Part of his men were on foot. Expect them in tonight. Guess I will send a few across the river soon.

July 22, 1864 - Hd. Qrs. 73rd Ind Infantry. (Friday) Weather has been very pleasant today, a cool breeze stirring all day.

A cotton train was burned by the guerrillas today we could see the smoke in the direction of Huntsville. Nothing of importance from Sherman or Grant.

July 25th 1864 – Triana. (Monday) The annual scare in Washington commenced a week or ten days ago but has finally subsided. Early and Breckinridge didn't make much out of this raid.

Grant still lies quiet in front of Petersburg. Sherman is making good progress towards Atlanta and indeed it is rumored that he now holds the city. I sincerely hope that it is true.

July 26th 1864 - Head Quarters 73rd Indiana Triana Ala. (Tuesday) The Boys at Stockade No. 8 captured a good horse last night. A squad of guerrillas tried to move several across the river but were interrupted during the night by our men and had to skedaddle leaving one of their animals behind.

Recd. a letter last night from Lt. Thomas Co. "I" He and the bal[ance] of 73rd officers are now at Camp Oglethorpe, Macon, Ga.

Rousseau our Div. General has started on a raid down

that way and hope that he will succeed in liberating them.

Weather has been very pleasant during the past few days. Should start a pontoon over the river soon.

July 28th 1864 – Head Quarters 73rd Indiana Infantry Triana Ala. (Thursday) A cool drizzly rain holds forth today and bids fair to dampen a little one of my schemes to "wake up" the enemy. If it don't rain too hard however I shall cross the river at Fletchers ferry and capture Somerville the county seat of Morgan Co. shortly after day break. Have ordered one day's provisions, 40 rounds of cartridges in boxes, and 20 additional rounds in haversacks. If Roddy's troops get in our way they will experience a difficulty. Have also ordered demonstrations to be made all along my line of 15 miles. 15 men will cross at Limestone Pt. and 3 or 4 at other Stockades. Hope we won't meet with serious disaster.

July 29th 1864 - head Quarters 73rd Indiana Infantry Triana Ala. (Friday) Was aroused by the orderly at 1 1/2 o'clock the AM. Dr. and self regaled ourselves with a cup of coffee but as the "night was dark" I postponed the march for one hour.

At 3 AM. mustered the men selected for the raid in front of quarters, they numbered only 50 all told. 37 privates and 13 non-commissioned officers. Two men were detailed to take the two canoes down the river and we commenced our march to Watkins ferry distant one & ½ miles below Triana. Surg. Meyers and Chaplain Frazier volunteered to accompany the expedition which all felt to be extremely hazardous and indeed it was. To cross so large a stream as the Tennessee, penetrate eight miles within the enemy's lines for the purpose of capturing the county seat of a large county was a bold undertaking for fifty men.

Only (a) few weeks previously 500 of the enemy with three pieces of artillery had crossed into our lines at the same place and made a successful raid. But bold undertakings are generally successful. We reached Watkins ferry about 3 1/2 o'clock.

I had previously ordered up one boat from Fletcher's Ferry which with two at this point made five canoes, our whole available means of crossing. Three of these were poor old things which would barely sustain two men. The others were better and would hold 3 apiece.

I ordered Co. "I" Detachment to cross at once and establish pickets on the other side. They made the fatal mistake of putting four men in one of the boats and had barely started before it capsized and three guns went to the bottom of the river and some difficulty was experienced in fishing out the poor fellows who were encumbered with their cartridge boxes. This disaster reduced our number [by] three men and occasioned some delay.

I pushed forward the crossing as rapidly as possible however and by 5 o'clock A.M. we were all on the opposite bank. The Sergt. in command of the stockade was instructed to allow no one to approach boats during our absence.

The river is not so wide but that our guns will come across and I did not anticipate that anybody would dare to come near enough to destroy them. We immediately struck south on an old road which did not exhibit much evidence of being traveled.

Crossed Little Cotaco Creek over the sleepers of an old bridge which had been burnt. The road leading for a while along the bank of Cotaco Creek. The river bottom extends back about two miles where the road crosses a range of bluffs not very high but rocky and rough. No signs of plantations on the bottom which together with the bluffs (are) thickly wooded.

We walked fast and at seven o'clock reached the plantation of Mr. Wm. M. McCarley distance 3 1/2 miles from the river. Here we refreshed ourselves with a good drink of water. Just before reaching the house his son, who is a rebel soldier, got sight of us and put out on the double quick. As we were on foot we could not capture him.

I search the house and found one double barreled shot gun which I presented to orderly McCoy, Co. D. Mr. McCarley had two good horses and his mules. I immediately confiscated the horses and one mule together with saddles, bridles etc. He attempted to scare us into turning back with huge storys of confederate forces encamped all around especially on Flint Creek.

But as one had started for Somerville I was bound to go through pushing on a mile and a half at 7 1/2 A.M. We came to Mr. Ely Allen's plantation. McCarley's son had been here before us and having procured a mule was acting as "avant courier" pushing on ahead at a break neck speed to alarm the rebel forces on Flint Creek and to warn the county that the "Yankees" were coming.

Found one shot gun here which we destroyed and also one good rifle which we brought with us to Mrs. McErland's. A search here revealed one gun which was destroyed.

Another mile at a fast pace and we stopped for water at Mr. Watkins' and brought away one good mule, saddle and bridle. We entered Somerville our destination in triumph at 8 ½ AM.

I ordered Lt. Sollan to take Co. H and search the houses while I stopped to have a chat and gain information from Mrs. Gill a union lady who has suffered much for opinions sake. She is very anxious that our lines should be extended soon that she may be able to save 83 bales of cotton the rebs threaten to confiscate. Quite a nice little property as it would realize now about $70,000.

I then took a stroll through the court house a good building but now neglected and going to ruin with its content. All the records of the old county are scattered around and many of them ruined or carried off.

Visited the Hotel next where I found a bevy of female rebels. At half past nine o'clock fearing that the enemy would muster in force and give us a tough fight I marched down Fletcher's Ferry road a half mile and camped at Mrs. Black-wells for dinner. On this place there is a beautiful cave spring.

Started shortly after 10 o'clock and traveled very fast to within one mile of Fletcher's Ferry where we captured a supposed bushwhacker with his gun, horse and ammunition. Nothing of interest occurred in the march from Blackwells to the point except the capture of two or three horses.

We were then within three miles of the boats, but from information obtained from someone who undoubtedly attempted to delay us until the Confed. Cavalry came up, we took the wrong road which led us three miles out of the way.

Reached Mr. McCarley's house about one o'clock and found that one scout had passed in search of us.

The men were very much exhausted. The sun very hot and from this point to the river had to stop and rest every half mile. 3 or 4 were partially sun struck and had to be held on the horses. I had walked every step of the way since crossing the river and apparently stood it much better than any of the men although it was the finest march on foot that I had made since entering the service.

Reached the ferry at 3 ½ o'clock P.M. and commenced crossing immediately. I found much trouble in swimming the horses, so much so that I could get five across although we had captured ten.

Came into camp before five o'clock all safe and sound but somewhat disappointed that we had "mish" [skirmish, Ed.]. The rear guard when four miles discovered eight or ten cavalry in our rear but they kept at a respectful distance and did not molest us. The fact of two other parties one crossing at Gillsport and one at Limestone helped us a great deal in bewildering the Rebs. and hearing of the parties they didn't know but what a whole army was at their heels.

Have occasion to be thankful that no lives were lost.

Remarks

Road forks at McCarleys the right leading to Decatur the left to Somerville. Good water at Allens, McErlands and Atkins. County generally heavily timbered and slightly rolling. Roads lead from Somerville to all points. Roads sandy in some places.

Road crosses Little Cotaco Creek. 200 yards from banks very steep. Impossible to cross with wagon, difficult with horses. Bridge burnt. Infantry crossed on sleepers. Road runs through bottom 2 miles, densely wooded there though bluffs not steep but road rough. Good well water Mr. McCurley's plantation.

Road good in dry weather. red clay soil and sticky when wet. County slightly rolling and open. Partly cultivated. Springs of good water one hundred rods above ferry landing. Very rough and rocky. The stockade is on a hill and commands the ferry.

Remarks Continued

Same road as traveled going to Somerville. No water between McCarleys and spring and on north side of ferry. Four men sun struck at this point slightly, not serious. Crops (growing) in route generally good. County is scouted by Rebels who are encamped on Flint Creek.

Turned to the right leaving Fletcher's Ferry Road. False information led the column 3 ½ miles out of the way. Nearest road to Atkins is by Fletcher's Ferry but not practicable for wagons. Road good, some what sandy. Water scarce

Road to Fletcher's Ferry nears north from Somerville. Camped for dinner at spring on Mrs.Blackwell's plantation. Good water. County still open and party cultivated. Decatur road cross at right angles. Road good, little sandy.

July 31, 1864 - Head Quarters 73rd Ind. Infantry Triana Ala. (Sunday) Lt. Kiersted Comdg. Co. "B" has sent in his report of operations on the 29th.

It seems the scouting party, 15 in number, crossed at 2 A.M. and were successful in procuring 60 bushels of corn and a beef. They were attacked by a party of 50 Rebel Cavalry and forced back to the river but succeeded in crossing without loss. They claim to have killed 3 or 4 of the Rebs.

A small party crossed at Gillsport but encountered a body of Rebel Cavalry and were forced to return.

Upon the whole I consider that the movement a success. It has thoroughly woked up the Rebs at least.

Aug. 2nd 1864 - Head Quarters 73rd Ind. Infty Triana Ala. (Tuesday) Yesterday Capt. Boyd's and Lieut. Grimes' resignations came back accepted "for the good of the service and for incompetency." I had the orders read on dress parade.

Took a ride down to Limestone Pt. and spent a pleasant hour with Becky Griffith.

Stockades at Watkins Ferry, Fletchers Ferry and Gillsport are about finished. At Bukton where Co. I is stationed will be up in a few days. Limestone Stockade is nearly completed. Drapens Ferry Stockade is finished and garrisoned and have commenced building three picket stockades at Limestone Pt (Triana I mean).

Weather pleasant. Had the ride from Limestone Pt. after dark last night.

Aug. 4th 1864 - Head Quarters 73rd Ind. Infty Triana Ala. (Thursday) Have recommended to Governor O.P. Morton of Indiana the following names for promotion.

Captain Wm. M. Kendall Co D to be Major, 1st Sergt. James M Beeber to be Capt., Sergt. Winfield S. Ramsey to be 1st Lieut, Sergt. Major Rufus M. Brown to be 2nd Lt. all of Company D.

2nd Lt. Otto H. Sollan to be 1st Lt. Co "F", 1 st Sergt. Alex Wilson Cmdj. Co G to be 2nd Lt. (vacancy in F) 1st Sergt. Wilson Dailey Cmdj. Co H to be 2nd Lt. (vacancy in K) 2nd Lt. Leander P. Williams to be 1st Lt. Co. K, Surgeon John S. Sack of South Bend to be Asst. Surg. If they go though all right shall have enough commissioned officers to command all the companies.

August 6 1864 - Head Qrs. 73rd Ind. Infantry Triana Ala. (Saturday) At last after urgent solicitation I have succeeded in procuring one piece of artillery, a six pdr. and caisson which is now on it. When necessary I can now cross the river under cover of its fire and also pay the Rebs back for their spiteful firing at our pickets and men while in swimming.

Got one recruit day before yesterday, an Alabamian named Nicholas Walker. I had him arrested for crossing the river and while held as a prisoner he concluded to enlist.

Have had a good deal of rain lately and it threatens another shower this afternoon.

Sent a scouting party north who made 52 miles.

August 9 1864 Hd. Qrs.73rd Indiana Infantry Triana Ala. (Tuesday) Yesterday two Rebel deserters, Homer L. Adams Private Co "A" 9th Ala. Infty. from Lee's army, and Joseph Hall Private Co. D 23rd Alabama Infantry, came across the river by the assistance of the patrols and gave themselves up. Also one citizen Albert S. Rutherford from Decatur Ga. They all say that the general feeling in the South is one of despondency and that the Confederacy is about played out.

No news of interest lately from Grant or Sherman except that our brave corps commander is rumored to take command at some other important place I suppose.

Aug. 10th 1864 Hd. Qrs. 73rd Ind. Infty. Triana Ala. (Wednesday) A Lt. and several men, members of the 3rd Ga. and 7th Ala Cav. came down with a flag of truce today. I sent Corp. Simons over. They wanted to exchange papers and letters and sent over quite a number, among them one from a son of Mrs. Laverty who is in the Rebel army. Have comm.-enced a secret correspondence with him in regard to sending a party over and effecting his capture. He is anxious to deliver himself up but does not like to desert.

I have my 6 pdr. so planted as to command the camp. Have detailed a squad of seven men to work it.

Aug. 11th 1864 Hd. Qrs. 73rd Ind. Infantry Triana Ala. (Thursday) Have just received a letter from Hon. Schuyler Colfax giving the sad intelligence of brother Robert's death on the 5th inst. Poor Bro. he has suffered so long and hopefully, that although painful to hear of his death yet perhaps it was a mercy to him. Robert's life has been checkered indeed. After ten years wandering he came home at last only to die. I wrote him a long letter a few days since to cheer him in his last sickness but am afraid that it came too late. Mr. Colfax says that mother and sister are nearly worn out as he did not seem to like for anyone else to take care of him.

Aug. 14th 1864 Hd. Qrs. 73rd Indiana Infantry Triana Ala. (Sunday) This morning a party of ten or twelve Rebs came down to the bank and hitched their horses and then without hoisting a flag some of them stripped off and went in swimming. I didn't care about firing at the men in swimming but the squad of horses presented too tempting a mark that I ordered Sergt. Harris Cmdj. the 6 pdr. to throw three shells at them as rapidly as possible. He landed the shells as scientifically as possible right in the midst of the clump of trees where the horses were hitched and no doubt killed a number of them. The Rebs skidaddled on foot, and on the double quick, some sans boots and clothes.

Aug. 15th 1864 Hd. Qrs. 73rd Indiana Infantry Triana Ala. (Monday) In accordance with plans previously arranged the men from each company not on duty (numbering one hundred) formed silently on the color line at 3 o'clock this morning with one days rations and sixty rounds of ammunition per man.

The night was pleasant but cloudy and dark. I marched the men down to river where one pontoon and one flat boat had been previously prepared. The pontoon would carry 15 men and the flat 20. I immediately sent Co. D across to picket the opposite bank and shipped the bal. over as fast as possible. The two boats silently crossing the broad Tennessee with their living freight looked in the twilight of morning very picturesque.

The crossing occupied nearly two hours before the last company had crossed. I pushed the column inland one mile and halted at the plantation of Major Ragland for the rear to come up. Here we found a corral of 30 good horses some of whom the rascally bushwhackers had run through our lines. Some belonged to soldiers and others to spies now in our lines who left their horses here. Major Ragland also had several among which was a very fine stallion. I left a corporal and six men with the horses and a squad men from Co. F.

The advance guard discovered rebel soldiers upon approaching the house who as soon as discovered ran for the woods. They were fired upon but not hit. Upon searching the house two other soldiers were discovered under a bed and brought forth much to their chagrin. One of them, W. G. Laverty, private in Wood's Battery French's Division (now at Atlanta) is the son of an estimable lady in Triana, the other denies belonging to any company. I sent these prisoners back to the river under charge of a corporal and six men with instructions to Adjt. Hagenbuck who was left in command .of the post to send over as many men as he could spare and take all the horses across.

I then marched south south west, passed the plantation of Mr. Draper, and at 6 ½ o'clock arrived at James Grantlin 3 1/2 miles from the river. Here I was informed by Walker, our new recruit from Ala. that a Salt Peter work was in operation belonging to the Confederate Govt. I left the main column in the road and taking ten men paid a visit to the work. The man left to watch it got away safe although fired upon. The kettles were very large and it was impossible to break them but I demolished the building and tore up the works as much as possible then sent a courier back to order the Regt. forward (I call it Regt. for I took the colors and music) and attempted to join it by a new road but got lost and spent an hour in getting together. One or two Reb. scouts were seen but failed to capture them.

We then pushed on to Valamosa Springs as rapidly as possible. Arrived at that place at 8 1/2 A.M.. Here our advance guard was fired upon by a squad of eight or ten Rebel Cavalry, but they retreated so fast after firing that I failed to get but one shot at them. Nobody hurt on either side.

The Springs is a lovely place and the fine hotel here and beautiful gardens have often delighted the southern chivalry. I was rather surprised to meet as proprietor of the house Mrs. Giens, whom I met a few months since while in command of Post LaVergne Tennessee. She is a very inteligent lady, vivacious and charming. While talking with her the soldiers invaded the parlor, kitchen & bed rooms and appropriated silver spoons and other property. As this is demoralizing to the troops. I called them into line and made them fork over the missing property. But permitted them to regale themselves out of a large water melon patch.

Here I found another saltpeter works and made short work of it. Breaking the kettles and burning the building. It was in flames when we left.

As all the conscripts in the county had been ordered to report to Somerville that day, deemed it prudent not [to] stay longer than necessary.

March back by the same route stopping for dinner at a spring 5 miles from river. Reached camp at 1 1/3 P.M. Results 25 horses, 4 oxen, 3 prisoners, 1 contraband, & no loss.

Remarks

Returned by same route. Camped for dinner at Spring and left by road.

Road good, country rolling and wooded. Good water at Mrs. Smith's, an excellent spring one mile from Vallamosa Springs. 200 yards on right of road.

Road good. Country rolling and wooded. No water on

the road. Draper's and Grantlin's houses off the road ¼ mile. In the bend of the road old school stands with 15 to 20 bales of cotton in it.

Arrived at James Ragland's plantation. Country open and level. Good water at the Raglands. Captured 2 soldiers & 22 horses at this point. Road good and straight.

Aug. 16th 1864 - Hd. Qrs 73rd Indiana Infantry Triana Ala. (Tuesday) Schuyler Colfax writes me the sad news that poor Brother Robert who has been confined so long to a sick bed by his injuries (received while struggling with a wild mule) has at last been released from his sufferings. He died Friday August 5th 1864 between 2 and 3 o'clock P.M. Brother Robert had been so long used to the active life of the frontier that it was doubly trying to him to be confined so long, almost perfectly helpless, and perhaps it is better as it is, than for him to have lingered on in that condition. Mr. Colfax writes that Mother is completely worn out with watching as well as sisters Jannie and Mary.

Aug. 19th 1864 - Hd. Qrs 73rd Indiana Triana Ala. (Friday) Nothing of interest has occurred on the past few days. Excepting a forage trip made to the other side of the river yesterday. I detailed 15 men and the six pioneers who went down the river ¾ of a mile with the teams. I planted the cannon so as to command Mr. Edwards corn crib on the other side and sent the men across in the flat boat.

Made three trips bringing three wagon loads each trip of com and fodder. Mr. Grantlin's family who live upon this side (in Triana) are in hysterics over it. At the application of Mrs. Grantlin, one of the family, I divided some of the hams and a barrel of salt with her which the boys had brought across.

Aug. 19th 1864 - Hd. Qrs. 73rd Indiana Infantry Triana Ala. (Also Friday) Have just completed an arrangement with H.

Blankinship, a deserter from the rebel army who is trying a crop [on] the river in Morgan Co., whereby he is to send me prompt intelligence of the enemy and to aid the Union cause generally. He is a perfect scoundrel if reports concerning him are true. But men of that character are generally the only ones that can be induced to enter the secret service. Three rebel deserters and one refugee came in yesterday and today. One of the soldiers was a sergeant just from Atlanta. He represents the feeling of the army as despondent and that if Atlanta falls it will be a death blow.

Aug. 20th 1864 - Head Quarters 73rd Indiana Infantry Triana Ala. (Saturday) Wm. M Lynch private Co. K 7th Ala. Cav., D.F. Hexter Sergt. Co. D 7th Ala. Cav., and Wyatt Blackwell Centrast Surgeon 7th Ala. Rebel deserters came in since last I wrote. Sergt. Hexter left the 7th Ala. at Atlanta only a short time since his company numbers only ten and the Regt. about 175.

A great quantity of rain has fallen lately since today.

There is a probability that the Regt. will return home to vote next month if it can be spared.

Triana security rather dull. I confine my visits to Mrs and Miss McIntosh.

A flag of truce came down to the river today and it proved to be a woman who wanted to cross, but would not allow it. Miss Wolina also sent over a note.

Aug. 20, 1864 - Hd. Qrs. 73rd Indiana Infy Triana Ala. 11 o'clock P.M. (Also Saturday) I have just started off an expedition of thirty men whom my heart will follow with anxiety till their return.

Blankinship reported to Sergt. Romig at Bricks Landing (Stockade No. 2) that Capt. White was opposite Watkins Ferry. At seven o'clock this evening he appeared on the opposite bank and showed a light. A boat was immediately sent across when he gave the information that Capt. Jourdan was at the Widow Troops with his company and immediately sent the information to me by courier. I've sent Lt. Sollan with orders to capture them. The Dillard family (where Head Qrs is established) are up and peeping to ascertain the object of our night move.

Aug. 21, 1864 - Head Quarter 73rd Indiana Infty Triana Ala. (Sunday) Sunday has passed quietly and with the exception of the return of our security party nothing of interest has occurred. Lt. Sollan left last night at 11 oc1ock with thirty men, in three Govt. wagons. They went the Mooresville road to Becks Landing a distance of 9 miles. At this point they crossed the river and guided by Blankinship (my secret service man) reached Widow Troops just before daylight where Capt. Jourdan & his 17 men were encamped.

Unfortunately the pickets discovered them and gave the rebs time to prepare. A lively interchange of shots was had when the enemy skeddadled leaving one dead horse, carbine, and equipment. Our loss one man slightly wounded.

Aug. 23rd 1864 Head Quarters 73rd Ind. Infty Triana Ala. (Tuesday) Have been maturing a scheme to be put into execution tomorrow night which I think will astonish the Rebs somewhat. Have got a stockade up which I shall pull to pieces, ferry it across the river, and before morning have it up and garrisoned. This will ensure an easy and safe crossing whenever desired. My artillery commands the point opposite completely so that I do not fear an attack on stockade.

Called on Mrs. Toney today and at Mrs. McIntosh tonight. My arrest of Mr. White for harboring Confederate soldiers within my lines created a furor amongst the citizens.

Has stopped raining at last.

Aug. 23rd 1864 - Head Quarters 73rd Ind. Inf. Triana Ala. (Also Tuesday) Made a mistake of one day in date of left hand page.

First numbers of Indianapolis Journal an Army and ... Journal for which I have subscribed came about the tenth of this month. 6 was for 1st and one yr. for 2nd.

Have concluded to change the position of companies and shall relieve A., E. and I who are on the N.C. and C.R.R. with F and K who number 100 men. Will send H to Limestone Pt. instead of B and let Co. "C" garrison Brickton Fletcher and Gillsport. This will gave the companies who have been away from Hd. Qrs. a chance to drill. Another letter from S. Colfax says we will probably go home to vote.

Aug. 24 1864 11 o'clock p.m. Triana Ala. (Wednesday) Have just dismissed the Regt. after being called into line by the long roll. 3 shots were fired on the picket line.

I completed a "brilliant idea" this morning. At ten o'clock last night I commenced moving stockade timbers (previously formed) across the river having sent 15 men over at nine to picket the opposite bank. The Pioneers worked with a will and before daylight this morning had completed the Block House. This ensures a safe crossing whenever necessary. The Rebel scouts watched the movement with interest and no doubt opened their eyes with astonishment this morning to see a strong permanent stockade where there was nothing last night. My 6 pdr. on this side commands the position completely.

Aug. 26th 1864 Triana Ala. (Friday) Last night at 11 o'clock about 20 Rebs attacked Stockade NO.9 on the opposite bank.

Regt. was in line before I got up but I dismissed them and took position with the six pdr. A straggling fire was kept up at and from the Block House for two or three hours but our garrison of four men bravely held their own and finally after I had sent two shells in close proximity to them the Rebs skedaddled whether with any loss or not is not known. None were injured in the stockade.

Genl. Granger a day or two since sent a complimentary letter thanking the Regt. and myself for courage and efficiency.

Aug. 26th 1864 - Triana Ala. (Also Friday) Called at Mrs. Tony's this eve and was treated to some good music by her handsome daughter. A fine plantation and a handsome house.

Hardly think that the Rebs will repeat their experiment of last night on Stockade No.9.

Have changed the Companies and have at Hd. Qrs. now Companies A, D, I, E, G and B. Companies F and K. are on the NC and CR. Co. H at Limestone Pt. and Co. C at Brick's Landing. Fletcher's Ferry and Gillsport shall change company. Drill into officers and non-cmd. officers drill tomorrow. I have about a month's work before me in drilling these companies who have got pretty rusty.

August 27th 1864 Triana. (Saturday) An attack was made upon the Stockade over the river this morning again and several bullets came in close proximity to the Garrison, but no one was hurt. This stockade by the way is an eyesore to the Rebs. and it aggravates them a good deal to think that they were so careless of their nights as to permit it to be erected. The companies that I have here now have never been under my immediate command for any length and therefore need drilling badly. I have commenced a system however which will soon bring them out all right. Had a very good battalion drill today and non-cmd. officers drill this a.m.

Aug. 28th 1864 Triana Ala. (Sunday) Three privates of Co. D at Stockade No.5 (Watkin's Ferry) were captured by the Rebs. this morning under the following circumstances.

Just at daylight a man appeared upon the opposite bank and helloed across that he wished to come over. Instead of asking him to hoist a flag of truce as I had expressly ordered in such cases, three of the boys started after him.

Arriving upon the opposite bank a party of 20 Rebels rushed out from behind a thicket and as our men had no arms they were compelled to surrender. They were marched back from the river in quick time.

As soon as I heard of the case I relieved Sergt. Shidler from command and reprimanded him severely.

In the hope of recapturing our boys and making a grand raid from Gillsport to Somerville and back to Triana via Valemosa spring, I mustered all the available mounted men (numbering 40) and left camp at 4 p.m. marching by the Morrisville road to Gillsport a distance of nine miles where we arrived after dusk.

Sent two men across to reconnoiter and then ten for picket. Had considerable trouble in loading up the horses but finally started off the first load of five. Before the boat had got 20 feet from shore it filled with water and its load of human and animal freight barely escaped drowning. Had to bail it out then to get our pickets over and abandon the expedition.

Aug. 31st 1864 Triana Ala. (Wednesday) Received an order late last night to concentrate my command at Triana.

Immediately dispatched couriers to the different stockades and the garrisons were all collected here by ten o' clock this a.m. I had received two days leave of absence for myself and seven others to go to Nashville for muster.

Shall start today and hope to get back before the Regt. moves.

Aug. 31st 1864 Decatur Junction Ala. (Also Wednesday) Came down to Decatur and while there an order was issued for the Regiment to march to the junction immediately. Am now at junction awaiting arrival of Regiment which is coming up under command of Capt. Eaton. Wheeler is playing havoc with the railroads.

Chapter Eight

September 1st, 1864 – December 31st, 1864 (Camp Life in Rebel Land)

Sept. 1st, 1864 - Elk River Bridge Tenn. (Thursday) At eleven o'clock today received an order from Genl. Granger to take special train and with the 73rd and a section of Co. "F" 1st Ohio artillery proceed to this place without delay.

The Regt. came in late last night. Companies F and K being placed on picket having arrived 1st. Arrived at this place at 2 P.M. and found Col Jackson of 9th Ind. Cav. in command of troops here consisting of 9th and 10th Indiana Cavalry and two companies of the 107 U.S. Col. Regiment.

I reported to him personally and to Brig Genl. Starkweather in writing and by telegraph. and then took positions on the bank of Elks River near pontoon bridge.

Sept. 2nd 1864 Prospect Tennessee. (Friday) We were aroused from our slumber last night about 11 o'clock by two or three volleys about half a mile from camp. The 73rd was roused immediately by the long roll and I wheeled them into line on the river bank and waited orders.

The cavalry pickets dashed in and formed line on my left. Col. Jackson came down and ordered me to remain in my position until a general engagement took place and then to retreat to the fort and support the artillery.

A train had just passed south and we knew that the firing was directed at it. But, although from a light in that direction it was supposed that they were burning the train, still no party was sent out. [We didn't] ascertain the fact until after daylight when we learned that a party of 200 of Roddy's Command had fired into the train (without capturing it however) and had then tom up and burnt the track for a short distance.

I blame Col. Jackson very much for not sending a party to drive them off.

Two or three hours after the first alarm there was some picket firing and I deemed it best to remove the Regiment 200 yards to the right in a commanding position. Which I did notifying the Col.

Genl. Starkweather came down today with 500 cavalry and we now feel perfectly safe against any attack. Even from Wheelers whole force. Starkweather is a young man but inspires confidence.

Sept. 3rd 64 Head Qrs. 73rd Ind. Infantry Prospect Fort Tenn. (Saturday) At 9 o'clock last night received orders from General Starkweather to move the Regiment to the fort and do so placing the men in the ditches and inside. A detail of 52 men was made for the Regiment for ground guard.

The General sent up word this P.M. that dispatches just received say that "Atlanta has fallen" Three rousing cheers went up for the 73rd upon hearing the news.

The General has just left with all the Cavalry except 50 and we guard the bridge alone.

Have been on short rations for several days.

3rd and 4th Tenn. Cavalry passed us this eve in search of the Elk River Road. Reported both up above.

Sept 4th 1864 - Prospect Tenn. (Sunday) General Granger passed us today with four trains of troops. The 6th Indiana was aboard going home for muster only. These are the first trains for two days.

Granger was terribly severe on Genl. Jackson for allowing the enemy to come so near the other night without attacking him and well he might be for it was shameful.

Rations gave out today and have sent some of the boys out to forage.

Quite a number have been taken with the ague lately and we are out of quinine.

There are two companies of Colored Troops here in

stockades and it seems to me that they could guard the bridge against any attack.

Sept. 6th 1864 - Prospect Tenn. (Tuesday) The Rebs were on the road five miles above yesterday and cut the telegraph wire.

General Steadman passed last night with his Brigade loaded on five trains. They have been patrolling the road for a week or two.

Col. Streight with the 51st Indiana is in that Brigade [The 51st Indiana under Abel D. Streight led the raid in which the 73rd was captured, Ed.]

Lt. Col. Chris Beck of the 9th Indiana Cavalry is in command here. Don't like him at all.

It is awful hot on this high hill and can't do much but lay in the shade all day long.

We have a fine view from the fort of the country for four or five miles around.

Hope we shall be ordered off soon as many men are getting sick.

Sept. 12th 1864 - Prospect Tenn. (Monday) The last six days have been over loaded with misery.

Haven't read a paper in 12 days but through other sources learn the charming news that Morgan has been killed in East Tennessee and his staff captured.

Wheeler however, although losing a good many men, has probably succeeded in placing the Tennessee River between himself and our forces. It is reported that he crossed at Florence, Chickasaw and Eastport.

McClellan and Pendleton have been nominated by the Peace Convention at Chicago for Pres. and Vice President.

There have been 70 cases of fever and ague in the Regt and have been quite sick myself for three or four days

Sept. 14, 64 Decatur Ala. (Wednesday) Orders were received from Pulaski this morning for the 73rd to return tomorrow and go into camp at Mooresville.

As I wished to ascertain the meaning of this order I came down on train today with the 102 Ohio who are to be stationed at Decatur.

Have visited both Brigade and Division (District) Head Qrs. but ascertain nothing as General Granger is at Huntsville. I shall go to Triana tonight and send for all the stores and baggage together with the troops to Mooresville. I regret leaving the river line very much as we have it well fortified.

Shall borrow a horse here and try to ride down although am very unwell.

Sept. 15th. 1864 - Head Qrs. 73rd Indiana Infantry Mooresville Ala. (Thursday) Attempted to ride to Triana last night but was so sick that had to stop at Limestone Creek on R.R. and send for ambulance. Reached Triana about 10 o'clock P.M. and immediately threw myself into some clean clothes. The first time I had enjoyed that luxury in more than two weeks.

This morning I ordered preparation for the march and started at one P.M. with everything, including our six pdr. drawn by four green mules.

The large star stockade at T commenced some time since had just been finished and we hated to leave it.

The citizens nine tenths of whom are secesh did not seem sorry to have us go however.

I brought away about 200 men a good many of whom were convalescents and consequently had to march slow but reached Mooresville before sun down where I found the balance of the Regt. who came down from Elk River Bridge today.

Established camp near the fine spring which is here and having appropriated two rooms in Dr. Thuches house have settled for a stay.

It is two weeks since a mail has been received at the regiment and it was a welcome sight this evening to see that two weeks accumulation come piling in upon us. The boys are a happy set tonight devouring the news from home. While I view my piles of Indianapolis Journals, weekly papers and my commission as Lieutenant Colonel with a complacent gaze.

Sept. 18th 1864 Head Qrs. 73rd Indiana Infantry Mooresville Ala. (Sunday) Mooresville is like all other towns in the South and not worth describing.

My Head Qrs. are very pleasantly situated in one of the best houses and we have the benefit of a furnished parlor and bedroom. The men are now living in sheltered tents and believe it will be good for their health. The officers have drawn wall tents.

The citizens of Mooresville have suffered comparatively little from the war although troops have been encamped almost all the time.

As have been appointed Lt. Col. by the Governor shall go to Nashville with other officers to be mustered into new grades.

Sept. 20th 1864 - Nashville Tenn. (Tuesday) Left Mooresville early yesterday morning and went to Limestone Bridge to flag the train and took seats for this place. There were no passenger cars and it was a weary day's ride on the hard seats of box cars. Reached here at 5 p.m. and put up at the St. Cloud.

Have worked very industriously all day today at the office of Capt. Eckels Commissary of..........for the 4th Div. and have concluded the muster of Alfred B. Wade from Major to Lt. Colonel,
Leander P. Williams from 2nd Lt. Co. K to 1 st Lt. Co. K
Otto H. Sollan from 2nd Lt. Co. C to 1st Lt. Co F
Alexander Wilson from 1st Sergt. Co. G to 2nd Lt Co. D
Wilson Dailey from 1st Sergt. Co. H to 2nd Lt. Co K
John Y. Slick from 1st Sergt. Co C to 2nd Lt. Co. C
Charles S. Arnold from 1st Sergt. Co. I to 2nd Lt. Co. I
also Pvts. Walker and Reprogle Recruits to Co. D and F

Sept. 22nd 1864 - Mooresville Ala. (Thursday) Arrived here from Nashville with my batch of newly made officers yesterday. Found that Company B has been ordered back to Triana.

With that exception everything was the same as when I left. Have now nine line officers on duty with the Regiment. There is some talk of the Regiment going home to vote but am afraid that it will only end in talk. The Cavalry Regiments appear to be certain of going.

The papers today speak of a victory by Sheridan in the Shenandoah Valley Virginia which appears to be of considerable importance as the enemy were driven many miles losing a number of Generals and many prisoners.

.

Sept. 23rd 1864 - Mooresville Ala. (Friday) A darkie came riding furiously into town from Decatur Junction two hours since with the information that the Rebs were advancing this way having burned some Govt. buildings on the other side of Decatur. I had the long roll sounded and sent out one company and the mounted scouts. They returned with the news that they were tearing up the railroad seven miles from here and that the Tenn. cavalry were after them. This is confirmed by gentlemen just in from the seat of war and quiet reigns in camp once more.

It seems that two plantations were burned and a stockade attacked. The rascals ought to be caught.

Sept. 25th 1864 - Decatur Ala. (Sunday) Yesterday morning at Mooresville, hearing heavy cannonading towards Athens I sent out scouts to the RR and went to work fortifying. During the forenoon Wm. S. Patterson Co. C 7th Ala came into the picket line and gave himself up. Says that the 7th only had 27 men left and they were about disbanding.

At noon received an order to march immediately for Decatur. Packed up and started at 2 p.m. Roads muddy and very bad especially over ...... Reached Decatur at 5 p.m. and went into camp.

Found Col. Given of 102 Ohio in command of Post. A part of the 102 and 18th Mich were captured today near Athens by Forrest about 350 men in all. Some apprehensions here of an attack upon this place.

Sept. 26th 1864 - Head Qrs. 73rd Ind. Infty Decatur Ala. (Monday) Excitement here is if anything on the increase, but I cannot believe that the enemy intends to attack this place.

Last night at 11 o'clock we were ordered to remove everything silently into camp. I placed part of the Regt. in S.W. angle Fort to support Battery F, 1st Ohio. Men were ordered to sleep with cartridge boxes on, a useless cruelty.

Today Col. Doolittle assumed command and if anything his movements were more ordered than Givens. He moved out 300 cavalry and the 102nd and 73rd two and four miles to ascertain if the enemy were near. A half a doz. men could have done the work just as easily and perhaps much better. Co. B captured a 7th Ala. man today (Sue Colliers brother.)

Sept. 27th 1864 Decatur Ala. (Tuesday) I have another admirable occasion to vent my spleen in regard to the ridiculous way in which military matters are carried on at this Post. Today Col. Doolittle of the 18th Mich. Cmdg. Post, wishing to ascertain whether the enemy were on the Moulton road or not, instead of sending out a company of Cavalry to reconnoiter detailed two Regts. of Cavalry, 3 Regts. of Infantry and one battery. The 73rd was unfortunate enough to be included in this detail.

Every man with the least particle of military sense knows that it is bad policy when the enemy is supposed to be near to tire out infantry before that enemy is found.

That this force was too small to cope with Wheeler even if we found him and too large to be scarified that if the enemy was really in the vicinity in force they could easily have come in on another road and taken Decatur in our absence.

We started about 11 a.m. The 73rd in rear of Battery

and by easy marches made ten miles by 5 p.m. and then finding nothing turned around and came back.

It soon grew dark and commenced raining. The road became horrible and the men groped along in the darkness falling into pits and mud holes constantly.

I attempted to keep up with the battery but the Regt. became so scattered that I finally halted it, placed a guard across the road, and allowed it to close up and found that our ambulance had broken down and had been left behind. Arrived in Decatur about ten o'clock

Sept. 29 1864 - Head Qrs. United States forces Athens Ala. (Thursday) Yesterday at Decatur 60 men were sent on picket and 30 up the river on board a gunboat.

In the evening received an order to move on special train to Athens, take the place and hold it. Pickets were called in and packed up everything. Left camp with 177 effective men of the 73rd and two hundred of the Tenth Indiana.

Crossed the river and after much trouble and crowding loaded the force on ten open cars.

As it was not known whether the enemy was in Athens or not, was ordered to take one hundred rounds of cartridges. Proceeded towards Athens very slowly and cautiously and arrived within one mile of town at half past one where we found the road tom up and could proceed no farther as it was quite dark. I concluded to go into camp by the side of the Rail Road.

At daylight started up the road with advance guard and found it was tore up badly in some places. The rebs had lined the road and by sheer strength turned it completely over. A fire engine and several cars had been burnt standing upon a bridge turning off to the left.

When within half a mile of town we struck towards the fort and soon began to see evidence of the late fight in the numerous debris incident to a battle field. We occupied the fort without meeting any enemy and found all the inside buildings and works burned but the walls remain entire and will afford great protection in case of attack.

The surrender by Col. Cameron is considered disgraceful although there was no boom proof in the fort & no protection against artillery.

I have a large and very handsome residence near the fort as Hd Qrs, for self and staff.

Rebs were here yesterday and are scouting the country in small squads. And under the impression that Forrest will come back this was and then for a fight.

Genl. Granger sent me up two rifled guns and 300 men of the 1st Tenn. Battery and 200 cavalry 2nd Tennessee today with my train of baggage and camp and garrison equipage.

Forrest I think has 12 pieces of artillery with him and that is all I dread. If he will only come without that I'll fight him with a will.

Sept. 30th 1864 - Head Qrs United States Forces Athens Ala. (Fridy) Reveille this morning before day break but no enemy appearing. We commenced the day's work by moving camp a short distance from the fort.

The news from Sulpher Trestle that a garrison of 800 men were compelled to surrender to Forrest simply because they could not withstand his artillery gave me some mental trouble in regard to my little band of three hundred and the open fort. This splendid Fort has been built with a great deal of trouble and expense but that fatal mistake was made of not building a bomb proof.

A happy thought finally struck me I had not the time to build one inside the Fort and whatever was to be done must be done quickly as I had no definite information in regard to the enemy and was liable to be attacked at any moment.

The outside ditch would serve my purpose admirably and I immediately set to work a force of men and all the teams available in hauling up logs from the old huts in the vicinity. These laid across the ditch makes it perfectly boom proof as any shot striking it will do so slantingly [sic] and must therefore glance off.

An entrance into this novel arrangement will be effected by a passage way dug under the gate of the Fort. If Forrest gives one until tomorrow noon I will fight his command artillery and all.

There are about 100 wounded here. One dead Negro soldier was found upon the battle field today and was buried.

A hard rain storm is now setting in.

Oct. 1st 1864 - Head Qrs United States Forces Athens Ala. (Saturday) I was heartily glad to see my wagon train come in this noon.

Huntsville was attacked last night and Major McBath with the 2nd Tenn. Cavalry had been ordered at midnight to proceed to that place and started this morning at day break but came tearing back this afternoon having met the enemy's advance guard 4 miles from Huntsville, coming this way.

At 3 o'clock P.M the pickets on the Huntsville road were driven in and at the same time a drenching rain storm commenced. I deployed one company of dismounted cavalry to engage the enemy who had taken position behind the Rail Road and commenced moving the baggage into the Fort.

Firing was kept up briskly on the skirmish line until dusk when I reinforced it with Co "G" of the 73rd to prevent the rebels from gaining possession of a cluster of houses near the Fort..

The cavalry dismounted fastened their horses and were stationed inside of the Fort.

The passage way under the gate leading into my boom proof was but a foot deep when skirmishing first commenced but I put all the men on to it that could work with instructions to dig away no matter how hard the fighting and by midnight it was large enough to be used.

My garrison now consisted of five companies of the 73rd Ind. Infty under command of Capt. Eaton, four companies of the 2nd Tennessee Cavalry under Major McBath, two companies of the 10th Ind. dismounted cavalry commanded by Capt. Gafferey, and a section of the 2nd Tenn Arty Battery "A" under Lt. Tobin, in all about 500 effective men.

Opposed to which was Brig. Genl. A. Buford's Division of Cavalry and a battery of four guns numbering four thousand men. His advantage was in numbers, ours was in fortifications, a good boom proof, and a better cause.

During the night the noise made by the enemy's guns enabled me to locate their position exactly and the two pieces in the Fort were brought to bear upon them ready to answer their fire as soon as opened. Three companies were moved into the boom proof. The balance placed in advantageous positions and we were ready to fight Buford and his whole command.

Oct. 2nd 1864 - Head Qrs. United States Forces Athens Ala. (Sunday) Half an hour before daybreak the men were aroused and stood to arms. From early daylight till 6 a.m., a brisk fire was kept up with small arms, principally upon the west side where a thick growth of timber approached to within short range of the Fort.

At six a.m. the enemy opened with one gun situated south west from the Fort on the Browns Ferry road which was promptly responded to.

Ten minutes after, three rifled pieces opened fire upon us in quick succession from a slight elevation (a) mile north. With such across fire there was scarcely a spot in the Fort but what could be reached by a shell and I immediately moved the troops into boom (sic) proof leaving a sufficient number as sentinels to watch for indications of an assault.

I had previously given orders to Lt. Arnold Cmdg. Co. E to halt any flag of truce that might approach some distance from the Fort in order that they might not discover our boom proof. After half an hour's practice the enemy guns obtained the range and threw shells into the Fort with great accuracy, I had planted the Regimental Flag of the 73rd on the parapet, and it suffered considerably, two shells passing through and tearing great holes. A caisson cover was tom off and set on fire within a few inches of the ammunition.

Private A. H. Kersey of Co I instantly put it out with a pail of water at the imminent risk of being blown to atoms. A tall chimney was tumbled to the ground hardly leaving one brick upon another. Thirty horses were killed or wounded which were fastened a few yards from the walls of the Fort. Five shells struck exactly at the position where company D of the 73rd had stood.

About 60 rounds were fired at us. 22 struck the Fort nearly all .inside - the balance bursting overhead or passing beyond. Our two guns returned this severe fire cooly and steadily. Had we remained silent the Rebs would not have wasted so much ammunition upon us.

At eight o'clock Genl. Buford concluding that we must be pretty well demoralized ceased firing and we soon saw a horseman approaching with a flag of truce.

I delegated Capt. Wm. C. Eaton of Co I to meet him and try to ascertain the disposition of their troops while I was answering whatever communication should be sent. While the flag was approaching I had leisure to examine the field with a glass and soon discovered that they were moving up a dismounted line in front of my weakest point. This was a violation of the flag but I concluded not to notice it and simply ordered out 3 companies and trained the artillery upon their line which had moved up within 200 yards of the Fort. Private Johnson who had accompanied the Captain soon brought in a sealed envelope which contained the following:

Hd. Qrs.in the Field
near Athens Ala. Oct. 2/64

Commanding Officer, U.S. Forces, Athens, Ala.

Sir: Having invested your place with a sufficient force to reduce it in a short time, for the sake of humanity, I demand the immediate surrender of the Fort, garrison, etc. Certain conditions will attend the surrender the bearer of this will acquaint you.

I am, sir, with much respect, etc.,

A Buford
Brig. Genl. P. A C. S., Comdg.

Buford's Adjutant, General Small, proved to be the bearer. I had some curiosity to know what conditions he would offer, but as that might lead him to think that we would surrender if they were liberal enough, I sat down on a cracker box and wrote the following:

Headquarters United States Forces,
Athens, Ala., October 2, 1864

Brigadier-General A Buford
Commanding Confederate Forces
In front of Athens, Ala.

Sir: I have had the honor to acknowledge the receipt of your communication of this date, demanding the surrender of the fort and garrison under my command. In answer I would say that having a sufficient force to defend the place I decline to surrender.

Very respectfully, your obedient servant,
A B . Wade
Lieutenant-Colonel Seventy-third Indiana Comdg.

and sending it out ordered the flag off and Captain Eaton to return immediately. It seems the cowardly rebels had basely taken advantage of this flag, and while I was engaged writing an answer stole six wagons and four ambulances directly from under my guns. I did not know this at the time, but because they had changed position under the flag I determined to teach them a lesson, and as soon as the flag disappeared ordered four companies and the artillery to open on their new line.

They fell back in confusion, leaving four dead. They continued to annoy us with their sharpshooters, who had taken possession of headquarters. I finally ordered eight shells to be sent through the building, which drove them out in hurry.

I then sent skirmishers out in every direction at 10 a.m. Suspecting that Buford had found a harder nut to crack than he anticipated and was leaving, which proved to be true, the cavalry immediately pursued, and found that they had retreated down the Florence road.

Our loss was only two slightly wounded. That of the enemy unknown, as he carried off all his wounded. This victory of ours has a great significance from the fact that a larger garrison surrendered this same fort when in better condition only a week or two since. I estimate the saving on casualties by our boom proof to be at least 50, as shells cannot explode in a small fort filled with men without killing somebody.

Oct. 4th 1864 - Hd. Qrs United States Forces Athens Ala. (Tuesday) Yesterday Genl. James Morgan's 2nd Division of the 14th Corps came down on the cars in nine trains. They are just from the front. The Div. consists of three Brigades composed of 18 Regts. and one battery. Genl Morgan and staff called at my Hd. Qrs and I was warmly congratulated for my successful defense yesterday.

The troops camped here last night and moved this morning down the Florence road. The Genl. called to bid good bye and leave some instructions. The 2nd Tenn. has been taken from my command but 150 of 102 Ohio and another of my own companies was added to it today.

A heavy rain has fallen.

Oct. 5th 1864 - Hd Qrs. United States Force Athens Ala. (Wednesday) A miserable rain storm has been drenching us for the past two days and no signs of abatement.

My courier returned who was sent after Genl. J. D. Morgan with the information that he could not cross Elk River. The 125th Ill. which started this morning will have to return.

Matters are quiet in the vicinity of Athens. Telegraph communication was established with Nashville via Stevenson this p.m. Received a dispatch from Genl. Granger inquiring for Forrest.

A small body of Rebs were in the vicinity last night.

Have appointed Lt. Williams Post Commissary. He has about 5000 rations.

About 100 of Genl. Morgan's sick were left behind.

Can't hear anything from Forrest but believe him to be making for the shoals on the west side of the Railroad.

Am afraid one of my couriers sent to Decatur is captured.

Oct. 6 1864 - Hd. Qrs. U.S. Forces Athens Ala. (Thursday) Telegraph working both ways today and many dispatches have come from Genl. Starkweather at Pulaski, Genl. Granger at Huntsville, and Col. Doolittle at Decatur for information in regard to the enemy, but as I have no cavalry can send them none.

One courier came through today from Genl. Morgan. He says that his comrade with dispatches from Genl. M. was drowned in crossing Elk. Sent Courier to him again today but he could not cross Elk.

Forrest is reported at Lawrenceburg. In which case he will hardly pay us a visit but am ready for anything that may turn up. The General must have a good deal of confidence in me as he continues to send me troops until now I find myself in command of a Brigade as follows:

73rd Ind., 6 Companies, Capt. Wm Eaton Comdg, 316
102 Ohio Infy, Capt. .... ,170

10th Ind Cav. Dismnted, 2 Cos., Capt. Gaffery Comdg., 116
125th Ill. Infty, IO Cos., Capt. Cook Comdg. 237
1st Tenn Arty. Batt. A, Lt. Tobin Comdg., 31
Total 870

Making quite a respectable force. Besides this there are about 200 sick and wounded in town under my command. Am well pleased with Athens and hope they will let us stay here.

A case of parents trying to force daughter Sarah to prevent her from marrying an officer came before me today.

Oct. 7th 1864 Hd. Qtrs. United States Forces Athens Ala. (Friday) The detachment of 102nd Ohio was ordered to Decatur last night. Starkweather has sent down several dispatches today making inquiries. Can't keep much of a picket force on and am full of anxiety for my command.

Have heard nothing from Forrest but expect he is across the river by this time.

Secesh citizens come infrequently but don't get much favor from the "Col. Comdg." I ordered one man to keep out of my lines today.

Weather was fine today and the boys engaged in a general "drying out" but it is blowing up another storm tonight.

Two more dead Rebs were found today killed by our shells.

Sent a man with and after mail to Nashville today. R.R. is being repaired as fast as possible. Genl. Rousseau and .... are in the field after Forrest.

Oct. 9th 1864 Hd. Qrs. U.S. Forces Athens Ala. (Sunday) Yesterday and today have passed off quietly. Have policed up the Fort and secured the debris accumulated during the last fights.

It seems that Gregory Cotton of Co C was killed accidentally a few days since at Beaver dam. Capt. Beckhart 111th Col. Infty reported to me for duty yesterday and I appointed him Provost Marshall.

Sheridan has gained another great victory over Early and the cause of the southern Confederacy grows everyday more gloomy.

Have departed from my rule in relation to granting safe guards in the one instance of the Female Institute at this place, Mad. J. Hamilton Childs Principal.

Am half sick and haven't scarcely even enough (strength?) to write up my journal. Capt. Eaton commands the Regt.

Oct. 10th 1864 - Head Qrs United States Forces Athens Ala. ((Monday) I telegraphed today to Genl. Starkweather and received permission to keep one company of the 9th Indiana Cav. here for security purposes. Am hopeful of getting the 73rd together at this place.

Recd. some late papers which after a two week suspension of the mail. Was a perfect god send.

There is much excitement over the coming Presidential election but I think there can hardly be a draft but that Lincoln will be the lucky man. The 73rd is almost a wait for him., McClellan having received but seven votes in the whole Regiment when an election was held a short time since.

Weather pleasant and citizens troublesome.

Oct. 11th 64 - Hd Qrs U.S. Forces Athens Ala. (Tuesday) Genl. Morgan's Division Commissary came in this P.M. and reports that the Div. will be here tomorrow. Last night Genl. Morgan telegraphed me to be ready to move at a moment's notice with my command. I telegraphed back and asked what my command meant. The answer was 73rd & 10th Ind leaving Balting & 125th Ill. here. But as the order has not come yet I guess their "scare" has subsided.

They are terribly sensitive about Decatur and concentrate a force there at the least sign of danger. When it is the least important point in the District either to us or the Rebs.

I believe Athens to be the strategic point of Nor. Ala. or at least this point. It is within ten miles of the place where raiders always cross and is the first point to be struck on the RR.

Knowing of Morgan's actions General Starkweather has ordered me to send back Capt. Walls and his Co. of the ninth (9th) Ind.

Beautiful weather now and although half sick I took a stroll this afternoon around the grounds connected with the beautiful mansion which I occupy as Hd. Qrs. Suddenly came upon family burial ground in the center of a orchard and wandering through many strange thoughts came to my mind. I noticed that the name of Coleman was upon all the tomb stones.

The Govt. of the citizens of this town would be no easy matter but I should like to stay here for some time to see what affect a little strictness would have.

Oct. 13th 1864 - Head Qrs. United States Forces Athens Ala. (Thursday) Yesterday Genl. Morgan's Division came in from Florence, will tend with their expedition. They did not stop but marched through town and two miles beyond and went into camp.

The General called to see me and when he left bid a hearty good bye. He looked worn and tired.

I issued 15,000 rations to the troops.

This morning several trains came down the track having been built so that the trains could run in. They have been going all day and the last of the 2nd Div. 14th Ala sped away Eastward at 4 o'clock this P.M. The 125th Ill went with them leaving me as a garrison the 73rd and 10th Ind. with the Battery.

Sent courier to Genls. Steadman and Rousseau yesterday with orders to move to Bridgeport.

Oct. 14th 1864 - Hd. Qrs. 73rd Ind Infantry Athens Ala. (Friday) Genl. Rousseau & Steadman (Maj. Generals) came in late last night. Their troops, about 6000, marched in today and camped in town and the vicinity. Genl. Rousseau left with an escort today for Pulaski.

My garrison is reduced down at last to my own Regt., six companies and the battery, the 10th Indiana being ordered to Decatur in the morning. The troops here now are to be furnished with transportation to Bridgeport.

Lt. Col Elliot, 102nd Ohio died last night and was buried today with full military honors. I commanded the six companies of my Regt as an escort.

I think that Forrest or somebody else will be up this way again on another raid soon. At least our Generals seem to court it in taking away all the troops from this vicinity.

Am anxious to hear the news in relation to the election in Indiana but nothing has come yet. I feel tolerably certain however that Morton and Colfax are elected as well as the state ticket.

Oct. 15th 64 - Hd. Qrs. United States Forces Athens Ala. (Saturday) Beautiful weather now and I enjoy evening rides around Athens hugely.

The 9th Ohio has been added to my garrison (about 300 men) Co. K has come up but are mainly all sick with the ague.

Nothing of importance has occurred lately except that all the troops have come in from the west and we are unguarded on that point. My 6 pdr. and Gun Detachment have been ordered to Triana.

Some of the 1st Tenn Arty. killed a hog belonging to the Govt after I had expressly ordered that there should be no more private foraging. And I made them pay for it as a punishment. It will have the effect to prevent this wholesale plundering of citizens in the future I hope.

Commenced drilling today and shall keep it up. The Regt. has improved very much and I am proud of 570 brave boys.

Oct. 17th 1864 - Hd. Qrs United States Forces Athens Ala. (Monday) The citizens of Athens and the soldiers therein have pursued the even turn of their way for the past two days with none to molest or make afraid. My efficient Provost Marshall Capt. Charles A Beckert has worked up a few cases of disloyal citizens and forwarded a bushwhacker or two but as a general rule everything is distressingly quiet.

By today's mail I get the first news from the elections and it is good. Indiana is union [the name of Lincoln's party in 1864, Ed.] by a handsome majority, Ohio ditto, and Pennsylvania although close yet safe. This is worth to our army a great victory and will depress the Rebs much.

Have but a small force available for drill now but am pushing it and the recitation in tactics with energy.

Called on Mad. J. Hamilton Childs today. She is principal of the Female Institute here and her buildings are admirably suited for that purpose and are fitted with great cost and expense. She invited me over to dine with her and think I shall accept the invitation.

Oct. 20 64 - Hd. Qrs. United States Forces Athens Ala. (Thursday) Sam Bartlett our sutler starts for So. Bend tomorrow and I shall send by him all my valuable papers that I do not need to keep by me and then I shall rest easier as to what may befall me in the varying fortunes of war.

A beautiful bouquet was sent me yesterday by an unknown friend who signs herself Mrs. R K. Smith. Of course am anxious to make the lady's acquaintance.

Military matters are extremely quiet now. Genl. Croxton and five or six Cavalry Regiments is down on the river near Florence and I feel comparatively safe now although have nothing here but my own Regt. and the battery.

Oct. 22nd 1864 - 3 P.M. - Head Qrs United States Forces Athens Ala. (Saturday) Just received the following by courier and copy for reference. By telegraph from Athens Ala near Florence Ala. Oct. 22nd 1864 - 3 P.M:

To Brig. Genl. Granger, Huntsville

Dispatched through Col. Wade, recd. on the 17th - General Thomas telegraphed me that the 9th and 10th Regts. Ind. Cav. and the 10th and 12th Tenn Cav. have been ordered to report to .... to assist in guarding the North bank of the river [Tennessee River, Ed.] and prevent the enemy crossing.

On the 19th he telegraphed as follows Genl. Granger will have the Tenn patrolled by the 2nd Regt until the 9th & 10th Inf. can be furnished also that he had ordered Genl. Granger to patrol the river from Decatur to La.:.... Ferry. So I depend on you to the latter point.

Respectfully, T. Croxton

Oct. 23rd 1864 - Head Qrs. United States Forces Athens Ala. (Sunday) The weather has become quite cool lately and underclothes and an extra blanket at night has become necessary for comfort.

The general situation is encouraging although movements near have come almost to a standstill. Hood and the main part of his army has been making desperate attempts to cut Sherman's communications between Chattanooga and Atlanta but has not accomplished anything serious.

Grant is still pegging away at Richmond and in due time will enter it in triumph. Nor. Alabama appears exceedingly quiet just now but I am apprehensive that Forrest will attempt another raid soon.

Oct. 27th 64 - Hd. Qrs U.S. Forces Decatur Junction Ala. (Thursday) The monotony of our camp life has suddenly been broken in upon. On the evening of the 26th I sent 100 men to reinforce Decatur which is threatened by an unknown force. Today I received an order to move the bal. of my command down, transportation being furnished by the R.R.

Spent the afternoon in loading the artillery on the cars and started just before dark. The wagon train having got off a short time previous. I left Lt. Williams in command at Athens with Co "D" and the convalescents. Cannonading at Decatur day before yesterday and yesterday was quite lively but the Rebs have not made a determined attack yet. Am laying here awaiting the wagon train. Have telegraphed to ask permission to camp here tonight.

Oct. 28th 1864 - Head Qrs. United States Forces Fort No 1 Decatur Ala. (Friday) Genl. Granger telegraphed me last night that I would have to slip into Decatur with my command before daylight as the enemy commanded the pontoon bridge and the river road with his sharpshooters.

Accordingly at midnight I ordered the artillery to be hitched up and commenced the march over that horrible corduroy road which was rendered almost impassable by the late rains. I ordered the train with eighteen mounted men as a guard to remain at the junction until further orders.

Arrived at Decatur about two o'clock and turning over the artillery took command of the portion of my Regiment here numbering about 150 men. The position assigned me was on the right and the men were distributed through the camp of the 18th Mich.

I had just laid down and was getting into a doze when the rattle of musketry on the picket line started me up and soon the cheers and yells of the Rebels as they charged the line convinced me that an assault was being attempted and I immediately formed the Regt. in position.

The 13th and 10th Ind Cav. Regts. were on the skirmish line in our front and were easily driven in. The Rebs contented themselves with this and did not attempt to assault the works. This same line had been driven in yesterday and was reestablished by a charge of the 100 men of our regiment sent here.

First daylight came on soon and I discovered that the enemy had dug rifle pits on the line gained this morning and that their line extended a distance of about three miles from the river above to the river below. The forenoon wore away and we were notified that an attempt to capture the enemy's skirmish line would be made and that we must be ready to support the charging party.

One of the company of the 18th Mich. filing out from an opening in the fortifications on the right of the 73rd succeeded in flanking their line and then charged down on it with a shout. The effect was instantaneous and ludicrous in the extreme. The whole Rebel line for half a mile broke to the rear without firing a shot. Our artillery opened upon them and must have killed & wounded a large number while over one hundred were captured. They belonged to the 8th Arkansas Cleburne Div. [of] Hardees Corps.

The enemy immediately advanced another line and we were ordered out to cover the retreat of the 18th Mich. I doubled quicked the regiment to the southeast sally port and pushed out under a heavy skirmish line, deployed and lay down. Remained here a half an hour and were then ordered in.

This P.M. the Regt. was ordered out to hold the extreme left rifle pits. I found the enemy in pretty good force in our front and a very lively skirmish was kept up all the afternoon. A man could not stick his head above the rifle pit without being shot at. I used up 80 rounds of cartridges per man but both sides were well protected and not much damage was inflicted. I thought at one time that my line would be driven back. A Regiment of colored troops (14th) was ordered to charge a battery of the enemy's on our left. Although numbering 500 men they were repulsed and driven back without accomplishing their object. They lost 40 killed and wounded in the charge.

The Rebs charged thru some distance to our left and rear and being flanked the left of our line which was very thin fell back. I soon reestablished it. The Regt. in our front seeing that our whole line on the left had given way advanced their colors and attempted to charge but a few volleys changed their determination and they fell back into their rifle pits and resumed sharp shooting. The battery in our rear when the

Rebel charge was made limbered up and went to the rear on the run.

About 5 o'clock P.M. I was relieved from the skirmish line and ordered into the fortification where I was placed in command of Fort Nash garrisoned by detachment from my Regt., the 18th and 29th Michigan and 181st Ohio and mounting eight guns belonging to 1st Ohio Battery F and 1st Tenn. Battery "A." Also one 24 pdr Howitzer.

100 men from my Regt. are detailed to perform the perilous task of establishing a new picket line tonight. Each man besides his gear carries a pack or spade and after the line is advanced as far as necessary rifle pits are to be thrown up. I sincerely hope that the boys will all come back alive. My command of the Fort prevents me from going.

Oct. 29th 64 - Hd. Qrs. U.S. Forces Fort No 1 Decatur Ala. (Saturday) Slept last night with Lt. Miller of the Battery. The Rebs cheered a good deal all along the line but made no other demonstration. I think from the looks of their campfires that they are slowly drawing off their forces. It is supposed the enemy's greatest force here at any one time was 20,000 men (there was 40,000). But only one division (Cleburnes) has made any active demonstration.

The loss of our Regt thus far is one dead (Flewellen Co I) killed and half a doz. very slightly wounded. The whole skirmish line charged this P.M. and drove the Rebs half a mile. The 73rd took two prisoners.. We are ordered to return to Athens tonight and I am anxious to get the Regt. settled as soon as possible.

Oct. 30th 1864 - Hd Qrs. 73rd Indiana Infantry Athens Ala. (Sunday) Left Decatur this morning on the cars in company with the 13th Wis. Arrived here at 9 A.M. and found things all safe but am very tired with my three day campaign.

Genl. Granger telegraphs me that reinforcement consisting of one Battery & 5 companies of Infantry would be sent to me coming from Lambs Ferry.

Came in tonight and report heavy cannonading at Florence. It is supposed that Hood's whole army is crossing there.

Genl Thomas telegraphs me from Nashville that Maj. General Stanley Comdg. 4th Corps will be here tomorrow.

Am very tired and sleepy but shall have to sit up till my reinforcements come in.

Oct. 31st 1864 - Head Qrs United States Forces Athens Ala. (Monday) Col O'David 181st Ohio came in last night with 450 of his Regiment also one section of battery.

1st Tenn Arty. Col O'Dowd refuses to take command of the post and very cautiously resigns in my favor, a proceeding whether arising from a fear of inability or as a matter of complement to me I cannot say. Certainly it is a very strange proceeding.

Major General Stanley and Brig. Genl. Wood my old Division Commander came in today with Wood's division. They are both soldiers and gentlemen and after a ride around town with them selecting a position for the 4th Corps I came to the conclusion that a more affable officer with his stars than Genl. Stanley did not exist. Genl. Wood also made himself agreeable although suffering from his old wound in the foot.

Orders came from Genl. Thomas this P.M for the 4th Corps to move to Pulaski immediately. I gave Genl. Wood's division one day's rations which took about all I had and they left about 3 P.M.

Am afraid that the Reb. Cavalry will be on to us tonight or in the morning. Hood is undoubtedly making a bold election evening movement.

After Genl. Stanley left matters had come to such a pass that I insisted upon Col. O'Dowd taking command of the Post and he did so. He had been in command but a short time however before an order was received to abandon the Post. And a more excited man I have seldom seem. He immediately issued orders that the enemy were within two miles of town and everybody must leave as soon as possible and in less than 40 minutes he was going it on quick time at the head of his Regiment for Decatur.

Nov. 1st 1864 - Head Qrs. 73rd Ind. Infty. Athens Ala. (Tuesday) The retreat and abandonment of this Post of the 31st was perfectly disgraceful. I have or soon shall represent the facts to Genl. Granger and ask to be relieved from under his command.

I arrived from Decatur Junction with my Regt. about noon and found the 2nd Div. 4th Corps in possession of the Fort and vicinity. I put my men in their old quarters and then waited three hours for the arrival of our valiant Col O'Dowd.

Col Walters in the absence of Genl. Whitaker is in command of the 2nd Div. I have delivered the orders left for them by Genl. Stanley to move at once for Pulaski and they will get off this P.M.

Nov. 2nd 1864 - Hd. Qrs. United States Forces Athens Ala. (Wednesday) General Wagner's Division 4th Corps came in today on the Rail Road and will proceed immediately to Pulaski.

What the movement of troops northward means I cannot imagine.

I venture the prediction that Beauregard when next heard from will be in front of Memphis Tenn. It is barely possible that he has crossed and is making for Nashville but the information I get leads me to doubt it.

Its not like Wagner at all and came near getting put under arrest for opposing his wishes to some extent. He wanted two of my wagons but I had been cut down so much already that I told him I could not spare them.

He appeared satisfied with this but soon after sent a staff officer and guard to take them, but I was determined not to let them go without a position and written order. And told the officer that I should defend them with my whole Regiment.

He concluded that he could not take them and reported to the Genl. who immediately sent his Adjt. Genl. who made the request in the General's name. I pointed to some paper and ink and told him if the General wanted the wagons he would have to get me a written order to that effect. He finally concluded to write the order and I gave two wagons.

Have issued rations to Division which exhausts the commissary.

Nov. 3 1864 - Head Qrs. U.S. Forces Athens Ala. (Thursday) Four trains arrived this AM. with 4 Batterys belonging to the 4th Corp and one Regt.

I dispatched cannons immediately to Genl. Wagner and he sent one regiment back to escort the artillery and everything belonging to the 4th Corps.

Left this AM. for Pulaski. The 174 Ohio also came in the AM. having marched from Decatur.

Four companies under Major B.G.C. Reed (formerly Capt. in the 3rd Ohio and one of my Libby Prison acquaint-tances). Am ordered to remain here and constitute part of the garrison.

The balance of the Regt. under Col Jones has marched for Elk River ford.

On the Florence road Col O'Dowd with his Regt., all but one company which was left here.

Am at that place having been sent there by Genl. Granger to get him out of the way after my protest against serving under him. My command consist of - at present the t
73rd Ind. Capt. Eaton Comdg., 338 men
174 Ohio Major R.C.G. Reed Comdg. 308 "
181 Ohio Lieut. Carpenter Comdg. 78 "
2nd Sec. Bat. "A" 1st Tenn Arty. Lt. John C Kridler 36 "
Total force with 2 rifles, 12 pdg 760 "

Have had considerable rain today and roads very muddy.

Nov. 3rd 64 - Head Qrs. United States Forces Athens Ala. (Also Thursday) Charles T. Heuitt, Lt. and AAAG., Sir,

I have the honor to submit the following report of the part taken by my regiment (73rd Ind. Infty.) in the late demonstration by the enemy against Decatur Ala. A detachment of 100 men from the Regiment under command of Capt. William Eaton arrived at Decatur at 10 o'clock P.M. on the 25th ult. and were assigned position upon the extreme right of the line.

At 2 o'clock P. M on the 27th the enemy having charged and drove in the pickets in front of the position a detail of 50 men was made from this detachment to reestablish the line. The men deployed as skirmishers under command of Lt. Wilson and moving forward upon the double quick, gallantly drove the enemy back although not without stubborn resistance.

At 2 o'clock A.M. on the 28th I arrived from Athens and took command of the Regt. At 3 o'clock the enemy charged and again our picket line was driven in. The regiment was formed at the parapet with two companies in reserve, but no further demonstration was made until the forenoon was well advanced when a small detachment of the 18th Mich. having gained the enemy's left flank gallantly charged with a yell driving the whole rebel line from the rifle pits and sweeping in something over one hundred prisoners. I was ordered to cover this detachment while it fell back and moved out on the double quick, drew the enemies attention and then having ordered the men to lie down deployed by companies. Yet were soon ordered in.

About 2 o'clock P.M. by order of Col. Doolittle I relieved the skirmishers of the 14th C. T. near the extreme left of the line, 3 guns having been in position in rear of the line.

Shortly after a charge was made upon my immediate left by the 14th C. T. and the enemy's line was driven but rallying they in turn drove the 14th back and threatened to double up my left flank at the same time an attempt was made by the enemy to charge in our immediate front and the Rebel columns advanced some distance but a few well directed volleys checked this movement and the line being established on the left.

The usual skirmish was resumed. The Regt. was relieved form this line about 5 o'clock and I was placed in command of Fort No. 1 which I retained until ordered to return to Athens at dusk on the 29th.

One hundred men from the Regt. in company with detachment from other Regts established a new line of rifle pits in advance of the fortifications under cover of night on the 28th. The next day the line advanced found the enemy weak and withdrawing. Ten prisoners were brought in by the Regt. at dusk when they were relieved and ordered to Athens.

Our loss was slight being one man killed and two wounded, a number were struck by spent balls but received no injury.

Very Respectfully, AB. Wade, Lt Col. 73rd Ind.

Nov. 4th 1864 - Hd. Qrs. United States Forces Athens Ala. (Friday) Have been ordered today to send two companies of the 174th Ohio to Col. Jones and Col. O'Dowd is ordered to return to Decatur with his Regiment (18th Ohio) a good riddance.

Everything muddy and disagreeable outdoors today.

Have developed a little domestic comedy in my military family today. Have had with me since leaving LaVergne a very excellent cook and exemplary mulatto woman whom I have never known as anybody else but "Aunt Betsey" All that I know of her history is that she formerly belonged to a wealthy family living in Culpeper County Virginia and as she was neat and clean and came well recommended I considered myself fortunate in possessing so good a cook.

She had with her an adopted daughter about 17 years old who is a fine girl, steady and industrious and her features and hair are but one remove from the pure saxon. It seems that my boy Toney who by the way is an excellent "man of all work" and who has been with me since leaving Nashville has struck up a match with the beautiful quadroon who assists "Aunt Betsey" in the kitchen department. And the "happy event" comes off tomorrow evening. The Chaplain to officiate on the occasion.

I have set apart one room at Hd. Qrs for the benefit of the occasion and in deep perplexity in regard to what shall be the present to the young bride (Dina).

Nov. 5th 1864 - Hd. Qrs United States Forces Athens Ala. (Saturday) The "interesting ceremony" before mentioned between my cook and black boy took place last evening. The hall of the large mansion occupied as Hd. Qrs. was detailed to that purpose. The Chaplain officiating.

Some firing yesterday and today in the direction of Florence but I do not apprehend an immediate attack here. Have been preparing for such an event, however, by strengthening the abatis around the fort.

The 174 Ohio Col. Jones Comdg. came up from Elk River ford today and will proceed to Decatur having been ordered there. It is rumored that Sherman has cut loose from his communications and is slashing things around in Ga. So mobile it is.

Nov. 7th 1864 - Hd. Qrs. United States Forces Athens Ala. (Monday) Genl. Granger has an insane idea that the enemy is going to march this way with his whole army and has ordered me to be ready to abandon the Post at a moment's notice. I telegraphed him that I would hold it against ten times my own number and begged to be allowed to do so. But no he says it is. Gen!. Thomas order and must be obeyed. I confess that I cannot see the strategy in it. The idea of holding a strong post until the enemy appears and then evacuating it is supremely ridiculous. However I sent off all my men, baggage on cars today and have been engaged pressing in teams this P.M. for five miles around and will save everything but some forage in case I have to go.

Nov. 8 1864 - Hd. Qrs United States Forces Athens Ala. (Tuesday) Have received official notification from 3rd auditor of the Treasury Dept. that my claim vs the U.S. as follows

For horse surrendered to enemy by order of Col. AD. Streight

Comdg. Brigade	$100.
Military Saddle Complete	30.
Military Bridle Complete	10
Total	$140.

has been placed on file. The number of the claim is 5258. The papers were returned to have a stamp affixed.

The latest news from the enemy is to the effect that Hood's whole army has crossed the Tennessee River at Florence, driven Genl. Croxton back and rapidly fortifying.

I am left here in a rather peculiar fix. With orders to return and abandon the Post as soon as the enemy advances. I don't like it at all.

Nov. 10th 1864 - Head Quarters United States Forces Athens Ala. (Thursday) The past two days have been dull indeed. Genl. Granger sent another train down yesterday and I shipped off all the sick and bal. of the baggage so that we are now in "..........time."

Enough states have been heard from to secure the election of Abraham Lincoln. I announced this tonight to the officers on dress parade. They announced it to the men who cheered lustily and indeed it is good news. The Rebels now will begin to believe that the north is terribly in earnest in regard to this war and if they court extermination they will surely get it.

One Division of Hoods army is across the Tennessee. But Croxton holds it in check. Another General has taken command at Nashville Brevet Maj. Genl. Wilson. I hope he'll do better than Rousseau who is brave in the fight but has not much administrative ability.

Nov. 11 64 - Hd. Qrs. U.S. Forces Athens Ala. (Friday) Everything is extremely dull in this vicinity. Genl. Croxton still keeps the one Division of Hoods Army which has crossed the river at bay and we are not excited by fears of an advance.

Lincolns election is insured which creates much joy in camps and will be a terrible blow to our "enemy Bros. and Sisters of the south" who have based all their hopes of late upon the election of Lincoln or rather McClellan I should say. I wrote to J. yesterday. The answer will be a turning point in my life. [this possibly is Jennie Bond, Wade's future wife, Ed.]

Played games of chess this eve with Lt. Arnold.

Visited one picket post. Surg. Wolf 181st Ohio who I appointed Post Surg. is relieved by Assistant Surgeon Force.

I have recommended Hosp. Steward Applegate for the vacant Assistant Surgeon in the 73rd.

Had a good skirmish drill with the Battalion today.

Nov. 15th 1864 - Head Qrs. U.S. Forces Athens Ala. (Tuesday) Matters in the Dist. of Nor. Ala. have again got into a fuddled state. A small body of the enemy's cavalry appeared before Decatur yesterday morning whereupon Gen. Granger although he has 5000 troops there gets scared and immediately tries to telegraph one to abandon Athens immediately but the line being down fortunately for us he has to send the order by courier who did not arrive until late yesterday p.m.

Genl. Granger also in the order frantically asks for reinforcements of 1000 men and directs one to telegraph Genls. Thomas and Rousseau at Nashville that the enemy have appeared before Decatur 500 strong. Supposed to be the advance guard of a larger force.

This would be exceedingly amusing if it were not such a serious matter to the morale of our troops and the effect upon citizens of the sign of our uncountable fear of the enemy. Genl. Granger in the same order also directs that the company at the mouth of Elk River shall march here immediately when transportation could be furnished them for Decatur. The same order to be sent to the company at Elk

River Ford.

When it is remembered that these companies are cavalry and that the time spent in putting the horses on the cars would suffice for them to make Decatur without the aid of the R. R. the foolishness of such orders becomes apparent but as I said fortunately these orders had to be sent by courier and during transition the mind of our General calmed down considerably and the wire having been repaired he telegraphed me not to abandon my post not to telegraph Thomas not to order Companies from Elk River but not having entirely recovered from his insane fears he did order 100 men to Decatur to reinforce his army of 5000 leaving me with 70 to defend this Post and two pieces of artillery.

To account for our small garrison here it must be remembered that Company B is at Triana, Company F at Limestone, Company C at Beaver Dam and a larger det. with the baggage.

Have not heard any canonading at Decatur yet and the demonstration there could not have amounted to anything. I am heartily sick of my Dist. Commander and its no use disguising the fact. He certainly hasn't the caliber to command any large body of troops and I doubt very much his ability to administer the ordinary affairs of his district with any degree of success.

Nov. 17th 1864 - Head Qrs. United States Forces Athens Ala. (Thursday) My "100" which a few days since were ordered down to Decatur returned today without having met the enemy simply because there was no enemy there as every sensible man knew at the time.

The baggage, rations, ammunition, and guards sent with it have also returned, so that I have my seven companies here.

The election news is glorious. State after state has nobly wheeled into line and emphatically endorsed "Father Abraham's" policy to crush the rebellion. Poor little Mac, the copperhead leader, can boast of but three states Kentucky,

New Jersey, and Delaware. This knocks the last hope from under the sinking cause of the Confederacy and I prophetize that next spring will witness the closing struggle.

I notice in the papers today an account of the capture of the Rebel Privateer Florida by one of our steamers, the Massachusetts I believe. If the papers have the true account of this affair I am afraid that it will lead to complications between the Brazilians and our Government.

It seems that the Florida was lying in the neutral port of Bahia when she was pounced upon by our steamer and carried off a prize with scarcely any assistance.

I have not noticed one word of condemnation for this act in the papers but it seems to one that we shall have to give up the vessel and prisoners or go to war with Brazil. Indeed I presume all nations censure the act as contrary to the law of nations.

I have succeeded in getting a few more appointments in the Regiment to fill vacancies. 1st Sergt. James Beeber is promoted to Captain Co. "D", Sergt. Winfield S. Ramsay to 1st Lieut. Company "D", Sergt. Major Rufus M. Brown to 2nd Lt. Company" F", Hosp. Stew. Charles H. Applegate to Asst. Surgeon. They are ordered to Nashville for muster.

The public or army have been able to obtain no news from Sherman since he "cut loose from civilization." I presume the first news we hear will come from southern sources.

I made out two monthly returns this p.m. simply to keep my hand concerning the Adjutants business.

My drill etc has been somewhat broken in upon lately but shall commence the regular routine tomorrow.

Nov. 18th 1864 - Head Qrs. United States Forces Athens Ala. (Friday) Have just received the following telegram

Hd Qrs. Dist. Nor. Ala.
Decatur Nov. 18th 1864
Lieut Col. Wade

Special Order No. 132

"Extract" II. Lt. Col. Wade 73rd Inda. Vol. Infantry is hereby assigned to the command of all that part of the Tennessee and Alabama and Memphis and Charleston Rail Roads now under command of Brig. Genl. Starkweather extending from Athens to Hurricane Creek by command of Brig. Genl. Granger.

Sam M. Krueland
1st Lt. 18th Mich. Infty
And AAAG

This will necessitate a trip over my new command which I shall take tomorrow if a pleasant day. Shall probably be gone several days.

Nov. 19th 1864 - Head Qrs. United States Forces Athens Ala. (Saturday) Have received a small addition to my force here in the shape of Capt. Gafney's Co. of the 10th Indiana Infantry, or rather cavalry I should say. His company is stationed here for courier duty.

Today has been gloomy enough. Nothing but rain from morning till night. I intended to make a circuit of my lines which extend from Athens to Huntsville thence south to Triana but as it is a two or three day trip the rain has decided me to postpone it indefinitely.

Glorious news may be expected from Sherman soon. He is undoubtedly moving to Augusta that is if rumors are true. It is perfectly impossible to get anything reliable just now.

Beauregard appears still to be in the vicinity of Tuscumbia Ala. What his intentions are is difficult to determine.

Nov. 21 st 1864 - Head Qrs. United States Forces Athens Ala. (Monday) Have been reading "English Traits" by Emerson, but .... by Mrs. J Hamilton Childs. Emerson is somewhat severe on English character but bestows some praise.

A telegram from General Thomas and Granger estimates an advance of the Army (Hoods) but I do not fear it much. Beauregard has undoubtedly heard from Sherman and is making back tracks to catch him as fast as he can.

The weather is not pleasant by any means.

Am daily expecting the advent of the Paymaster and shall welcome him right morally as we are four months behind.

Athens and its inhabitants are in a fever of suspense in regard to the military situation.

Nov. 23rd 1864 Limestone bridge M and C. RR Alabama. (Wednesday) Major Martin came up today on the cars and paid off the seven Cos. here They received four months pay but several settled up a two year clothing account which cut it down considerable.

I had Co. C's (who is stationed at Beaver Dam and Indian Creek) rolls with me and the Co. money was paid over to me and I sent it down by Sergt. Cole with 12 patrols. I

Escorted the Major as far as Beaver Dam and thereafter inspecting the Block House, kept up the RR with four men. Lt. Williams with the balance escorting the Paymaster to Triana.

Reached this place where Co. F is stationed about dusk and shall stay all night. Inspected Little Limestone stockade on the route and forded Big Limestone which is rather high.

Nov. 24, 64 - Head Qrs. United States Forces Decatur Junction Ala. (Thursday) Left Company F stockade early this morning and came to the junction.

Telegraphed Granger that I could not locate my command and while waiting an answer heard that Athens was ordered to be evacuated. I hastened on in hopes of reaching there before the order was carried into effect but met the

Regt. and artillery about 6 miles out under command of Lt. Hagenbuck. Made a short halt and then came on here where I have gone into camp.

Took up the garrisons of three stockades between this place and Athens. They are composed of three different detachments of the106 and 111th U.S. Colored Infty. and 174th Ohio and are now under my command. The order is to march to Huntsville and take up all garrisons on the R.R. including Triana.

Nov. 25th 1864 - Head Qrs. 73rd Ind. Infantry Huntsville Ala. (Friday) Arrived here about 10 o'clock tonight after a fatiguing march of 27 miles interspersed with many annoying halts. Left Decatur Junction with the 73rd in advance, the artillery and wagon train next, and the Colored troops in rear.

At Mooresville, distance four miles, the men were compelled to wade Little Piney creek. Soon after we took up Company F. At Beaver we made a halt of one hour and pressed in a wagon for Co "I". At Madison Station we found Co " B " from Triana with the 6 pdr drawn by oxen. Also Major Martin with his chest containing $50,000.

Night overtook us long before we reached Huntsville The Major's wagon broke down. The battery wagon stuck in the mud and we had a hard time generally. I brought the motley train safe in at last except for the battery wagon.

Nov. 26th 1864 - Head Qrs. 73rd Ind. Infantry Huntsville Ala. (Saturday) Have lain in camp today but have been re-modeling the train and preparing for a march to Stevenson.

Huntsville and the whole county is to be evacuated. The troops are leaving Decatur today. Train after train of cars came in from the east empty and go out heavily laden with troops, guns, stores, refugees and contrabands.

Amongst the latter there is much excitement and thousands are preparing to leave. Called on Genl. Granger and learnt the meaning of the move. Hood's army is in the vicinity of Pulaski. Thomas has fallen back to Columbia and of course this country can be of no use to us until Hood is driven South of the river. [Tennessee River, Ed.] It is policy to draw him as far north as possible.

Russell's Cavalry is threatening the road and I sent down 50 men to look after him.

Nov. 27th 64 - Head Qrs. United States Forces Cedar Gap Camp Ala. (Sunday) Commenced our long march of six miles about 11 o'clock this A.M. Our wagon train is a monster one about four miles long. The 73rd was detailed as rear guard and did not leave H [Huntsville, Ed.] until several hours after the head of the train got under way.

While behind this long train there is another of at least 100 wagons belonging to refugees and contrabands who could not get railroad transportation. The Negroes old and young male and female swarm the roads by thousands and impede the rear guard greatly.

Marched within half a mile of Brownsboro, distance ten miles from Huntsville when I received an order from the Genl. to take the 73rd, the Colored Troops and Capt Wheelers company of cavalry and return to this place to guard four or five trains of which were stopped by a break made by the Rebs this P.M.

Nov. 28th 1864 - Head Qrs 73rd Ind. Infantry Paint Rock Ala. (Monday) At daylight this morning I sent back to Huntsville 115 of the Colored Troops on a train to bring up some empty cars. While engaged in the business the Rebel Cavalry attacked the train. The engineer got frightened and ran it off an open switch and the troops had to abandon it and march back. They joined us here.

Shortly after daylight I broke camp at Cedar Gap and marched to Brownsboro where we found the balance of the 1st brigade (18th Mich. 102 Ohio. 13th US and Batt. A 1st Tennessee Arty.

Was assigned next to the 102nd and continued the march to this place which we reached after dark over bad roads. Had to ford Coal Creek which was 3 feet deep. The troops however crossed on the R.R. bridge. Today's march was fatiguing and the train not being up, our camp is cheerless.

Nov. 29th 1864 - Head Qrs 73rd Indiana Infantry Larkinsville Ala. (Tuesday) Was assigned the middle of the train in today's march and had a tedious time. The country is very rough and hilly and there was a halt about every five minutes. The weather however is pleasant which helps matters some.

The enemy made a slight attack on the rear today and a few of the refugees getting frightened cut loose from their teams and consequently lost them. The rush of Negroes to the front was highly amusing..

We are in such a position that we can get no news from any point. My anxiety to hear from Sherman is intense. Undoubtedly he is hewing his way to Savannah. God speed him I say.

As for Hood if he will only wait until we get to Stevenson he may attack us as hard as he pleases. My opinion is that Thomas will give him enough employment north.

Nov. 30. 64 - Camp near Bellefonte Ala. (Wednesday) March at the head of the column today and was therefore not bothered with the train but the roads were wretched and I had to detail a pioneer squad to improve them and make new ones in many places.

We struck across the country in hopes to find a better road but did not make any thing with the exception of going several miles out of our way. About 60 of the Regt. are mounted now and can do good service when called upon.

Made a long halt at Scottsboro for the train to close up. This village as well as all others we have passed through are utterly ruined and present a pitiable aspect. Truly war is cruelty and cannot be refined.

We are making the rail fences suffer tonight. Thousands of cheerful fires dotting the hillside and valleys.

Dec. 1st 1864 - Camp in the Field. (Thursday) The Regt. was rear guard again today and did not leave the camp until late in the forenoon.

Passed through Bellefonte and was delayed several hours while the train was crossing Mud Creek. The train went into camp early but we did not get in until after dark.

The Contrabands are encamped in every direction. I understand there are about 3000 besides the large number carried on the Rail Road.

At last we have heard form Sherman. He has taken Macon and .Milledgeville Ga. and no doubt is in Augusta by this time. There is a rumor that Thomas has beaten Hood and taken several thousand prisoners but it is not confirmed yet.

Paluski is evacuated by our forces and there has been some skirmishing at Columbia.

Dec. 2 1864 - Head Qrs 73rd Ind. Infantry Stevenson Ala. (Friday) At last we have reached our journeys end. The train cannot cross the creek between it and S. but the Genl. ordered the 73rd in to hold the place until the arrangement could be completed to bring the wagons in by RR. I swam my horse and crossed the Regt. on the R. R bridge.

Stevenson is a god forsaken place sure enough and the muddiest hole I ever saw when it rains. But it is of considerable military importance and therefore I suppose we shall remain here for a time.

The 58th New York a German Regiment is stationed here and the Col. Commands the Post. Have gone into camp near the excellent spring with which the place is blessed and now await our wagons which the cars are bringing in as fast as possible.

Dec. 4th 64 - Hd Qrs. United States Forces Redoubt "Harker' Stevenson Ala. (Sunday) Yesterday the balance of the Brigade came in and Genl. Granger has assumed command of the Post. Col. Lyon commands the Brigade in the absence of Col. Doolittle.

I have been assigned to the command of Redoubt Harker with my Regiment and Company "K" 1st Ohio Artillery as a garrison. The Redoubt mounts six guns and is provided with a good stockade inside, but could not stand a heavy bombardment.

The road and telegraph is cut between here and Nashville and we are isolated from the rest of the world but we have 150,000 rations here and can stand a long siege without starving provided we do not have to furnish Chattanooga and Knoxville.

Thomas is reported to have fallen back to Franklin. Hood will find himself in a tight place soon.

Dec. 5th 1864 - Stevenson Ala. (Monday) Was detailed as Brigade officer of the day today and had a tedious time in posting pickets and inspecting the lines which is about..... miles long and over very rough ground. Visited it twice during the day and made the grand rounds at 12 o'clock tonight or rather last night for it is nearly 4 o'clock now and must soon count drowsy herd or daylight will catch me not napping.

Wrote to Couz. J. today on important business.

Hood has cut the RR and is between us and Nashville. I feel like fighting for delaying this of all other letters.

Am having considerable trouble with Co. "E." They are a rough set of boys and almost entirely deficient of discipline. The easiest remedy I think will be to advise Lt. Chas. H. Arnold to resign.

Dec. 8th 1864 - Qrs. 73rd Indiana Infanty Stevenson Ala. (Thursday) Yesterday and today has been very cold The men, having nothing but shelter tents and some of them being destitute of overcoats, have suffered somewhat. ·As for myself I managed to procure a stove for my tent but stove pipe is something unknown in Stevenson and consequently I had to cut a hole in my tent and set one half of the stove inside and the other out. This is an excellent plan to make a stove smoke and consequently I've been moderately miserable for the last 48 hours.

The details are excessive. Keeping the men on duty nearly all the time and allowing no opportunity to build quarters. Have organized a "fatigue squad" from the stragglers on our late march in. I think it will have a good effect.

No news from Hood today or Sherman either.

Dec. 9th 1864 - Head Qrs. 73rd Indiana Infty Stevenson Ala. (Friday) A dull dreary day today. Cold, raining and muddy, and to crown all the mismanagement in this Brigade is insufferable. No one knows from the orders received what is expected of him and everybody is expected to [do] everything just or rather just according to the ideas of the General Comdj without orders.

No news from the north yet and none expected for several days. I would give almost anything if I was with Sherman on his grand campaign through rebeldom. Should not wonder if Hood was attempting to intimidate him by striking north of Nashville. He will go far enough north to satisfy himself this time. Perhaps we are staying here because no orders can reach us. At all events I hope we will move soon.

Dec. 10th 1864 Head Qrs. 73rd Ind. Infantry Stevenson Ala. (Saturday) Nothing of interest in the military line to chronicle today. Have just finished reading "Russian Shores of the Black Seas" by Oliphant a book lent me by Mrs.Childs at Athens and which the adjutant packed up with my things when the Regt. left. It is rather dull I think and would hardly be readable except under the circumstances in which I am now situated.

Am also reading another work lent me by the .... "Poets and Poetry of the Bible" by Gilfillan which promises to be of some interest.

Today have been engaged in changing the guns in the Redoubt - substituting rifled pieces for smooth bores - and also in pushing the work of erecting an abatis around it.

The rain has ceased and the ground is drying slowly.

Dec. 10th 1864 – Stevenson. (Later Saturday) Having nothing better to do tonight, have made a rough sketch of our position.

It seems that the General expects an attack and if one is made on our position in Redoubt Harker it will be anything but pleasant. No attempt has been made to fortify the position in our fort and the enemy can take possession of it and shell us to death as the fort affords but little protection to the men. It is decidedly a poor place to defend I think.

Dec. 11th 1864 - Head Qrs. 73rd Ind. inf. Stevenson Ala. (Sunday) Clear but cold and windy. The Genl. has foolishly prohibited the men from building winter quarters and consequently there is much suffering. Even if we were to occupy them but for a week the men would gladly build them.

The General rode up today to examine my abatis. He told me that the last news from Hood was that he was fortifying in front of Nashville. If he stays there very long he will reduce us soon to short rations and we shall have to get out of this by way of .... valley.

Have taken a horse and mare from the Govt. appraised at $125. Granger has been making a general impressment of southern citizens, refugees and negroes, to work on fortifications, a policy which I heartily approve.

December 12 1864 - Stevenson Ala. (Monday) Today old Sol showed his cherry face and gladdened our shivering hearts much. A rumor in camp that Sherman has taken Savannah which I hope will prove true. Everything indefinite concerning Hood's movements as yet but we shall soon know all about it.

I still prosecute the work of encircling my Redoubt with

an abatis and shall have it completed tomorrow.

The men are busy putting up more comfortable quarters than shelter tents and I am having the police squad of men who have been absent without leave put me up a fire place which will be more comfortable than my stove without a chimney.

Dec. 13th 1864 Stevenson Ala. (Tuesday) Weather pleasant. Today I have completed a capacious and cozy looking fireplace to my tent and am now quite reconciled to Stevenson.

The 61st Illinois came down from Murfreesboro today on a train. They left that point at 3 p.m. yesterday and had worked their way down by repairing breaks. Although M is but 15 miles from Nashville yet they have been cut off from that place and have not heard a word of news for 14 days.

Occasional fighting was going and one battle had taken place near Franklin in which rumor places the loss of the Rebs at 2200 including seven Generals.

There is a rumor also that 4000 of the enemy have succeeded in crossing the Cumberland. There appears no likely hood of an attack here very soon.

Dec. 15th 1864 Head Qrs. 73rd Indiana Infantry Stevenson Ala. (Thursday) Yesterday was quiet and monotonous. Today bids fair to be the same.

By direction of the General I sent Lieut. Williams and thirty men on special train to Paint Rock to guard that point.

Weather fair although the mud from the last sprinkle has not dried up yet.

7 o'clock p.m. Took a ride with Adjt. Hagenbuck today around the city and its environs. I have grown quite reconciled with Stevenson and could even see during our ride some of the grand beauties which cling to its mountain sides.

Our fighting chaplain has been up to the lookout three successive times after turkeys but as yet has signally failed to procure one. The Chaplain has been added to our mess lately. He is a genius for a chaplain.

Dec. 17th 1864 - Head Qrs. 73rd Indiana Infantry Stevenson Ala. (Saturday) Raining and disagreeable. The inspection was postponed on account of the weather. Our dainty inspector could not "turn out" for fear of soiling his boots.

Some of the Company "C" boys got access to liquor today and got extremely jolly. Private Lario got into a fight and I had him bucked and gagged which is an effective method of treating a drunken man.

I've thought it rather strange the "boys" should never get angry with me when I [am] compelled to punish them in this or some other way but attribute it to the fact that always after punishment I call them up and give them a short lecture upon the evil of their ways and I do not believe that there is one out of the 560 which the Regt. now numbers but what would do anything to serve me.

Dec. 18th 1864 - Head Qrs. 73rd Indiana Infantry Stevenson Ala. (Sunday) I feel like shouting "Glory Hallelujah" Genl. Sherman - I would say Thomas - has captured thou. [thousands, Ed.] Divisions of Hood's Army and that doughty General is falling back with the remnant of his army.

That is all the news that we have up to date but the construction trains are at work on both ends of the road and I presume we shall have communications soon.

For twenty days I haven't seen a newspaper. It seems awful and is extremely aggravating at this particular time. After such momentous events are occurring.

Stevens Brigade inspector inspected the Regt. or rather what there was of it in camp today. The details are excessive and we cannot finish them but will have to keep the men on every day.

Dec. 19th 1864 Head Qrs 1st Brigade 4th Div. 20th Ala. Caperton's Landing Ala. (Monday) Col. Wm. P. Lyon with his Regiment was detached and ordered to Huntsville today by RR The General then ordered me to take command of the Brigade. The staff consisting of Lt. Charles Hewilt 18th Mich Asst. Adjt Genl., Lt. Wilkins Aide de Camp, and Capt. Stevens Inspector reported to me and I am fairly installed in my new command.

This afternoon was ordered to move the Brigade to this place with five days rations 100 rounds of ammunition per man and as much baggage as could be loaded on five wagons to each Regiment.

At three o'clock p.m. I broke camp and commenced moving out in the following order 73rd Ind. Capt. Beeber Comdg. in advance, Capt. Black Battery "A" 1st Tenn Arty next, then the 102nd Ohio Cpt. Scott Comdg., and the 18th Mich Major Comdj. in rear with the trains in rear of each Regiment and Battery.

Although our destination was only four miles yet the roads were in such a horrible state that the rear of the column did not get here until after dark.

Genl. Granger started here for Bridgeport before we left and was to have come down with steamboats enough to take the Brigade,.but he has not yet made his appearance and I have ordered the Regts. to bivouac for the night in the following order 18th Mich on the right, 73rd Ind. right center, Battery "A" left center & 102nd Ohio on the left, wagon trains in rear.

The ground is very wet and the troops will be uncomfortable tonight. Each Regt. pickets its own front. I do not anticipate that there is any force in the vicinity but have selected the best position to sustain an attack.

The Tennessee River very narrow at this point and if there should be any force on the other side they could bother us a good deal with artillery & even muskets.

Dec. 20th 1864 Head Qrs 1st Brig. 4th Div. 20 A Corps. Steamer Chattanooga. (Tuesday) Reville at daybreak and soon after I ordered the Battery and wagons to be hitched up in readiness for the boats. I set one company from each Regt.

to work leveling a fortification which had been thrown up across the road and which prevented teams from reaching the river.

Five steamers hove in sight from above about 3 p.m. and as soon as the gunboat Stone River landed I went aboard and reported to the General.

After considerable delay the 18th Mich. was put aboard the Stone River. The 73rd on the Chattanooga and the 102nd on the Gunboats and the Chattanooga.

I have established Hd. Qrs. on the latter boat and the fleet is about to start down the river. It was impossible to load the Battery or any of the wagons and they will have to be left behind until more boats come up.

A Regiment of colored troops were disembarked to guard them.

Dec. 21th 1864 - Head Qrs. 1st Brig. 4th Div. 20th AC. Steamer Chattanooga Whiting Ala. (Wednesday) A dreary uncomfortable night truly. The weather has turned quite cool which with a drizzly rain at times makes it exceedingly uncomfortable for the men four hundred of whom are stowed on this boat and such a boat!!!

It was the first boat built at Chattanooga by the soldiers during Rosecrans campaign and is the greatest curiosity. The cabin accommodations are miserable. Capt. Samuels however does everything he can for me and we discuss war and his Indian experience over cold turkey. He is formerly of the 1st Wisconsin.

The fleet travelled downstream until late last night and then tied up near Bellefonte until 4 o'clock this a.m. when they put on steam and felt their way cautiously down to this point where they landed at dusk during a slight snowstorm. Shall probably remain till morning.

Col. Gregory 29th Ind. called over to see me.

Dec. 22, 64 - Head Qrs. 1st Brig. 4th Div. 20th AC. Steamer Chattanooga off Limestone Pt. Ala. (Thursday)
Last night I received a written order from the Dist. Adjt. Genl. desiring my presence on board the Stone River Gunboat as soon as we reached this point to confer with the General and Adjt. Hagenbuck and myself.

Turned in on the cabin floor and slept comfortably till daylight. We lay under the lee of a high bank and the men slept warmer than usual. I kept one company out as a picket and allowed as many to go to shore as wished to for the purpose of building fires.

At daylight the Gunboats weighed anchor and the transports swung off from shore and started down the river. Came in sight of Limestone Pt. a little after noon and landed above Indian Creek (I was stationed at this point last summer and built a strong stockade here and interspersed my military duties with the agreeable pastime of making love to fair Becky Griffith.) but now everything has changed. Her mother is dead and the family having removed from the house it is occupied by a stranger.

As soon as we landed I had a long interview with the General. He detailed to me his plan of attack as follows, the troops were to land two miles above Decatur and make a night assault. The 18th Mich. to storm the works, next the river bank and capture the redoubt in the center of the fortifications. The 102 Ohio followed by the 29th Ind. are to enter at the southeast sally port and capture fort No 2. The 73rd Ind. and other troops were to act as reserve or as circumstances should direct. But he had received information of a larger force at Decatur than anticipated and his decision in regard to attack was deferred until fresh information could be had.

The men from the transports were allowed during the afternoon to go on shore, make coffee and rest themselves.

About dusk Genl. Morgan called a council of war of his Brigade and Regimental commanders to decide upon the expediency of making the attack tonight. The following officers composed the council,

Col. Given 102 Ohio - indisposed & no command - came late & no of troops not given.
Lt. Col A B. Wade Comdg 1st Brigade 4th Div. 20th A,C.
Major H. ......18th Mich Infty, 300
Captain Scott, 102nd Ohio Infty, 300
Lt. Col. Gregory, 29th Ind Infty, 425
73rd Ind Infty, 250
And Col Beach Chief of Artillery
Total Force 1275

The General stated to the council the following facts. The enemy has nine pieces of artillery at Decatur and his force was reported at 2000 men. He however only estimates it at 1500. He was extremely anxious to make the attack but if it failed it would be the annihilation of the Brigade and he wanted an expression of opinion before proceeding further.

Nearly all of us knew the works and their strength intimately and were competent to decide, with the fact before us at least 1500 men garrison, whether they could be carried by assault.

A long conference ensued. My mind was already made up and it proved to be the unanimous opinion of all present that in view of rapid approach of Genl. Steadman with 9000 men and no important military necessity for taking the place at once that it was inexpedient to attack tonight. This settled the matter and the transports were at once ordered to Whitesburg while the gunboats ran down to canon the enemy with a few shells.

Dec. 23rd 1864 - Head Qrs. 1st Brig. 4th Div. 20th A.C. Whitesburg, Ala. (IFriday) Arrived here during the night and this morning landed the Brigade and baggage and have gone into camp.

The fleet now here consists of five gunboats and the transports Chattanooga, Bridgeport, Kenesaw, Kingston, Missionary Ridge and Lookout. The Chickamauga was disabled and turned back.

The General left for Huntsville with an escort and placed me in command of everything here. I inspected the picket line and the ground in vicinity of camp and rested quietly until dark.

The weather is very pleasant and a general feeling of relief is experienced by the officers when the decision not to attack Decatur became known. Everybody considered it madness. The men, who of course knew something of what was in the wind, experienced the greatest reluctance in attacking works which they had held against Hood's whole army only a month or two before.

Beach's Battery came up today on a transport and the Colonel's troops were sent back. The 29th Ind. Col. Gregory Cmdj. is temporarily attached to the Brigade. Lt. Col. G is a fine officer. At seven o'clock Div.. Adjt. Genl. Kuerland came,riding back post haste with an order from the General for me to move the Brigade to Huntsville immediately as Forrest was in the vicinity and would probably attack before morning.

I gave the Regiments an hour to get ready and then moved out in the following order: 18th Mich. in advance, 73rd Ind. next, 29th Ind. next and 102nd in rear. The distance was only ten miles and on a good pike but the men carried their knapsacks and being in marching time did not reach Huntsville until 1 o'clock the next morning. Left 50 men with the boats which were ordered to anchor in mid stream.

Dec. 24th 1864 - Head Qrs. 1st Brig. 4th Div. 20th A.C. Huntsville Ala. (Saturday, Christmas Eve) Settled down into camp about one o'clock this morning. Made temporary Brigade Hd. Qrs. with the Lt. in Comdj. of Fort.

This a.m. called on General Granger and Col. Lyon Post Commander and had a long conference at noon [and] dined with them. It seems that Forrest is not in the vicinity and that there is no danger whatever. Train after train is arriving bringing Genl. Steadman's command of 9000 men.

About one p.m. the Brigade was ordered to return to

Whitesburg but my Regt. was selected to remain with it which suits me exactly. Shall go on Post duty here and probably remain for some time. Sent one team with a cavalry escort to bring up what baggage was absolutely necessary.

Have selected an excellent camping ground.

Dec.. 25th 1864 - Head Qrs 73rd Ind. Infantry Huntsville Ala. (Sunday, Christmas day) Have procured three rooms in the mansion of Mr. White near camp for my Hd. Qrs. which are very comfortable.

The men are tearing down a large number of unoccupied houses in town and are building up comfortable quarters.

Genl. Thomas' victory over Hood was signed and completed . A few details have reached us. Steadman's troops were in the fight and are now pushing as fast as possible to head off Hood's army or what is left of it.

The first Brigade, under command of Granger I presume, has gone down the river and undoubtedly taken possession of Decatur without a fight.

Weather today rather chilly and unpleasant.

We are now waiting patiently for our months accumulation of mail.

One company is detailed as Provost Guard and one at the Depot.

Dec. 27th 1864 - Head Qrs. 73rd Ind. Infantry Huntsville Ala. (Tuesday) Yesterday although a damp disagreeable day the men proceeded with the work of building quarters and in a short time we will have a splendid camp.

My rooms are very comfortable and the soft feather bed which Mr. White's consideration has furnished me with is a luxury truly.

Spent the evening last night with Col. Lyon and a few officers in cards, wine and conversation. Today is pleasant.

The Chaplain came up and reports Qr. Mr. Hubbard and the transportation at Whitesburg. The boats having brought him up that far.

Wrote mother this p.m. Am at a loss for something to read and look anxiously for the mail. For want of something better am pouring over the History of Alabama by Pickett, an ordinary work with a southern touch of egotism and "blood."

Dec. 29th 1864 - Head Qrs. 73rd Indiana Infty Huntsville Ala. (Thursday) I get quite discouraged at times with the many impediments thrown in the way of improving the Regt. in drill discipline etc. The detail is down so that we have no more than 100 or 150 men in camp at one time.

Have sent Companies E and I to guard Indian Creek and Beaver Dam and a detachment of 40 men to Limestone and Piney Creeks. Company "C" came in from Stevenson last night.

The men have nearly finished their quarters which are very comfortable. Weather is pleasant. The R.R. is not repaired yet and have received but one mail since our arrival here.

Sent forage train out today and gathered a large quantity of corn. Had Battalion drill this p.m. Its only a vexation to have it with so few men. Haven't heard from Hood lately.

Dec. 31st Brownsboro, Ala. (Saturday) I arranged yesterday for a thorough and searching inspection of the Regt. at the regular muster today but like almost all my plans for the benefit of the Regt. it was broken in upon by an order for me to proceed to Decatur and take command of that important post and also the 1st Brigade.

I had an interview with Genl. Granger for instructions when it was decided also to send the Regt. down at 3 o'clock this p.m. when the order was countermanded and I was ordered to take 150 men and proceed to this point. Keep 100 of them here and send 50 to Hurricane Creek Bridge as reinforcements for these points.

It seems that two companies of the 13th Wis. and some cavalry numbering 118 men were surprised this morning and nearly all of them captured together with one piece of artillery.

The Bridge was burnt which will interrupt our communications very much. From all accounts it is a very disgraceful affair.

We came in here at dusk and Capt. Cobb 13th Wis. who is in command of the garrison here very kindly stowed the men away in his company quarters and took all the officers to his own quarters.

Later (Saturday)

Train just in from Huntsville with orders to send the hundred men I have here to Paint Rock immediately but for myself to remain at this Post which is rather strange. Have called in the pickets and the men will get off in half an hour. Brownsboro is a scattering village of three or four houses about a mile apart but the country is beautiful.

Journal

Date	Hour	Weather	Distance	Route
1864	4.30 P.M.		20½	TRIANA
			5	
	2.30 P.M.	Hot		
			2½	
	12½ P.M.	Very Hot		
	11 A.M.		4	
		Very Warm		
	9½ A.M.			
	9 A.M.			SOMERVILLE
Jul 29th			9	

TRIANA
STOCKADE
WATKINS FERRY
COTACO CR.
LITCOTIA
WM. McCARLEYS
FLETCHERS FERRY
STOCKADE
TENN RIVER
D.E.S.E.
DECATUR ROAD
CAMP
SPRING
MRS. BLACKWELLS
KENT FERRY ROAD
SOMERVILLE

P.M. Results several & no lose

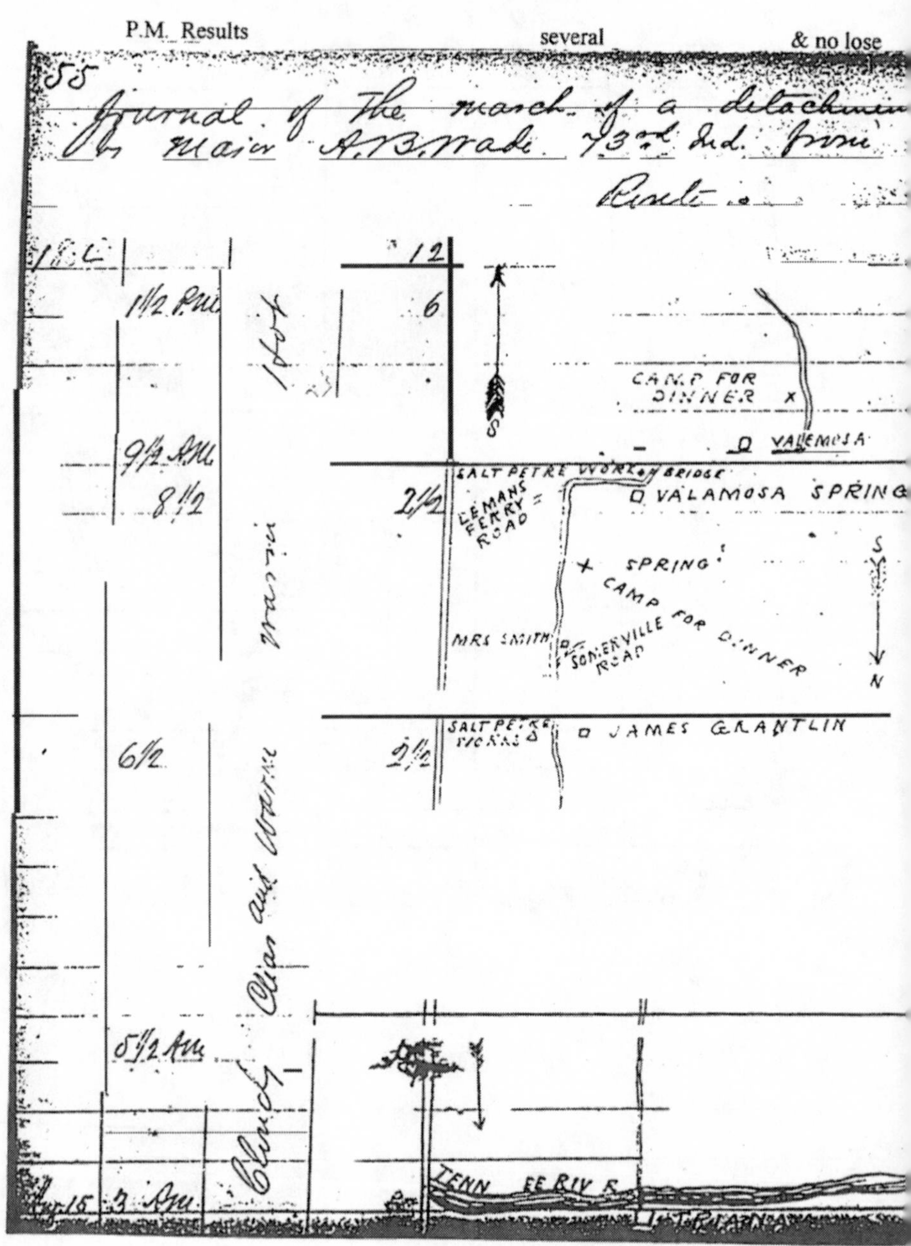

38

Journal of a march of detachments from numbering 47 men from Triana Ala. to

Date	Hour	Weather	Distance	Route
1864	8½ A.M.		9	SO ERVILLE
			4	ATKINS HOUSE
				MRS. MCERLAND
		Warm		
				E. ALLEN S.S.W
				ROAD TO DECATUR
	7 A.M.		½	WM MCCARLEYS
		Cloudy and pleasant		BLUFS SSW LIT. COTACO ROAD COTACO CREEK
				REVERSED
	5½ A.M.			
	3½ A.M.		1½	WATKINS FERRY XSTONE ROAD SPRINGS WATKINS HOUSE ROUTE N
		Cool and		
Feb. 29th	3 A.M.	foggy		TRIANA

Chapter Nine

January 1st, 1865 – September 5th, 1865 (End of War, Home Again at Last)

Jan. 1st 1865 - Head Qrs. 73rd Ind Infantry Huntsville Ala. (Sunday) It seems rather strange to write those figures "1865" but shall soon get used to it.

Came up from Brownsboro along this a.m. and called to see the General. I told him that although much gratified at the important command which he tendered me yet I felt that it was my duty to remain with the Regt. for the present at least. It is scattered around in so many different squads that I am fearful unless someone stays at the head to oversee matters that they will go on from bad to worse. The books and records as well as the and baggage is scattered from Nashville to Decatur.

By the way I've forgotten to mention that Decatur was retaken without a fight. The Rebs evacuated it upon the advance of Steadman's 9000 men.

Weather like Indian summer here.

Jan. 3rd 1864 - Head Qrs. 73rd Indiana Infantry Huntsville Ala. (Tuesday) Another mail came in today and my daily papers have full details of the late glorious campaigns under Sherman and Thomas.

I render the prediction that August 1865 will smile upon a peaceful united "United States." The moral effect of Sherman's march through the "Corn-fed-eracy" will be great especially on foreign countries.

The President has called for three hundred thousand more troops which will have an exhilarating effect on loyal people and a correspondingly depressing effect on the Chivalry.

Hood appears to be pretty well used up and he will trouble u but little this winter. Sherman is rushing his army and will soon be heard from in South Carolina (thank God for that) while Grant is quietly watching his opportunity and will strike before long.

.... is attacked by a naval force.

Jan. 6th 1865 - Head Qrs. 73rd Indiana Infantry Huntsville Ala. (Friday) The 4th Corp. commanded by Genl. Wood came in yesterday. I went out to the 3rd Division Camp to see Col. Streight and Capt. Scorce. Lt. Col. Lasselle of the 9th Indiana passed the night with me.

It is not yet settled what duty the 73rd will be put in and I am in anxious suspense.

The joyful news that Capts. Mull, Westlake and Ricbley and Lt. Callahan have been exchanged and that Lts. Thomas and Brown had escaped has just reached the Regt. They will all get a thirty days leave of absence and then return to the Regiment where they will be warmly welcomed after nearly two years imprisonment.

Weather is delightful for this season of the year and if the Regt. was only settled I could enjoy myself.

Thomas will probably halt and reorganize his army for the spring campaign.

Jan. 7th 1865 Head Qrs. 73rd Ind. Inf. Huntsville Ala. (Tuesday) Have just finished reading one of the Waverly novels, The Well of St. Ronaus, which my worthy host lent me to beguile the tedious hours. I consider it a .... affair.

Col. Lasselle called today. There are rumors in camp that our Brigade is ordered east to join Sherman but have received no official notice yet.

Time passes heavily. Co H and I [are] the only companies here.

January 8th 1865 - Huntsville Sunday. A dull day. The baggage from Nashville came up and I also received a box from Major Myers and his estimable lady full of canned fruit etc., together [with] an assorted lot of liquors which I knew the Dr. is capable of selecting. Can entertain my friends now when they call with something more than corn pone and fresh pork of which I am getting heartily tired.

.

January 13th 1865 - Head Qrs. Post Larkinsville Ala. (Friday) Yesterday received orders to move on the railroad east. The 18th Mich. came up from Decatur last night to take our place. Moved down to the Depot at 8 am. and by noon had loaded on the horses, mules and wagons together with Regt.baggage on train and started.

I left the several companies as follows:

Company "G" at Hurricane Creek, Companies H and E at Gurley's Tank, Companies D and A at Paint Rock and Companies B, C, F, I and K at Larkinsville, Ala.

Larkinsville is a pretty place and if they will only let us stay here I shall be well satisfied.

.... Brigade which has been here to intercept the Rebels leaves tonight.

All of Head Qrs. horses stampeded us soon as we unloaded and am afraid the bushwhackers have got them.

January 15th, 1865 - Head Qrs. Post Larkinsville Ala. (Sunday) Am well pleased with Larkinsville but have to keep up a strong picket as guerrilla bands ranging from 50 to 500 are in the vicinity. Reports from loyal citizens are continually coming in in relation to them.

My command here consists of the following: 5 companies

73rd Indiana Infty	192
Co M 11th Ind. Cavalry Capt. Givens	82
Co. E 110th U.S. Col. Infy. Lt. Smart	19
Co of Home Guards Capt. Flowers	25
Total	318

I am also promised a section of the 1st Tenn Artillery Battery "A." I have one smooth bore 12 pdr. [cannon] manned by my own men and which will do execution when the time comes. I am building a log house as out defense to be garrisoned by Company K which will strengthen me somewhat.

January 16th 1865 Head Qrs. Larkinsville Ala. (Monday) Matters are progressing quietly at our new Post. The excitement occasioned by the capture of Savannah and the defeat of Hood's army has subsided and the people are awaiting further developments.

A great and irrepressible desire for peace is spreading over the whole south and will sooner or later engulf the secession leaders in utter ruin.

Some of my men made a heavy forage from Mrs. Brown today. I returned 11 hogs which they had killed and am investigating the matter.

A train is off the track at Scottsboro and no mail came in today.

Have appointed Lt. R. M. Brown Provost Marshal and Lt. Winfield Ramsey Commissary.

The boys have erected good winter quarters and are very comfortable.

One of the 11th Cav. shot himself bad tonight.

January 18th 1865 Head Qrs. Post Larkinsville Ala. (Wednesday) Sent Lt. Swartz Co. E of the 100th U.S. Col. Infty to Scottsboro today to report to Capt. Henry for duty in the "Brown" affair.

Yesterday I became acquainted with Maggie Brown an enchanting little rebel [and] also Miss Atkinson.

Weather pleasant and military affairs extremely dull although I can hear of various squads of Rebs 5 and 10 miles off. Four deserters from Genl. Lyons command came in today.

Jan. 19th 1865 Larkinsville Ala. (Thursday) Eleven more deserters came in today and gave themselves up. They belonged to Co. A and B ..... Kentucky Battalion. They brought their horses in with them and I shall use them to mount my men.

Fort Fisher is taken by Gen. Terry. This will kill Butler as a military man as it shows that it could have been taken before just as well as not.

Jan. 20th 1865 Head Qrs. Post Larkinsville Ala. (Friday) Col. Lyon came down on special train today and paid me a visit in company with the Asst. Inspector of Block Houses. I had a sharp discussion with the latter in relation to the best means of defending Larkinsville which ended in obtaining permission to build a Block House according to my own ideas.

Company K will go down to Woodville Station tomorrow and fortify the depot at that point.

The weather here is very mild and pleasant and resembles somewhat our Indian summer at the north.

Have commenced mounting a few of my men

for scouting purposes.

A regular flood of citizens still sets in from morning till night.

Shall have to cut down my picket force to agree with the garrison.

Received a letter last night from the dear friend J.B.

Jan. 23rd 1865 Head Qrs. Post Larkinsville Ala. (Monday) Have been principally occupied for the past two days in answering the enquiries of the War Dept. in relation to my late musters of officers. My pay has been stopped in consequence. I forwarded a report today however which I think will explain the matter.

Weather cold and muddy.

Jan. 24th 1865 - Larkinsville Ala. (Tuesday) Weather cold and ground frozen hard.

Everything is so very quiet just now that I begin to think we shall wake up some of these mornings with the enemy close at hand and have therefore ordered morning patrols.

Capt. Givens of the 11th Ind Cav. is somewhat out of humor with some of my details and threatens wondrous things.

Some of my officers have Govt. horses which I must issue an order against as it is contrary to regulations.

January 27th 1865 - Head Qrs. Post Larkinsville Ala. (Friday) Weather quite cold and ice has frozen strong enough to bear a man.

Established a post Counsel of Administration today and instructed them to fix a schedule of prices at which the citizens must sell their produce at this point. Produce comes in quite frequently and we have plenty of butter eggs poultry etc..

Became acquainted with Mrs. Smith a very lady like woman who lives near town.

Appointed 2nd Lt. John Lebanon Post Commissary. Whereat Capt. Givens Comdj. Company M of the 11th Cavalry, and amazingly the discharge of Beeber and Brown as enlisted men having been revoked, I have appointed 1st Lt. Winfield S. Ramsey Provost Marshall of the Post.

Have orders to send one commissioned officer and 25 men to Nashville to build Block Houses. Have taken them from each Company and placed Lt. Arnold in command.

Jan. 28 1865 Head Qrs. post Larkinsville Ala. (Saturday) All the talk in the daily papers is now peace! peace! I think it does harm to our cause attempting in any way to negotiate with the enemy. We will have peace when we whip them, not before.

Sent Col. Streight some hasty memoranda of prominent events connected with the history of the Regiment for a sketch in the Indiana Roll of Honor.

Have been placed by Genl. Granger in command of the RR defenses as far as Stevenson. Must make the trip on the road and find how many garrisons I command.

Capt. Givens Company M of the 11th Cavalry are ordered to join their Regiment and will get off tomorrow I suppose. The home guards were also disbanded, so that I have no forces here except 4 companies of very own men.

January 301865 Head Qrs M and C RR Defences Larkinsville Ala. (Monday) Am blessed with the responsibility of these three different Hd Qrs. the RR Defences, the Post, and the Regiment.

Lt. Thomas who has been a prisoner for 19 months came up today. He will take command of Company "C."

Lt. Slick has been detailed as Assistant Commissary of Subsistence.

Weather cool.

Feb. 2nd 1865 Larkinsville Ala. (Thursday) Delightful weather as one could wish. The atmosphere is as soft and balmy as May.

Lt. Brown Co. "E" came up and has gone to his Company at Woodville.

The guerrillas are evidently stirring up some development and perhaps they will show their hand soon.

The great talk in the papers now is peace! peace! I sincerely hope that it will come soon but place little faith in negotiations.

Feb. 5th 1865 Head Qrs. Post Larkinsville Ala. (Sunday) Everything is very quiet in this vicinity. I hear of 60 guerrillas 9 miles from here but have not got enough mounted force to pursue them.

Stevens [Stephens] Hunter and Campell Peace Commissions have arrived at Fortress Monroe from Richmond but cannot think that they will accomplish anything.

Mother was kind enough to send me a box of good things from home.

There is much hope now of the exchange of the 73rd officers as Gov. Morton is currently at work trying to effect it and has sent Col. Coburn to Washington for that purpose.

Have received a six pdr. gun [cannon] and cassion from Battery D, First Missouri and am prepared for the Rebs should they give us a call.

Weather pleasant.

Feb. 7th 1865 Head Qrs. Post Larkinsville Ala. (Tuesday) Last night at 9 o'clock the Rebs made an attack upon 15 home guards who were quartered just outside of the pickets. The enemy numbered about 50 men well motivated. They killed two and wounded four of the home guards. I immediately sent out an ambulance and guard to bring the wounded in but for want of mounted men could not pursue them.

The Rebs in the meantime skirted around my picket lines and appeared upon the other side of town where they fired into a train which had stopped to wood up. The engineer put on steam and escaped them.

I thought this was getting rather bold and as soon as the second firing commenced had the long roll sounded and the troops fall in. I then sent five mounted men up to reconnoiter who found the enemy gone.

Today I thought that measures ought to be taken to put a stop to their fun and issued an order to press into service enemy horses in the country which was fit for cavalry service, thereby serving two ends - punishing the citizens who are responsible for these guerrilla outrages and mounting my men. Eight smooth faced oily tongued quasi union citizens rode into town today but footed it home much to their chagrin.

I think the plan works admirably and only fear that Genl. Granger may rescind my order. The four home guards who were severely wounded I sent to Huntsville today.

Abram Finney Company C shot himself yesterday by accident on picket and died in a few moments.

Weather rather cool and muddy.

Feb. 8th 1865 Head Qrs. Post Larkinsville Ala. (Wednesday) The good work of picking up all the horses in the country still progresses.

Miss Maggie Brown an enchanting little rebel came in today and begged hard for her pony but I couldn't listen to the siren and she departed in a pout.

A circumstance occurred in connection with the guerrilla attack night before last which smacks a little of the romantic. One of the men, Dave Washburn I believe was his name, [Pvt.David Washburn, Co. F, 73rd Indiana, from Plymouth, mustered out July 1st, 1865. Ed] was courting a young lady who lives one mile out of the picket line when suddenly Rebs surrounded the house and demanded of her how many men were there. Our heroine denied the presence of her lover and while they were hitching their horses ran back and forced him into a large chest which she locked and kept the key.

The Rebels for a wonder neglected to search this chest and Dave came forth afterwards stretching like a ....

Feb. 12th 1865 Head Qrs. Post Larkinsville Ala. (Sunday) Yesterday and today have been very pleasant. We unfurled the stars and stripes yesterday afternoon from our new flag staff and tis quite a feature at "our post."

Peace negotiations have failed and the new campaigns are being commenced. Grant has gained five miles of ground on his left flank and Sherman has stopped the R.R. between Augusta and Branchville. He will be at one of the two places in person in a short time.

Our army under Thomas is laying quietly at

Huntsville and Eastpoint but will probably move soon although it has been weakened a good deal [with] the 23rd Corps having gone east and other troops west.

Guerrillas still independent in this vicinity but I shall soon have a good squad of mounted men.

Feb. 13th 1865 Head Qrs. Post Larkinsville Ala. (Monday) The guerrillas 150 strong camped within five miles of us last night. They captured a man by the name of Dowdy who had been discharged from our army and murdered him in cold blood.

I have ordered two dwelling houses (burned?) in retaliation for this brutal murder. I expect them to attack us tonight or in the morning and am prepared for them.

Feb. 15th 1865 - Larkinsville Ala. (Wednesday) The home guards had a skirmish with the enemy five miles from here this morning losing one man killed and wounding one of the enemy.

I have got 1st. Sergt. Merrill of Company K up here and am building a good stockade.

There is a perfect reign of terror now through the country on account of guerrillas. The Union citizens are preparing to fly the country.

Feb. 17th 1865 Hd Qrs. Post Larkinsville Ala. (Friday) Our boys of Co. H and the Pioneer Camps at Gurley's tank gave the Rebs a taste of their mettle yesterday. 20 them were out guarding a forage train when they were attacked by about fifty of the 4th Ala. Cav. The boys fought them for half an hour, killed one, wounded one badly (taking him prisoner), and brought their wagons off in triumph.

It was supposed that more of the enemy were wounded but it could not be definitely understood. We did not lose a man. In the confusing incident in the first charge of the enemy two of our boys were captured but while the fighting was going on they escaped and came in without their guns.

The Rebs raided Woodville where Co. E is stationed day before yesterday and cut off a wagon which was not guarded.

I have issued an order to the citizens here and shall burn them out unless the guerrillas are stopped.

Feb. 22nd 1865 - Head Qrs. post Larkinsville Ala. (Wednesday) We just finished a salute of thirteen guns in honor of the flag raised over Fort Sumpter yesterday.

A dispatch from the Secretary of War which I received half an hour since contains the glorious news that Charleston is in our possession and ordered a salute from all posts in honor of the event.

Some excellent target practice was made.

Feb. 24th 1865 Head Qrs. Post Larkinsville Ala. (Friday) Yesterday I received telegraphic orders from Huntsville to send down a resolute officer and a detachment of soldiers to quell a meeting amongst the negro troops at Boyd's Station.

I sent down Capt. Eaton with fifteen mounted men who reports today that no trouble was apprehended.

It seems that Lt. Gibbs of the 13th Wis. who was in command of them got frightened and basically surrendered his authority deserting his troops at a time when there was some dissatisfaction amongst them in regard to the small amount of ammunition on hand. He desires to be dismissed [from] the service.

Weather for the last two days rainy and very muddy.

Trains will commence running on M & C R.R today on account of track in the Decatur road.

March 1 1865 - Larkinsville Ala. (Wednesday) Appointed Albert H. Kersey Co. I Corporal for brave and gallant conduct at Athens Ala. Oct 2 1864.

The several companies of the Regt. are now located on the railroad as follows

Co. A, Geo. S. Clark, Paint Rock Bridge
Co. B, Lt. J. H. Kiersted, Larkinsville Ala.
Co. C, Lt. Alex N. Thomas, Larkinsville Ala.
Co.D, Sergt.James Beeber, Paint Rock Bridge
Co. E, Lt. L. Brown, Woodville Tank
Co. F, Lt. Otto H. Sollan, Larkinsville, Ala.
Co. G, Lt. Alex Wilson, Hurricane Creek
Co. H, Lt. Wilson Dailey, Gurley's Tank
Co. I, Capt. Wm. E. Eaton, Larkinsville, Ala
Co. K, Sergt. Job Barnard, Camden Ala.

Military matters rather quiet here and elsewhere just now but we may expect stirring times in the east soon. The Spring and Summer campaign in the west however will not be very exciting.

March 7 1865 - Head Qrs. M & C RR Defences Larkinsville Ala. (Tuesday) Several bridges are down between here and Nashville and no mail has been received for several days.

Very hard rains have fallen lately and the country is flooded to such an extent as to stop citizens from bringing in produce.

My stockade at this place is progressing finely and will soon be completed.

My present command is equivalent to a Brigade and embraces thirteen posts from Huntsville to

Stevenson a distance of sixty miles. The garrisons are composed of the following troops

All of the 73rd Indiana Infantry
Three Companies 189th Ohio Infantry Detachment
101st U S. Colored Infantry Detachment
106th US. Colored Infantry Detachment
110th U.S. Colored Infantry Detachment
111th U S. Colored Infantry Detachment
18th Michigan Pioneers
Detachment 102nd Ohio Infantry
Three companies Alabama Cavalry acting as scouts

March 16th 1865 Head Qrs. Main & Charleston RR Defences Larkinsville Ala. (Thursday) I did not properly assume command of the Defences until yesterday when Col. Lyon 13th Wis.Volunteers abdicated his Regiment having been assigned to the 4th Corps. The 4th Corps is now being moved through to Knoxville by railroad.

I have moved Head Quarters from Huntsville to this place and appointed J. Rolfe Uptigrove Acting Assistant Adjutant General.

The garrisons have not been changed since I enumerated them March 7th.

March 23rd 1865 Larkinsville. (Thursday) The guerrillas were robbing at will last night. They met six boys from Company C and wounded two of them, James Hall through the shoulder and William Brewer through the arm. Brewer's arm will have to be amputated.

Apr. 1st 1865 - Head Qrs. M and C RR Defences Larkinsville Ala. (Saturday) Mrs. Kirby who lives on the opposite side of the river came through the lines a day or two since and obtained a pass from Genl. Granger to Nashville.

She wanted to go back but would not take the trouble to get a proper pass and I told her that if she attempted to go out of the lines without a pass I should have her arrested upon her return from Nashville.

Therefore she came back only as far as Scottsboro and tried to get away from that point but the wide awake Lt. Bickens Comdj. that Post promptly arrested her and sent her here.

She now has the mortification of being caught in evading the regulations and subjected to a vexatious delay and now wishes that she had obeyed orders.

Apr. 8th 1865 Larkinsville Ala. (Saturday) A skirmish occurred today near Paint Rock Bridge between fifteen men of Co. D of this Regiment and about forty guerrillas.

Francis Bradberry of Co. D was killed and Metcalf wounded severely. Three of the enemy were killed and three wounded as the men claim and the statement is confirmed by negroes.

Our boys were compelled to fall back to camp, when receiving reinforcements they went out and brought in the body of their comrades.

Captains Richley and Westlake have returned to the Regiment.

Letters from charming Jeannie bring me good news.

The news from Grant is glorious, Richmond the Capitol of the bogus Confederacy is ours and the rebel army fleeing for its life. The Army of the Potomac has done a good thing.

Apr. 14th 1865 Larkinsville Ala. (Friday) Glory Hallelujah. Lee's army surrendered, the greatest event of the war, whipped badly when it had the advantage of fortifications.

Nothing was left it but to surrender upon taking the field and pursued by our army. The surrender was made on the ninth inst. and the War Department ordered a salute of two hundred guns to be fired at every post in the Union for that and the raising today of the old flag over Sumpter.

I am making these grand old mountains reverberate with shot shell and canisters from my six pounders.

The great rebellion is now virtually over and had I a better pen and paper to write upon I'd grow enthusiastic over the event. But my satisfaction is too great to be expressed.

Apr. 19th 1865 - Larkinsville Ala. (Wednesday) Today alas our flag is at half mast for the death of our beloved President. He was assassinated at Ford's Theatre Washington on the night of the 14th. I received the news on the 15th and my flag has been at half mast since yesterday. I fired a gun every half hour from sunrise to sunset.

Today is the funeral and the War Dept. has ordered all labor to be suspended at Military Posts and twenty one minute guns to be fired at 12 a.m. J. Wilkes Booth is the assassin.

The deed is chargeable upon the whole southern people however for it is the national fruit of rebellion failing to stand up against freemen in the open fight. They resort to this banal and cowardly manner of venting their passions.

May 2 1865 – Larkinsville. (Tuesday(An organization of citizens has been formed in this vicinity to protect themselves against guerrillas.

I have appointed Moses A Morgan Captain of the Company.

Military matters are extremely quiet along the line. Many of the guerrillas are coming in and delivering themselves up. Dr. Brown and four men came in today. The men were in the last fight near Paint Rock Bridge a few days ago.

Weather warm and pleasant.

It is probable that we shall be mustered out about the 1st of June and hope that will prove true.

Am reading ……… and like his poetry very much.

Recd a letter from A D. Streight a day or two since.

Had serious inspection and muster on the 30 April.

May 4th 65 - Hd. Qrs. M. & C. RR Defenses Larkinsville Ala. (Thursday) Col. Norwood formerly of the 55th Ala. now commanding an independent battalion sent in a communication asking to surrender on the same terms as Lee.

General Granger has authorized me to accept his surrender on those terms and have authorized Capt. Westlake at Bellefonte to notify him of that decision. He has a number of horses taken from citizens on this side which he wishes to return.

I have been quite unwell yesterday and today but am feeling better now.

Johnson has surrendered to Sherman and there is now no longer Confederate forces east of the Mississippi.

100,000$ reward is offered for Jeff Davis for

complicity in the murder of Lincoln.

May 14th 1865 - Larkinsville Ala. (Sunday) General Granger has just telegraphed me that Jeff Davis and staff was captured on the 10th, Greenville, Ga. by Col. Pritchard 4th Mich. Cav. Glorious news. Now when he is hung the last act in this bloody tragedy of civil war will have ended.

He will undoubtedly be first tried for complicity in the assassination of President Lincoln but he should be hung for treason.

This is no time for false sympathy with traitors and we cannot afford to make treason respectable.

Lieut. Booher Co I lately Prisoner of War has returned to the Regiment and we expect several officers tomorrow.

Took a long ride this P.M with Surg. and orderly McCoy. Rode over the mountains for twelve miles but did not roust any guerrillas.

Weather pleasant.

Wrote coz. J on 12th this month.

May 17th 1865 - Larkinsville Ala. (Wednesday) The balance of our officers from southern prisons arrived safe and sound yesterday morning. They were in fine spirits and we had a jolly time celebrating the reunion.

Wm. M. Kendall will be mustered in to date May 16th as Major. This will be Beeber's opportunity to muster as Capt. of Co. D for which I am heartily glad.

Another special order has been issued by the War Dept. in relation to Co. A. It musters in Fry as 1st Lieutenant and revokes the muster of Upthegrove as 1st leaving him 2nd Lt.

Lieut. Cotton came in with his company and surrendered to Lt. Brown at Woodville Tank. He brought in his arms and they will be turned over to the Govt. AAAG.

Upthegrove has returned and assumed his duties again.

Have made an application to go to Nashville on business.

June 3rd 1865 – Larkinsville. (Saturday) On Monday the citizens of this county hold a convention at Scottsboro for the purpose of inaugurating civil law again.

Thus far I've taken no action whatever in any of these measurements as I think it best that the people quietly await until a Governor is appointed for the state and then uniformity of action can be had.

Weather is hot and sultry making the drill somewhat burdensome. One man came on dress parade tonight with is pants in his boots and punished him by making him stand in front of the Regiment at a present arms till the parade was ended.

Wrote yesterday to Mother and Coz. Jeannie.

Don't know why it is but I take no Interest in my journal nowadays and can scarcely have patience to write even a page.

D. H. and E. along the RR all ·present here.

June 18th 1865 - Head Quarters M. & C. RR Larkinsville. (Sunday) My commission as Colonel 73rd Regiment Indiana Infantry Volunteers came today. It was forwarded by Gov. Morton sometime since but was lost in the mail. It is dated July 6th, 1864. So that I have been Col. for nearly a year without knowing it.

Wm. M. Kendall's Commission as Lieut. Col. also arrived.

There are rumors afloat that we will go to

Nashville this week but I hardly believe it. General (Brt. Major Genl.) Granger in his recommendation stated that I was the bravest and most efficient officer on duty in the district which is saying a good deal and 1'm thankful for his good opinion as there are two Brt. Brig and half a doz. Cols. in the dist. It places me rather high.

June 20th 1865 - Head Quarters M. & C. RR Defenses Larkinsville. (Tuesday) Have just received Special Orders 55 from Department Head Qrs. ordering the73rd Indiana to report to Nashville Tenn for muster out and also a telegram from Brt. Major General Granger stating that troops will be sent from Huntsville to relieve us. This is good news for me and the whole Regiment and we're all jolly at the idea of going home. Do not expect that we can get off from here however in less than two or three days and will probably remain in Nashville several more.

I don't feel much regret at the idea of leaving Nashville or Larkinsville. I would say, for its about the dullest place just now that I've ever been in.

July 1st 1865 - Head Qrs. 73rd Ind. Nashville. (Saturday) The 73rd Indiana was mustered out of the service today and all its members are citizens once more. We are entitled to pay however until our arrival at home.

One hundred and fourteen recruits were left behind to make up term of enlistment and they have been assigned to the 29th Indiana.

We shall start tomorrow afternoon in an extra passenger train for Louisville and thence to Indianapolis where final payment will be made.

Am heartily glad that the end of our obligation to Uncle Sam has arrived at last.

Received a dear good letter from Jennie today and one from Mother yesterday.

Weather warm and oppressive.

Have sent Major Kendall and Lt. Williams to Louisville and Indianapolis to make necessary arrangements.

July 3rd 1865 - Head Qtrs. 73rd Ind. Louisville Ky. (Monday) Left Nashville yesterday. Was escorted through the streets by the brass band of the Ist Brig. 1st Div. Dept. Guard stationed at N [Nashville] which discoursed sweet music and smight the city..........to witness our march.

Marched by the flank from the Exchange Barracks to Broad St. and then by Platoons to Cherry, down Cherry to Commercial Hotel, thence to the left to College Street, and down College to Depot.

Left on an extra passenger train at 6:45 p.m. and arrived here at 5 a.m. Shall march through Louisville with our own band cross Ferry to Jeffersonville and take cars immediately for Indianapolis.

Weather extremely warm.

Shall be at our State Capitol in time to spend the 4th.

July 4th 1865 - Head Quarters 73rd Indiana, Indianapolis. (Tuesday) I write while the inevitable firecrackers and "squibs" are in active operation on all sides.

After a pleasant ride over the Jeff Railroad where all along the road the good Hoosiers welcome us with shouts and the waving of handkerchiefs and at Seymour passed under an arch with the inscription "Welcome home brave soldiers."

Arrived here at 6 p.m. and the men were quartered at the "Soldiers Home." All the officers are stopping at the Spencer Hotel.

Tomorrow we have a reception at the State House.

Turned over our arms today and moved the Regiment to Camp Carrington.

Weather very warm.

We are all anxious to get home as soon as possible. Hope to start on Friday.

July 5th 1865 - Head Quarters 73rd Inda., Indianapolis Inda. (Wednesday) This A.M. called on Genl. Pitcher, Provost Marshall General Indiana. Recd rolls and Major Hendricks Paymaster was assigned to pay the Regiment at 12 o'clock P.M.

General Mansfield arrived at Camp Carrington and conducted the 73rd and 80th Inda. and 13th and 17th Battery to the Soldiers Home where a good dinner was given the troops.

From there we marched under the escort of a fine band to the State House where a pleasant and agreeable reception awaited us. Governor Morton made an excellent address during which he made a short sketch of the Regimental History of the 73rd.

He was preceded by the Chaplain Dozier who sang the "good old Union wagon," and was followed by Major General Henry in a good address. The chaplain then sang Glory Hallelujah.

When the Gen. called me out and introduced me to the large assembly and "hoped that Col. Wade would address us" I was perfectly dumbfounded never having yet had an opportunity to "try my powers" in oratory. But after a moments silence I rallied somewhat and attempted to express thanks for the kind reception given us but suddenly came to a stop and "bestirred by confusion" for the want of something to say I was as much amused at my "magnificent failure" as anyone and didn't take it to heart much as I feel a presentiment that I'll yet make a passable speaker but not extemporaneously.

July 11th 1865 - South Bend. (Tuesday) Home again! After three years experience in the tented field and well satisfied am I to be again at rest and well rid of the worry and confusion of the past thou. weeks.

So. Bend has changed a great deal since I was here. It has been incorporated as a city and the late fire and improvements of the business part of town just in .... of erection make the town look very rugged.

In the course of a year however the new houses will be completed and a great improvement will be visible.

Attended quite a social party at Mr. Hendricks this eve and met an array of wit and beauty to which I've been a stranger for the last two years.

MARRIED!!!

At the residence of the bride's father in Niles Michigan **(Tuesday)** Sept. 5, 1865 by Rev. T. Dwight Hunt - Alfred B. Wade late Colonel 73rd Indiana to Jennie Y. Bond.

<u>and</u> so <u>ends my journal</u> ---- Alf B.

"All is well that ends well"
Yours Truly
Jennie Y Bond.

GLOSSARY

Michael P. Downs

As explained in my Introduction to the Diary, I have added this Glossary to help a reader better understand the military terms which Colonel Alfred B. Wade employed in his writing as well as differences in language usage found in documents of the 1860's.

AAAG. - Acting Assistant Adjutant General- The adjutant was the right hand of the commanding officer. They would write up the orders, see that they were delivered and complete whatever military matters needed to be taken care of.

Abatis or Abbatis - A fence-like obstacle of sharpened stakes or timbers used to stop, or at least delay, attacking soldiers.

Ague - An illness with symptoms of high fever and chills.

A Q.M. - Acting Quarter Master. This individual was the source of supplies for the armies during the Civil War.

Army Organization - A *company* was made up of 100 men initially. A *regiment* would usually have ten *companies.* There were three to four *regiments* in a *brigade*... three to four *brigades* in a division... and two to four *brigades* in a *corp.* Later in the War, after battles were fought the units were generally smaller in number, often much smaller.

Battery - A unit of six guns (cannons) and made up of

155 men when at full strength.

Brevet - During the Civil War a soldier could be promoted for a special reason (such as battle field bravery) but the promotion would still have to be approved by the Department of War and/or Congress.

During the time he was awaiting the approval he would not be paid at the new rank, however he would probably assume the responsibilities of the new level.

Bivouac - An encampment of soldiers in the field.

Boom Proof or Bomb Proof (Colonel Wade referred to them as a boom proof) A deep hole usually with several layers of logs for a roof used to protect soldiers from cannon bombardment.

Castle Thunder - A prison in Richmond, Virginia used to house civilians.

Chase, Salmon P. - The head of the Department of the Treasury. His creative ideas went a long way toward paying for the-cost of the Civil War.

Chivalry - The Southern upper class that Colonel Wade feels led the South into the war.

Christian Society - A religious organization formed to aid and proselytize to the soldiers.

Colfax, Schuyler - During the Civil War he was the Indiana Representative to Congress from the Ninth Congressional District (which included South Bend) and Speaker of the House. He arranged for Colonel Wade's exchange from the Confederate Libby Prison and also was a good friend of the Colonel.

Later Colfax became U.S. Grant's Vice-President during his first term but was caught in the Credit Mobilier scandal and retired to South Bend in 1873. He was also the publisher of the influential South Bend newspaper The Register.

Colors - The flags of the regiment - one represented the United States and the second the state and regiment.

Contrabands - Slaves that had been freed by the Union Army or had escaped from a plantation as the Union Army neared.

Copperhead - A northern supporter of the Confederacy during the Civil War.

Corduroy road - A road that used wooden logs as its base with dirt thrown on top to smooth it out.

Cousin Sallie - A nickname for the Confederate government used by Union prisoners-of-war. (A take off on the nickname Uncle Sam.)

Forrest, Nathan Bedford, Confederate Cavalry Lieutenant General. – Famed as the most aggressive, effective, successful cavalry officer from either side in America's Civil War, he was born into a rather poor family, the eldest of twelve children. His father William Forrest, a blacksmith, died when he was 17 and Forrest found himself head of his family.

A big man for the era, 6'2" tall and 200 pounds Forrest discovered himself to be an outstanding farmer and businessman. By the time of the Civil War, Forrest owned three plantations and was one of the richest men in the South, worth $1,500,000, taking good care of his mother and siblings, and educating his brothers.

In Memphis, Forrest served as an elected city official. And for a time there, as a merchant, he also conducted a slave trading business, an enterprise which, sadly, was then legal in both Northern and Southern states.

However, Forrest is said to have been a kind plantation manager, conducting his farming labor in such a way that kept black families together.

In fact Forrest was respected well enough by those who worked for him that blacks from his farms joined his cavalry regiments as fighting men.

Forrest promised them their freedom if they did so, and in fact, before the end of America's Civil War, he freed all the slaves from his plantations.

There were a number of black Southerners who fought with Forrest in his Confederate cavalry units. He praised them as being among the best soldiers he ever led.

It is estimated in historical records that about 50,000 black men joined and fought for their homeland in the Confederate army. Many others, of course, fought with distinction on the Union side as described in the books "The Boys From Lake County," "The Official History of the 73rd Indiana Volunteer Infantry Regiment," and this Diary.

As the Civil War began Forrest joined a cavalry regiment as a Private. Soon, seeing that Confederate forces were greatly in need of equipment, he offered to provide money to equip a full cavalry regiment. As such he was promoted by the Governor to Colonel and Regimental Commander.

By the end of the conflict he was recognized by General Robert E. Lee as the best cavalry officer of the Confederacy. His battle tactics were so fierce and effective that they are still taught in the U.S. Army's battle strategy classes.

Forrest and his cavalry troopers captured Colonel Alfred B. Wade and the entire "Provisional Brigade" during Colonel Abel D. Streight's raid across northern Alabama in the spring of 1863. The captured officers of the Brigade all reported Forrest to be truthful and honorable in his treatment of them as Prisoners Of War.

[It is claimed by some today that Forrest, after the Civil War, was the first leader of the Ku Klux Klan.

However, in a personal interview given a newspaper reporter Forrest avowed that he'd never been a member of the Klan. He acknowledged, however, that he had been in sympathy with its original aims.

The original intentions of the organization were to protect Southern homes, women, and children from murderous or destructive rampages feared after the War's end. Within a year or so - as with Gen. Robert E. Lee and other key Southern leaders - when Forrest saw that the organization had been taken over by those who evinced far more vicious purposes he separated himself completely from it and worked diligently to disband it. Publisher]

Fort Sumter – The firing upon the fort by Confederate forces during a non-military resupply attempt is considered to be the beginning of military hostilities and our Civil War.

Greenbacks - The currency of the United States during much of the Civil War, they were a dark green color on the backside.

Hardtack - A very hard cracker issued to troops as

food rations during the Civil War.

Instant or inst. - Often used in writing during the 19th century to mean an event which occurred in the present month.

Irish or Irish Hoist - A dressing down of someone or a "kick in the pants."

Levies - The new draftees brought in to the ranks of the army.

Libby Prison - A Southern prison located in Richmond, Virginia that housed Northern officers. Colonel Wade spent ten months there. Libby Prison has been nearly forgotten in present times. However, it was widely known and written about in newspapers during the years of America's Civil War.

Line of communications - The military term given to the supply line of the armies during the Civil War.

Mess - A group of soldiers organized to supply and cook the food of its members.

Morton, Oliver P. - The Civil War governor of Indiana and a strong supporter of President Lincoln. He also issued Alfred .B. Wade his commission as major in the 73rd Indiana Volunteer Infantry Regiment.

Parole - During the Civil War a captured soldier might be allowed to sign a parole which was his pledge to return home and not take up arms again until exchanged for another soldier.

Pickets - Soldiers on guard duty out front of the

military lines as a protective measure.

Potomac Army – (Army of the Potomac) The primary Union Army fighting in the eastern theater of the war mainly against Robert E. Lee's Confederate Army of Northern Virginia.

Quadroon - The term used during the 19th century for any person of at least black ancestry.

The Register - The South Bend, Indiana newspaper for which Congressman and Speaker of the House, Schuyler Colfax, was owner and editor.

Sanitary Commission - The civilian organization formed to provide food and medical care to soldiers during the Civil War.

Secesh - The abbreviation of the term secessionist and used to indicate an individual (or group) who was a supporter of the Southern cause.

Seward, William H. - The Secretary of State during the Civil War. He later would be involved in the purchase of Alaska from the Russian government.

Skedaddle - This slang military term meant to retreat very rapidly.

Skirmishers - Soldiers sent out from main unit lines to discover and locate opposing troops. When they engaged in limited, initial, rifle fire, sounds of the guns would alert the main force, giving them time to prepare for battle. These small outer defense forces were also called pickets. They would not risk losing many men by standing to fight, but would quickly fade back into the main force prepared for battle.

Stanton, Edwin M. - The Secretary of War (now called the Defense Department) during the Civil War and into the Johnson administration.

Streight, Abel D. – Colonel, 51st Indiana Volunteer Infantry Regiment and leader of the "Provisional Brigade" which included the 73rd Indiana Volunteer Infantry Regiment. Colonel Streight led that Brigade on the raid through northern Alabama in the spring of 1863 until captured by the cavalry of General Nathan Bedford Forrest. Abel D. Streight was also the man who formed the 51st Indiana. Before the end of the Civil War, he was promoted to Brevet Brigadier General in the Union Army..

Sutler - A civilian who followed the troops with supply wagons selling all types of goods to the soldiers.

Teams - Made up of horses or mules and used to pull wagons, caissons, artillery, etc.

Train - The wagons that carried supplies, baggage, etc. of the armies during the Civil War.

Ultimo - Often used in writing during the 19th century to mean that an event took place in the month preceding the present time.

Bibliography

"A History of the 73rd Indiana Infantry." West Chester Tribune. Chesterton, IN. Published in series. Jan 1, 1897 through Aug 16, 1897.

Anderson and Cooley. (Eds.) "South Bend and the Men Who Have Made It." The Tribune Printing Co. South Bend, IN. 1901.

Cist, H. M. "The Army Of The Cumberland" Scribner's Sons, New York, NY. 1882.

Civil War Center. Internet Homepage of the Civil War Center of Louisiana State University. Web site: www.cwc.lsu.

Connolly, James A. "Three Years in the Army of the Cumberland." Indiana University Press. Bloomington, IN.1987.

Connelly, T. L. "Civil War Tennessee, Battles and Leaders". The University of Tennessee Press, Knoxville, TN. 1979.

Cozzens, Peter. "No Better Place To Die - the Battle Of Stones River". University of Illinois Press, Urbana, Ill. 1990.

Domer, R. G. "Rebel Rout of Streight's Raiders." America's Civil War mag. Sept.1996, Pg 30-36.

Dyer, F. H. "A Compendium of the War of the Rebellion." CD-ROM (Windows Vers.) Available from: Guild Press of Indiana. 1997.
Fox, W.F. "Regimental Losses In The American Civil

War (1861-1865)" CD-ROM (Windows Vers.) Available: Guild Press of Indiana, 1997.

Gallagher, G. W. (Ed.) "War at Every Door - Partisan Politics and Guerrilla Violence in East Tennessee, 1860-1869." University of North Carolina Press, Chapel Hill, NC. 1997.

Grimsley, Mark. "The Great Deceiver - The Life of Nathan Bedford Forrest." Civil War Times Illustrated. November/December,1993. Pg 33-38.

Hartpence, W. E. "Of The Fifty-First Indiana Veteran Volunteer Infantry." The Robert Clarke Company, Cincinnati, OH. 1894.

Hess, Earl J. "Banners To The Breeze, The Kentucky Campaign, Corinth and Stones River." University of Nebraska Press. Lincoln, Neb. 2000.

Hom, S. F. "The Battle of Stones River." Eastern Acorn Press, 1991.

Hurst, Jack. "Nathan Bedford Forrest, A Bibliography." Alfred A. Knopf. New York, NY. 1993.

Lamers, W. M. "The Edge of Glory, A Biography of General William S Rosecrans. U.S.A." Harcourt, Brace. New York, NY. 1961.

Liggett, Kris and Larry. Letters from the 73rd Indiana Infantry. Copyright 1999. Web site: Indiana In The Civil War. Web address: www.thnet.com.

Long, E.B. with Barbara Long. "The Civil War Day By

Da, An Almanac 1861 - 1875." Da Capo Press, Inc., New York, NY. 1971.

Longacre, E. G. "Mounted Raids of the Civil War." A.S. Barnes & Company, Cranbury, NJ. 1975.

McDonough, J. L. "Stones River - Bloody Winter in Tennessee." The University of Tennessee Press, Knoxville, TN. 1980.

"Obituary of Alfred B. Wade." South Bend Tribune. Mar 1, 1877. Pg 4.

"Proceedings of the Eighth Annual Session of the Survivors of the Battle of Stone's River. (Note: No Author or Publisher listed.) 1898.

Roach, A. C. "The Prisoner of War And How Treated." The Railroad City Publishing House, Indianapolis, IN. 1865.

Smith, W. H. "Schuyler Colfax - The Changing Fortunes of a Political Idol." Indiana Historical Bureau. Indianapolis, IN. 1952.

Terrell, W. H. H. "Report of the Adjutant General of the State of Indiana (8 vols.)." Indianapolis, IN 1869.

Thombrough, E. L. "Indiana in the Civil War." Indiana Historical Society, Indianapolis, IN. 1965.

Varhola, Michael J. "Every Day Life During The Civil War." Writer's Digest Books, Cincinnati, OH. 1999.

"War of the Rebellion: A Compilation of the Official

Records." CD-ROM (Windows Vers.) Available: Guild Press of Indiana. 1997.

Willett, Robert L. "The Lightning Mille Brigade, Abel Streight's 1863 Raid Into Alabama." Guild Press, Carmel, IN. 1999.

Williams, Leander; Job Barnard; John Caulfield, Edward Jernegan, Wilber Gorsuch, and Henry Morgan. "History of the Seventy-third Indiana Volunteers in the War of 1861-65." Carnahan Press, Washington, DC.:1909.

Womack, Bob. "Call Forth The Mighty Men" Colonial Press, Bessemer, AL. 1987.

Michael P. Downs

Biography of Transcriber, Michael P. Downs

Michael P. Downs was born and reared in South Bend, Indiana...the same city so loved by the author of this Diary of America's Civil War years.

Mike Downs was educated in South Bend schools through completion of his High School years. He then earned both undergraduate and graduate degrees from Indiana University - Bloomington.

From 1970 through 1976 he served in the United States Navy and is a "Vietnam Era Veteran."

Downs enjoyed an Elementary Education career of thirty years in the South Bend Public School System where his specialty was in history. During that time he was recognized by his peers as "Teacher of the Year." Additionally, in 2008 Mike Downs was selected by the Indiana Daughters of the American Revolution as the outstanding United States History teacher for the State of Indiana.

Recently retired, Downs is currently active in several "Civil War Round Table" groups, as a Camp Commander for the Sons of Union Veterans, and as a noted historian of the 73rd Indiana Regiment. He is completing research on a new book about eastern Tennessee during the Civil War.

Downs' Great-Great Uncle, William H. Downs, fought as a Private in Company G, 73rd Indiana Volunteer Infantry Regiment, the Regiment commanded by Colonel Alfred B. Wade, author of this Diary. Pvt. Downs successfully completed the entire three years of his Civil War enlistment, and mustered out with the 73rd Regiment, July 1st, 1865.

For forty years, Mike Downs has been married to his lovely wife Carol who shares his great love of history, as well as their five Maine Coon cats who go with them on all of their travels.

Historical and Genealogical notes:

Historical and Genealogical notes:

:

LaVergne, TN USA
24 August 2009
155703LV00001B/50/P